Artistes of Colour

ETHNIC DIVERSITY AND REPRESENTATION IN
THE VICTORIAN CIRCUS

Steve Ward, PhD

Modern Vaudeville Press
PHILADELPHIA, PA

By Steve Ward.

Edited by Helen Gould (Salt & Sage Books) & Thom Wall.

Cover by Thom Wall.

ISBN: 978-1-7339712-7-0

Library of Congress: 2021900060

Modern Vaudeville Press
113 E Mayland St
Philadelphia, PA 19144
United States of America
www.ModernVaudevillePress.com

Ordering Information:
Quantity sales. Special discounts are available on quantity purchases by corporations, associations, and others. For details, contact the "Special Sales Department" at the address above.

Artistes of Colour: Ethnic Diversity and Representation in the Victorian Circus. —1st ed.

For justice, recognition, and equality
Black Lives Matter

CONTENTS

ACKNOWLEDGEMENTS

In compiling this book I have received help and support from many people. I would especially like to mention the following;

The National Fairground and Circus Archive; The Leeds Library; Helen Skilbeck at the Leeds City Library; Joe Williams of Heritage Corner; Claire Pickering at the Wakefield Library; Erin Sullivan and Terence Rowe for additional information on the Christoffs; John Wynne and David Tonkin for additional information on Joseph Hillier; Kay Vetter Winter and Jessica Kerwin Jenkins for additional information on Leona Dare; David G Marks for additional information on Miss La La; Gifty Burrows of the Africans in Yorkshire Project; Martin Hale for additional information on Albert May; Alison Young of the British Music Hall Society - and finally, Linda, my wife, for her constant support and understanding.

Foreword - Professor. Ron Beadle

Circus is an ethereal artform, its achievements disappearing in the moment of their creation. Those who research it face several challenges – records are scarce, often contradictory, artistes' own accounts are all too often aimed at entertainment rather than truth and their names, acts, partnerships, employers and relationships change with remarkable frequency. Despite these obstacles, Dr Ward has produced five volumes of circus history and his sixth is his most challenging project yet.

It tells the stories of Black and Ethnic Minority artistes in the Victorian era. As Dr Ward points out, much of what is supposedly known of their histories is false, the victim of romanticism, poor research or unchecked assumptions. This text is a necessary corrective and could only be the work of someone whose knowledge of circus is only exceeded for his love of it. It contextualises circus stories within the wider history of BAME people (BIPOC) in Britain but is thankfully unencumbered by the forced theorizing of much contemporary circus writing.

Dr Ward draws on a wide range of archival sources to carefully piece together the lives of a small number of artistes and directors for whom documentary evidence is available. They were stars in their day, but amongst their tragedies was the forgetfulness of a once adoring public when age or injury ended their careers.

Students of circus will learn much here and so will students of injustice. The courage, dexterity and athleticism of BAME artistes could either challenge or reinforce the racist tropes of the era; Dr Ward evidences both. White racism, outside the ring, is recorded in all its ugly stupidity but so are accounts of its opposite. Dr Ward shows how circus enabled BAME people to be celebrated in Victorian times. It is a story worthy of being told.

Professor Ron Beadle
Northumbria University
Newcastle upon Tyne, England, 2021

FOREWORD - AMITY STODDARD & SELLAM OUAHABI

My husband is always telling me that there is no writing things down in the circus.

"In traditional circus there is no taking notes," is usually how the conversation begins. On this particular night, Sellam is lighting his third cigarette as he cracks the window of our aging silver Hyundai. We're headed out to see a student show, and we're late. "A real coach just remembers. You see an act in your mind; you tell it to your troupe. You teach it in an afternoon."

He pauses to fiddle with the defroster, which works on his side, but not for the passenger seat. A clear circle of glass appears above the steering wheel, while my portion of window remains covered with a crystal mosaic of frost. Outside, the sky is bruised looking, ominous clouds push down along the horizon line. Evening is near, snow will fall overnight. I was born in New England, and tend to read the skies like an ongoing conversation. Sellam is from Morocco, but in reality, he is not very Moroccan; he is not from anywhere. He would tell you he is a traveler. He is a student of the road, having lived with traveling circuses since he was a child.

"Each night," he leans back in the driver's seat and continues, giving up on clearing the glass for me. "You go to the performance, you watch it. A real coach does that – a proper coach, they watch the show. Every show. And they know . . . not just where the mistakes happened. They see the mistake coming before it happens. They can tell. An experienced coach will run into the ring to catch that mistake before it falls and gets injured. How can you write that down? Are you going to read your notes while you run through the tent?"

He laughs, his voice gravelly and thick, the sound of his voice makes the car feel warm. I think to myself, again, how his voice makes our whole life feel warm. When he begins to talk, it's like a fire starting, and I curl up near him, warming myself, drifting with his elliptical stories that somehow flow together, one feeding the other. I put my hand and on top of his, where it rests on the stickshift. He gives me an amused sidelong glance, then flicks my hand away.

"You want to drive now?" he chastises, and we giggle together, our exhales freeze into thin clouds, and rise.

***

Whenever Sellam tells me there is no writing in the circus, I can't help but complete the sentence, silently, in my mind: There is no writing about him, or people like him, in the circus. No writing, or very little, about his experience of being an artist of color, about his experience of being a featured act - often chosen because of the "exotic" cast of his skin, or the technique specific to his culture – and then being paid half the salary, while expected to do twice the physical show labor, for the very same reasons.

Sellam was taken on by his first acrobatic troupe when he was just twelve years old; at that point, he was already a professional. Moroccans are natural acrobats; traditionally, they train in the loose sand of the beaches, reaching impossible heights. They are special currency in the circus world – the unsung heroes of the human pyramid, which they are sometimes credited with inventing. Far from entertainment, the human pyramid was created as a war technique; a way to see far across the desert for signs of intruders.

That first troupe didn't leave Morocco; it was a local act that traveled throughout Tangier, Casablanca and Rabat, popular during First and Second Eid celebrations, when the sheep are slaughtered. During the time of Eid, throughout Morocco, festivals fill the boulevards and marketplaces, people rejoice with music and set up tables along the narrow streets. They eat together, laugh together, and of course, there are acrobats.

These were the old festivals, Sellam explains, a time that now seems long ago, and forgotten. At the old festivals, there were fakirs, charming the snakes out of their baskets. There were storytellers, and breathers of fire. And the food! All around, the smell of fresh, hot kefta; triangles of sweet chicken basteeya; griwach and roasting nuts. The food was enough to drive him mad, his stomach churning with hunger. But watching the acrobats, it's like a tiny bell began to sound in his mind. The sound of this bell was high and faint, the vibration permeated his body and his sense of gravity changed. Sellam explains, it was the feeling of mektub: The feeling of his destiny. The best acrobats of the city performed for these festivals, tumbling on the stone streets, forming towering human pyramids, and working the crowds for money. Sellam watched as the smaller boys climbed onto the bigger boys' shoulders. Those boys bent at the waist and reached down, hoisting even smaller boys up, until they were three- and four-men-high. It was always the smallest, most fearless boy who climbed to the top. As he watched, Sellam knew that he could be that boy.

Sellam began to sculpt his acrobatic style on the local beaches of Tangier, tumbling with the gangs of boys after school, and in the mornings, he practiced by himself when the others attended classes. They called him "Sellam Tanjawi" – Sellam the Tangier Boy – out of respect. There were no circus schools then; circus was something you were born into. If you were a boy like Sellam, your chance of being selected for a troupe, and from there, making it out of Morocco to a proper tented show, was nothing short of a miracle. In Sellam's mind, it was the only choice, a decision he made for himself that would take him away from his family, first to Spain, and then to Europe.

***

We arrive just before the show begins, and already, a nervous student has flagged him down for an emergency lesson, backstage. Sellam is laughing and smacking the student's legs; she is struggling to find the right position upside down. They are several handstands in, and he won't let her go, even as the ringmaster has begun to greet the audience, beyond the curtain.

"Squeeze! Tight your stomach!" Sellam commands, and the student is giggling, now, too.

"Stop that," warns Sellam, his voice stern but his eyes sparkling with mischief. "Focus." And the student bites her lip, stifling a round guffaw deep in her chest.

"Hands too far apart," Sellam says. He holds her ankles and uses his shin to nudge her elbows toward her ears. The girl adjusts the width of her hands, brings them directly under her shoulders, palms flat, fingers reaching, and a transformation takes place: She is suddenly a straight line, an arrow of human, her ribs and buttocks tucked neatly inward, toes pointed and reaching for the ceiling, she is breathing easy.

"That's the one," Sellam growls, satisfied. "That is called 'the stack'."

I am watching and remembering that feeling of finding alignment, that incredible sense of place when your body settles into an acrobatic position, and you realize you are designed for so much more than sitting and standing. The first time I felt it, as a novice young gymnast, my entire world changed. I gained control over my body, and by extension, my life. A feeling like that can reveal your path, your destiny. One small triumph, one discovery of your own ability, changes everything. You realize: If we can stand comfortably on our hands, then we can surely defy gravity in other ways.

***

When he was seven years old, Sellam tells me, his mother had led him to the neighborhood school. They were met at the door by the headmistress, who pulled the heavy gate shut in front of them.

"He is too old," the headmistress pronounced. Sellam stood behind his mother and watched the woman's face, the poison in her hard eyes, the way the vines of black metal in the gate blended with her shadowed complexion. To my husband, whose eyes were now blurring with anger, the metal work looked like thin black snakes, rising upward to disappear into the nest of hair obscured by her silk scarf.

As he tells me the story, I can see his young face, a face that seems blank and impenetrable, until you find his eyes. Now, without school, Sellam drifts through the streets, invisible. He slips out at dawn, to gather the water for his mother. The neighborhood well is a half-mile trek uphill, and he carries four buckets at a time. Two 10-gallon buckets in each hand, running, plastic shoes flapping where they are split at the toe. Once the blue plastic barrel in Mama Fatima's kitchen is full, he is free. He navigates the alleys of the Casbah, down the hillside to the beach, to join the gangs of older men who are practicing their side somersaults, their pyramids. He is careful to avoid the freshly washed and combed friends his own age, as they march to their classes with books under their arms. As they pass by, he squints, unseen, at their book covers. On the beach, exhausted from practice, he finds a stone and scrapes the shape of the book titles he has seen them carrying, into the granite of the breakwater. Writing back then, he tells me, was the practice of remembering shapes. He held the shape in his mind, carved it into rock, watching for someone to happen upon his work and pronounce the word, so he could know what he had written. He would never ask.

While he was performing in a festival at Second Eid, Sellam was seen by the leader of an international troupe. That man came to his family home on Rue Bougasse and asked for permission to take him away. He wanted that little boy: The one he had seen at the top of every pyramid; the one who was already leaving the ground before the last man had settled into place. I imagine what Sellam's mother must have felt, answering the knock on the door. Fatima has her son's red-brown eyes; her son's strong and dimpled chin. She doesn't open the door wide; only just enough to see this man, who is respectful and has his hands clasped in front of his waist, his eyes cast downward. When he reveals his purpose, she invites him in for a traditional mint tea. Ahmed and Absellam, my husband's older brothers, appear in order to talk business alongside their mother. I imagine little Sellam in another room, listening. Perhaps he is outside, clinging to the deep window sill on the side of their three-room, cement house. Perhaps he is by the sea, on the sand, practicing, just feeling the conversation, seeing it in his mind.

When asked, Sellam tells me that he mostly felt shame about his dream of circus – something he wanted so badly, that he would leave Tangier, live as a child among strangers in foreign countries, fighting his way into the ring. Who would fetch the water for his mother, when he was gone, he wondered? The sharp point of guilt pricked him behind the ears. The guilt of getting what he wanted, the answer to his prayers. Please, God. Take me away from here; give me a different life.

The man tells Fatima that Sellam is special, that his talent will take him far. For starters, he tells the brothers, it will take him to Spain, where the troupe has signed a contract with Circo Russo. Fatima is looking into the man's eyes in that way only she can; her eyes are divining tools. The man can feel them cutting deftly through his story, her gaze is steadfast, diamond hard. He has seen that look in the young face of my husband. It's the look that convinces him to take Sellam into the troupe, the look that knows and accepts pain, cuts through to the next order of business: How to become stronger; how to fix a mistake in the air. She does not say yes right away. But they all know it is the only choice. The schools have refused Sellam.

Now the leader of the troupe rises, smiling, and shakes the brothers' hands, giving blessings. The deal is settled. He raises his right hand to his mouth, kisses is it, then presses the hand to his heart, nodding at Fatima. Sellam's mother remains seated, she blesses the man, raising her own hand and kissing her own knuckles, and then the brothers leave, and she is alone, silent. Her heart is already shaping itself around the empty space that her son will leave behind. In the morning, the man will come to collect Sellam, who will clutch two shirts and two trousers in a plastic bag.

Fatima will press a sack of raif into her son's hand as he leaves – a layered, chewy crepe that will last for a few breakfasts, at least. They will not look at each other as he passes through the door, squeezing past her solid body. It will be the beginning of 30 years away from home, the beginning of a life belonging to no country.

***

What we can't speak, or solve for ourselves, we write across the hearts of those we love.

"But where did you sleep, when you were so little?" I ask him.

"Wherever I could. Sometimes, I slept in the zoo," he chuckles. "They gived me a trash bag to pull over my body and keep away the water, and I use the hay for my pillow, my blanket."

"The zoo?" I ask, not quite comprehending.

"The animals. There was a big tent where they sleep at night. Sometimes I slept near the lions, and the tigers, and the bear cages. Sometimes I slept with the horses and the elephants. Other times, I go under the bleachers, or the semi trucks. I slept on the ground, and cover myself with hay."

"Alone?" I ask him, blinking.

"Yes – alone," he says, and when my eyes widen with shock, he chuckles, and recants.

"Well," he says. "Not really alone. Especially when I was with them – the animals. It's like, they were looking out for me. And they were frightened too. We begin to understand each other."

***

In my husband's world, there is no writing, only story upon story, each folded on top of the other, compressed into a hard knot in his abdomen. So often, one breaks free, fluttering like insect wings behind his eyes, as he tries to sleep, as he smokes and walks with me in the evenings for coffee, the stories pour forth, and I try desperately to catch each one, to order and file them mentally for later recollection. I scramble for a pen, a tape recorder, I tell him to slow down. I have begun to understand that as unusual a man as he is, his experience is not. There are many stories like his . . . and none seem to be written down.

"We are writing this for your son," I tell him. "We are writing this for your family. So they can understand where you went. So they can travel with you. So they can remember you."

"I want to write this for the one that punished me, too," he smiles mischievously, his eyes hardening. "I want to say the truth, what really happens."

***

In my life, the written word has always been my solace. Sometimes it feels like my salvation, the only way I can make sense of my path. I fumble through my waking life, befuddled and distracted; when I sit down to write, I gather the fragments and create a whole. I exist. Writing is the cathedral I enter for meaning. In my husband's life, there are no records, by his own hand, or anyone else . . . his story is buried deep inside his own chest, and the story of others like him are also unmarked, unknown. Despite centuries of circus tradition in Morocco, indigenous circus companies are rare. Spanish and French companies cross the borders and set up shows and training facilities; they hire Moroccan troupes and apply for grants from the government. They receive attention from local television and radio stations. Neighborhood boys like Sellam train in jeans and tee-shirts and bare feet, on the beach, on the stone pavement, and dream of leaving Morocco so that they can earn a real living; so that they can see the world, and be seen by the world. I wonder, how does it feel to live without a written history? Without a trace.

***

Sellam takes another drag, blows out smoke in a thin stream, it spreads and fills the car.

"There are times," he concedes. "I wish I could write my story. It bother me very much. It bother me so deep, when I can't spell a word, when I can't find the meaning, when I can't say what I am carrying." He tells me that when he sees others writing and reading, it is like they are sitting in a room he can't enter.

That night, I lie awake, listening to him sleep. I am still hearing his voice, remembering the smoke swirling near the crown of his head. His voice entered my life ten years ago, now. I was running the kitchen of a small traveling circus. We worked two- and three-day stands, it was a rough, sweet company – you could call it a mud show. There were two windows in the pie car; those were the windows that I passed food through, to the children and adults that performed the show. Deeper in, where the exhaust fan roared, eight propane burners and the sun beating down on the roof heated the kitchen to 120 degrees. I cooked in tank tops and relieved my assistants constantly to wander outside and cool off. Passing cups of hot coffee to my husband, who was not yet my husband but still a strange, small jewel of a man who told stories in a clipped and honeyed accent – British expressions pronounced with rolling R's and other hints of multiple origin – was the highlight of my day. I leaned forward, bent at the hip, my elbows balanced on the counter, and listened to his observations of these strange Americans, and I pieced together his story of circus, the story he seemed both reluctant and eager to tell, his fascination fighting with some aspect of his modesty. At night, I closed the door to my tiny bunk, by coincidence next to his, and I tried to sleep, but I could only hear his voice. The image of his hands floated above me: Those hands clasping each other, water flowing over them as they washed for prayer, the thick rough fingers folding around each other. His hands seemed to carry an extra length and joint, at the thumb. I knew without asking that his hands had stretched to handle enormous weight, relentless work. When one of those hands flattened out and clasped my shoulder, the strength was almost frightening. I could feel the way he must temper his touch, restrain the full might in those hands. Later, I would watch him heft the ends of tent poles and swing sledgehammers as if they were toys.

He used every inch of his body, all the parts seemed to connect into one muscle, a single force of execution. How many things I never had to ask him . . . how obvious that his enormous strength and will alone had taken him around the world. My husband would tell me later, it was God; everything I have, from God and I would nod silently, but I couldn't help the nagging feeling that his strength had grown to fill the spaces where God was absent.

***

Over the years, the sound of Sellam's voice has somehow become my own voice talking, in my head. I tell stories to myself, in his voice. I write his travels against my own eyelids. I dream his memories, I talk to the people in his past. In those dreams, I travel backward through time as a dragon, a wolf wife, and I defend his life against those who have injured him.

I have the luxury of knowing a voice can enter me, and travel out again, onto a page. I can put things right on paper. But I still worry: I wonder, will he be remembered. If I don't write his story, who will. What if I don't tell his story the way he wants me to tell it. What if my voice cancels out his voice. What if my words are not strong enough to portray him. What if I am too weak. What if I fail. When we met, he was a man who didn't sleep much, he walked a living road of dust and memory. I must remember him properly. Isn't that our duty, our promise to those that we love? And to that which we hold sacred?

Amity Stoddard & Sellam Ouahabi
Biddeford, Maine, 2021

Philip Astley: silhouette from the frontispiece of his book *The System of Equestrian Education* 1802. *(Reproduced with permission of the National Fairground and Circus Archive).*

INTRODUCTION

By the time that Queen Victoria came to the throne in 1837, the 'modern' circus was almost seventy years old. Founded in 1768 by a retired cavalry officer, Philip Astley, it became a highly popular form of entertainment for the masses. If we examine how this popularity arose we can see that the social conditions within Britain during the late eighteenth and early nineteenth centuries facilitated the growth of a nationalistic pride. This was reflected and reinforced by how and what the circus, in its early stages, presented. Its popular appeal would serve to influence how the British came to see their place in an expanding world.

Largely equestrian in nature at the beginning, skills were forged on the battlefields of Europe and then translated into displays of horsemanship for a new paying audience. During the late eighteenth and early nineteenth centuries, Britain had been embroiled in military conflicts around the world, particularly in Europe. The war horse was the exemplification of a mythical heroic quality and epitomised military might. From the beginning, Astley's demonstrations of military riding and his interpretation of how the 15th Dragoons charged the French fed the public patriotic zeal. Astley was a hero, the embodiment of the loyal patriotic soldier prepared to lay down his life for his country. His swashbuckling performances portrayed an heroic indestructibility. Lavish hippodramas (plays specifically written for the inclusion of horses, blending horsemanship and popular melodrama), spectacular pageantry, and reconstructions of famous battles, all involving many men and horses, pandered to public nostalgia and enthusiastic nationalism. So the circus was to reinforce Britain's view of itself in the world and its attitude towards foreigners and a perceived 'evil'.

The addition of other physical skills, such as rope-dancing, acrobatics, feats of strength, and clowning created the embryonic form of circus that we might recognise today. It was truly a popular form of entertainment that embraced all social classes. By the mid nineteenth century it was well established and many towns and cities around the United Kingdom had permanent circus amphitheatres, and many more had semi-permanent structures erected as and when needed. Some of these amphitheatres could seat several thousands of people.

The interior of Astley's c. 1810. One of a number of colour plates reproduced by the Dutch Dairy Bureau in the 1950s for the album *The Colourful World of the Circus*. *(Author's collection).*

During a period of rapid industrial expansion and with the rise of Capitalism, underpinned by the philosophy of Utilitarianism, the working classes found themselves in a new state of oppression. 'To work' became the social mantra; it was a commodity driven society in which the role of the individual became diminished. Painful poverty prevented its victims from enjoying all but the cheapest entertainments. 'Penny gaffs', street entertainers, peep shows, and cock fights were amongst the popular common entertainments. There was little time for play but the circus provided one escape from the drudgery of everyday life. As Mr Sleary, the circus owner, says in *Hard Times* (Dickens, 1854);

> People must be amused … they can't be always a working … they aren't made for it … You must have us.

The circus provided a contrast between the harsh reality of life and the world of the imagination. But this imaginary and illusory world of the circus seemed to exist beyond the bounds of social laws; it was a self-contained world in which the individual was prized. It had an 'otherness' about it that both attracted and repulsed people at the same time. It was a world of the exotic, disorder, inversion, and anomaly (Stoddard, 2000:89-90). The circus consciously perpetuated this 'otherness' throughout the Victorian period. Examine circus advertising of the time and you will often find adjectives such as exotic, beautiful, unrivalled, novel, antipodean, dangerous etc. This all added to the idea of the Otherness of the circus and as escapism from the ordinariness of everyday life for the audience.

Part of the Exotic Otherness of the circus lay in its inclusivity and diversity. The circus empowered women, it allowed opportunities for those in society who we might now label 'disabled', and it provided a platform for ethnic minority performers.

However, open any book on the history of the circus and you will be informed that Pablo Fanque was the first black circus owner in the UK (Davies, 2017), or that Miss La La was a female performer of colour (Toulmin, 2018), and perhaps you may find a mention of Martini Maccomo the black lion tamer (Frost, 1874:360). But Fanque was not

"Carolina Twins,"
MILLIE AND CHRISTINA.

the only black circus proprietor; Miss La La was not the only female performer of colour; and Maccomo was certainly not the only black lion tamer during the Victorian period. In fact there were many artistes from a range of ethnic minority backgrounds performing in the circus, and other places such as Music Halls and other performance venues, both before and during Victoria's reign, and I have taken the liberty to embrace those parameters within the context of this work. Yet somehow their stories seem to have been glossed over, almost expunged from the history. Why is this? As we shall see, the 'modern' circus was a very British institution. From a tiny green space in London the circus rapidly spread its tentacles throughout the world. I believe that because the early circus had its roots in displays of military equestrianism, as presented by the patriotic military heroic figure of its founder, Philip Astley, it became a political vehicle for jingoistic equestrian performances that promulgated the idea of a British national supremacy, to the detriment of anything 'foreign'. To a certain extent this was true, and many circus programmes contained re-enactments of victorious British battles, where Britain was at first triumphant over its neighbouring European enemies. Later, depictions of conquests over other ethnic 'enemies' such as in India, China, or Africa appeared. All depicted 'white man good – black man bad', where the word black was a term used at the time to cover any skin tone that was not Anglo-Saxon white. It has to be remembered that at this time British society was also framing its own Colonial narrative that would create an ethnic hierarchy, with Anglo-Saxon at the top and sub-Saharan African at the bottom. Newspaper articles, such as the one that follows, only fuelled this ideology.

The negro of Africa is among the inferior races of men, without by any means being the lowest, for he is superior to the Australian and several other races … the negro … is still at best a barbarian, sometimes a cannibal, and often indulging in human sacrifices … The African negro submits to enslavement with a patience unknown to any other race of men (*The Daily Post* 15 October 1866)

Fundamental Christian views and Darwinism were to play an important factor in this, and xenophobia turned into something more sinister based on ignorance and racial stereotyping. An additional fact is that information on these performers is often difficult to unearth, especially at a time when an 'exotic' sounding *nom de plume* did not always indicate a true identity. Occasionally some of these individuals are quite well documented but others may have only a brief mention in a newspaper. By researching old cuttings, posters, photographs, and other accounts it is possible to piece together the wealth of ethnic performers at this time.

In dealing with historical records and materials they are very often written in the language of the time. Today we may find some of it offensive. However, when directly quoting material, I have not redacted this language in order to maintain the integrity of the sources. It is not my intention to cause offense or harm.

I hope that this book goes some way to redressing the balance of circus history by acknowledging the many performers from ethnic minority backgrounds. It is intended to be a celebration of those artistes, not just a catalogue, because they are an important part in the history of the circus. I hope that it will be entertaining as well as informative. For all the research that I have undertaken, I know that there is a lot more to discover. It is a work that will never be finished.

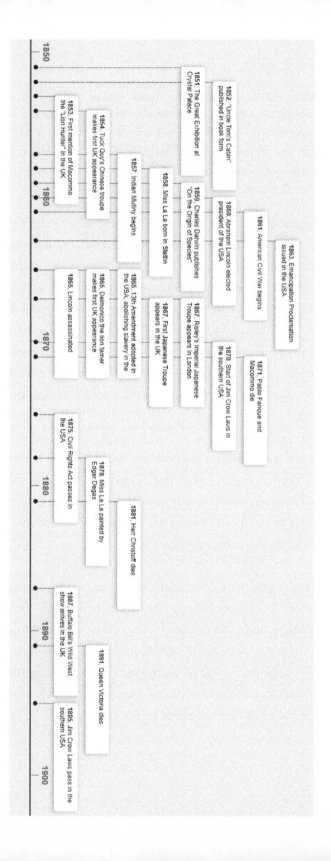

1850

1851. The Great Exhibition at Crystal Palace

1852. "Uncle Tom's Cabin" published in book form

1853. First mention of Macommo the "Lion Hunter" in the UK

1854. Tuck Quy's Chinese troupe makes first UK appearance

1857. Indian Mutiny begins

1858. Miss La La born in Stettin

1859. Charles Darwin publishes "On the Origin of Species"

1860

1860. Abraham Lincoln elected president of the USA

1861. American Civil War begins

1863. Emancipation Proclamation issued in the USA

1865. 13th Amendment adopted in the USA, abolishing slavery in the

1865. Demonico the lion tamer makes first UK appearance

1865. Lincoln assassinated

1867. First Japanese Troupe appears in the UK

1867. Risley's Imperial Japanese Troupe appears in London

1870

1870. Start of Jim Crow Laws in the southern USA

1871. Pablo Fanque and Macommo die

1875. Civil Rights Act passes in the USA

1878. Miss La La painted by Edgar Degas

1880

1881. Herr Christoff dies

1890

1887. Buffalo Bill's Wild West show arrives in the UK

1891. Queen Victoria dies

1895. Jim Crow Laws pass in the southern USA

1900

28

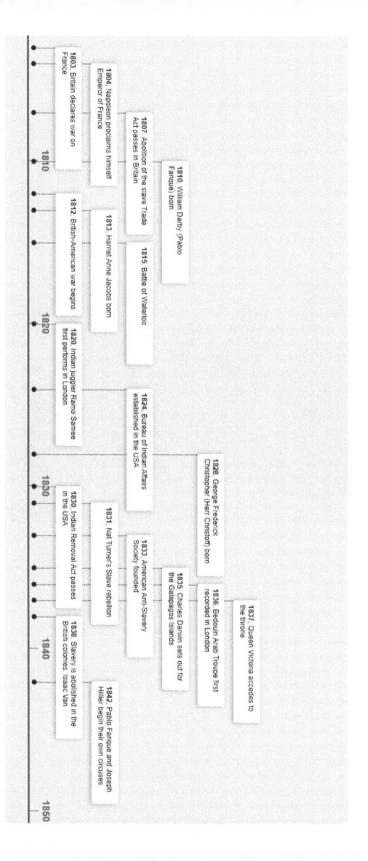

1803, Britain declares war on France

1804, Napoleon proclaims himself Emperor of France

1807, Abolition of the slave Trade Act passes in Britain

1810, William Darby (Pablo Fanque) born

1812, British-American war begins

1813, Harriet Anne Jacobs born

1815, Battle of Waterloo

1820, Indian juggler Ramo Samee first performs in London

1824, Bureau of Indian Affairs established in the USA

1828, George Frederick Christopher (Herr Christoff) born

1830, Indian Removal Act passes in the USA

1831, Nat Turner's Slave rebellion

1833, American Anti-Slavery Society founded

1835, Charles Darwin sets out for the Galapagos Islands

1836, Bedouin Arab Troupe first recorded in London

1837, Queen Victoria accedes to the throne

1838, Slavery is abolished in the British colonies. Isaac Van

1842, Pablo Fanque and Joseph Hillier begin their own circuses

1810

1820

1830

1840

1850

Slave auction 1856 *(Library of Congress)*

CHAPTER 1
THE VICTORIANS AND RACE

It was the best of times, it was the worst of times, it was the age of wisdom, it was the age of foolishness, it was the epoch of belief, it was the epoch of incredulity, it was the season of Light, it was the season of Darkness (Dickens, 1859)

Although Dickens' novel *A Tale of Two Cities* is set in London and Paris before and during the French Revolution of the late eighteenth century, the opening lines above could equally well have been written about the Victorian period. This was a period of great social and industrial advancements but it also had a much darker side that is often glossed over. It was a time in which many of our great national institutions were founded by wealthy patrons, but it was a wealth obtained through the trafficking of human beings – the 'F'. Mercantile families and land owners, such as the Gladstones of Liverpool and the Lascelles family of Yorkshire accrued vast sums of money through the forcible shipment of African people to the British sugar plantations of the Caribbean. Between 1700 and 1808, it is estimated that around 3 million men, women, and children were removed from their homes in Africa and transported to the Caribbean islands by British and American ships (Rediker, 2007). Other European countries such as France, Spain, Portugal, and Denmark were also involved in this inhuman trade, and shipped enslaved people to their own dependencies in the Caribbean, the Azores, and Brazil. The British ports of Bristol and Liverpool became immensely rich as 'slave ships' returned from the Caribbean laden with sugar. This trade was to provide the financial platform upon which all the great Victorian institutions were to be built.

Early activists against the trade in enslaved people formally came together in May 1787 to create the Society for Effecting the Abolition of the Slave Trade. At the first committee meeting it was resolved that 'the said Trade was both impolitick [sic] and unjust'[1]. Religious groups, notably the Quakers, parliamentarians, and freed slaves, were all active and vociferous in their condemnation of trade in enslaved people and sought to engage public opinion towards abolition. Women were also very active, and the Leeds Anti-slavery Association was very progressive in that it was the first association to allow women to become members, in fact most members were female. Ironically, by the turn of the century Britain had become the largest proponent for the abolition of slavery having previously been the largest 'slave trading' nation. After years of campaigning, and often in the face of stiff opposition from those with vested interest in the trade, the *Abolition of the Slave Trade Act* was passed by the British parliament in March 1807. The Act made it illegal to trade in enslaved people throughout the British colonies but did not ban enslavery *per se*. A clandestine trade in enslaved people still continued after this date until an 1811 Act made it a felony to deal in such within British colonies. Britain lagged behind some other European nations; Denmark had passed a law in 1792 and Sweden a few years later in 1803. Neither country allowed any further trade in enslaved people (Armistead, 1853:35). It was not until 1833 that the *Slavery Abolition Act* was finally passed in Britain, coming into law the following year.

> All slaves in the British Colonies, shall become, and be to all intents and purposes, free and discharged, from and of all manner of slavery, and slavery is hereby for ever abolished, and declared unlawful. (Act of Parliament, 1833)

This law did not only apply to European Britain but also to the twenty British colonies at that time, seventeen of which were in the West Indies and three in the East Indies. Enslaved children under the age of six years old were to be freed, whilst those over the age of six were redesignated as apprentices, without pay, and eventually freed in two tranches, 1838 and 1840. In Jamaica alone there were 331,000 enslaved people (Armistead, 1853.Tract 80:4). Government compensation was paid to former 'slave owners', but notably not to those who had been enslaved. Parliamentary records show that absentee 'slave ownership' (those who resided in Britain but who owned enslaved people in the colonies) was not restricted to the landed gentry. Members of the Clergy, military personnel, bankers, and others of the middle classes were all represented in the 46,000 claims made to the Government. What is surprising is that it is estimated that 25% of claimants were women, given that women at this time were socially unequal to men and considered as the 'weaker sex'. The claims ranged from ownership of a small number of people up to those, like the Lascelles, who owned over 2,500 enslaved people. Claims could exceed 26,000 pounds sterling (equivalent in 2020 of over 1.75 million pounds sterling). It was one of the largest state pay-outs in British history and which necessitated the government of that time to take out a 15 million pounds sterling loan, which was only finally repaid in 2015 (Manjara, 2018). The cancer of the trade in enslaved humans permeated the very structure of British society during the late eighteenth and early nineteenth centuries.

British history is interlaced with invasions; the Romans, the Vikings, the Angles and Saxons, and of course the Normans. Add to this early immigrations such as the twelfth century Jews, the Lombards, Flemish weavers, and the Huguenots (not to mention the later immigrations of the twentieth century) and it becomes difficult to define exactly what 'Britishness' is. That there have been persons of colour in Britain for many centuries is a matter of record. As a maritime nation, historically Britain has traded with many countries from around the world, and the presence of seamen from a wide variety of ethnic backgrounds was common in the major ports. We know that the Romans stationed black auxiliary units in Britain after Hadrian's Wall was built. Public records show that there were black people in Britain in Tudor times, and although an embryonic trade in enslaved people had begun in the 16th century, Queen Elizabeth I had expressed concern that people should be carried off without their own free will;

> It would be detestable, and call down the vengeance of Heaven upon the undertakers (Armistead, 1853:17)

Some of these were retained as servants, some were employed, and others lived on their own means. Importantly, none of them were officially enslaved because no statute was ever passed to codify slavery in British law (Kaufmann, 2017). This formed the basis for the 1772 case of James Somerset, an enslaved African, who ran away from his master Charles Stewart who had brought him to Britain from America in 1769. Somerset was recaptured and imprisoned on a ship that was due to sail to Jamaica. Stewart directed that he be sold as a plantation labourer. Whilst in Britain Somerset had been baptised as a Christian and his Godparents made an application of a writ of *habeas corpus* and the case was brought before the Court of the King's Bench to determine whether his imprisonment was legal. After lengthy consideration and debate Lord Mansfield, the Chief Justice, decreed that;

> The state of slavery is such a nature that it is incapable of being introduced on any reasons, moral or political, but only by positive law, which preserves its force long after the reasons, occasions, and time itself from whence it was created, is erased from memory. It [slavery] is so odious, that nothing can be suffered to support it, but positive law. Whatever inconveniences, therefore, may follow from the decision, I cannot say this case is allowed or approved by the law of England, and therefore the black must be discharged. (Usherwood, 1981)

And so in 1772 Somerset was freed - but the case only ruled against his forcible removal from England. However, this was a landmark case and Lord Mansfield did raise the deeper moral question of the 'odious' practice of enslavery that gave fuel to the Abolitionist Movement. After the 1772 court judgment James Somerset disappeared from public view and is presumed to have died in Britain shortly after.

Although Britain has always been endemically xenophobic, particularly towards continental Europeans, a person was more likely to be judged upon their religious belief or their social standing rather than the colour of their skin (Kaufmann, 2017). For many, travel beyond parish limits was an occasion. So anyone beyond that sphere of acquaintance was treated with some suspicion; they were 'strangers', irrespective of their ethnicity. It was only with the growth of the industrial revolution that the rural population became more mobile. Nineteenth century urbanisation, focused around industrial centres, saw the emergence of a social stratum of working class people. Eric Hobsbawm (cited Harris, 1993:7) refers to this as 'a distinctive, national, homogenous working-class rooted in a common experience of advanced mass production.' Of course, there had always been a form of class structure within Britain from very early history; there had been the ruling class of royalty and nobility, and the peasantry, with the clergy and academics sitting somewhere in between. But with the arrival of the Victorian era the class structure became more distinct; the working, middle, and upper classes (with some further stratification within each band). People identified within their own perceived social group and whilst there may have been aspirations to move socially upwards people tended to be judged upon their social standing rather than ethnicity.

Harriet Ann Jacobs was born into enslavement in North Carolina in 1813. After enduring many years of abuse she eventually managed to escape to the North in 1842. Her owner, Norcrom, earlier placed an advertisement in the *American Beacon* newspaper in July 1835, offering a reward for her capture and return[2]. After her escape she became an ardent abolitionist and in her 1861 autobiographical work *Incidents in the*

Life of a Slave Girl (under the pseudonym of Linda Brent) she describes a visit to England in 1845;

> For the first time in my life I was in a place where I was treated according to my deportment, without reference to my complexion ... Indeed, I entirely forgot it [skin colour] till the time came for us to return to America (cited Dickerson, 2008:60)

Her experience led her to claim that there was no colour prejudice in England. Because of the way that she dressed, spoke, behaved, and carried herself she moved in social circles that openly accepted her as an equal. Had she found herself in a different social class, amongst less polite society her experience may have been otherwise. Such was the case with two Bombay naval architects who recorded their experiences in their 1841 work *Journal of a Residence of 2 ½ years in Great Britain*. After a visit to some of the minor theatres in London, and specifically of Astley's Amphitheatre, they wrote;

> ... always to go to the boxes, which are frequented by a respectable class of people, and there they will receive much civility and attention, but never for the sake of economy go to the pit or gallery of any of them ... because these places are always resorted to by the humbler classes, as well as by rogues, thieves, and pickpockets, and should a stranger happen to be there, he is often teased and insulted with gross and abusive language by these fellows ... we state this from the treatment we once experienced at Astley's Amphitheatre, but on our discovering the error, we immediately left the place ... And here we would inform our countrymen that the majority of the lower orders in England are very rude in their manners and behaviour towards strangers, whom they do not like to see in their own country. (Nowrojee & Merwanjee, 1841:109-110)

Clearly, Nowrojee and Merwanjee were in the wrong place with the wrong crowd. They were teased and abused, not specifically because of their ethnicity but because they were perceived as being of a different class. By their own admission, when mixing with the 'respectable class' they were treated with civility. One can imagine that if Harriet Jacobs had moved outside of the social circles into which she had been accepted, she may well have experienced the same as Nowrojee and Merwanjee. As we have seen, there had been a non-white heritage population within Great Britain for many centuries that had been generally accepted. So at what point did the socio-xenophobic attitude prevalent within British society become more focused upon skin colour and race rather than just 'foreignness'?

The Abolition of Slavery left Britain a divided country. There were those, chiefly the capitalists, who remained against it, as much of their income and wealth had been derived from the sugar plantations in the West Indies. Mill owners continued to trade with the cotton producing plantations of the southern United States, still worked by slave labour. Only on 22 September, 1862 did Abraham Lincoln declare;

> That, on the first day of January [1863] – all persons held as slaves, within any state – shall be thence henceforward and forever free. (cited Wilson, 2016:377)

In the early part of the American Civil War, Confederate flags were seen on display in some areas of Lancashire, England, and ships were built for the Confederate navy on Merseyside. As the import of American cotton declined during the American Civil War, so mill owners were forced to sourced cotton from elsewhere: India, China, and Egypt.

Many notable members of British society; politicians such as William Pitt and William Wilberforce; members of the clergy such as John Wesley; artists such as Joshua Reynolds; and writers such as William Wordsworth and Alexander Pope all backed the pro-abolition movement. But some, such as Leeds born Wilson Armistead, a Quaker, recognised that post-abolition society still had not fully embraced the notion of the equality of man.

England has given to the nations a noble example, in abolishing, at a great sacrifice, a system of great injustice and cruelty in which she had long taken a guilty part ... Yet notwithstanding the evils of Slavery are becoming increasingly felt and acknowledged, it is evident that there still exists in the minds of many who deprecate the whole system as unjust, a strong delusion with regard to the moral and intellectual capacities of the Coloured portion of mankind, and as regards their proper station in the scale of intelligent existence. (Armistead, 1848:3-4)

Charles Dickens, that notable proponent of social reform, reflects the sentiments of Armistead's comments in his own writing. In an article entitled *The Noble Savage,* he launches into an oxymoronic diatribe against the sentimentalism shown by some towards the idealised concept of the wild human uncorrupted by civilisation;

To come to the point at once, I beg to say that I have not the least belief in the Noble Savage. I consider him to be a prodigious nuisance and an enormous superstition ... I call him a savage, and I call a savage a something highly desirable to be civilised off the face of the earth ... Mine are no new views on the noble savage. The greatest writers on natural history found him out long ago. BUFFON knew what he was, and showed why he is the sulky tyrant that he is to his women, and how it happens (Heaven be praised!) that his race is spare in numbers ... It is my opinion that if we retained in us anything of the noble savage, we could not get rid of it too soon ... To conclude as I began. My position is, that if we have anything to learn from the Noble Savage, it is what to avoid. His virtues are a fable; his happiness is a delusion; his nobility, nonsense ... and the world will be all the better when his place knows him no more. (Dickens, 1853)

The Victorian era, 1837 – 1901, was the era of the enquiring mind. There was a fascination with the outside world, especially other cultures and the 'exotic'. Travel was Anglocentric, in the sense that the focus of travel was on the 'Britishness' of the travellers with little regard for the countries or cultures being visited. They travelled within their own British 'bubble', a trait still witnessed today when many British tourists seek out the 'British' pubs and cafes, eat 'British' food, read 'British' newspapers, and have very little contact with the local people. As the British Empire expanded it opened up a knowledge of ethnic diversity. This fascination with the 'exotic' embraced all classes and was central to how the Victorian British tried to make sense of their place in the world (Assael, 2005). Post-abolition Britain had a degree of national guilt over slavery, even if sections of society still had not come to terms with it. Attitudes towards race, especially towards people of colour, were varied. There were those who displayed an 'avuncular' attitude, in the same way as an adult might feel towards a child. There were others of a more enquiring mind who viewed them with genuine, if objectifying, interest and then there were those, the nationalist and foreigner-hating, who treated them little more than a spectacle. But embodied in all of these attitudes there was the underpinning ideology that the white Anglo-Saxon was superior to other races. In actual fact, defining exactly what 'race' is has always been a hot discussion point for both modern sociologists and geneticists. Rutherford (2016) makes the point;

> There are plenty of genetic differences and physical differences that emerge from those genes between people and peoples, but none that align with the way we talk about 'race' … The great irony is this; the science of genetics was founded specifically on the study of racial inequality, by a racist [Francis Galton]. The history of my field [genetics] is inextricably entwined with ideas that we now find toxic: racism, empire, prejudice, and eugenics. (Rutherford, 2016:215)

There were those who sought justification in Old Testament references to the 'curse of Ham'. Ham was cursed by his father Noah and is held by some to be the antecedent of African peoples. His curse was that he left the Ark black skinned and therefore the curse fell upon him and his descendants. Others felt that the bible supported the notion of master and slave. In the United States, this was echoed in a later published statement by the Missionary Society of the South Carolina Conference of the Methodist Episcopal Church;

We denounce the principles and practice of the abolitionists, *in toto* ... We believe that the Holy Scriptures so far from giving any countenance to this delusion, do, unequivocally authorise the relation of master and slave (Armistead, 1853. Tract 8:23)

Yet others were ready to interpret (or perhaps misinterpret) the new scientific theories of Charles Darwin who, amongst other ideas, promoted the thought of 'natural selection' and 'survival of the fittest'. Although an ardent abolitionist all of his life, Darwin believed in the superiority of the white races and shared contemporary views on 'savages' (Bethencourt, 2013). As early as 1839, in his collection of notes and diaries which he published as *The Voyage of the Beagle*, he was making reference to natives he came across in Tierra del Fuego with the comment, 'one can hardly make oneself believe that they are fellow creatures'. In *The Descent of Man* (1871), Darwin had written 'the civilised races of man will almost certainly exterminate, and replace, the savage races throughout the world'. Even liberal reformers such as Henry Fawcett clung to the notion that there were inferior races;

The lot of the whole human race might be improved if inferior races were gradually enlightened and elevated, by bringing them into contact with the ideas and institutions of a high civilisation (cited Harris, 1993:23 3)

But few were ready to acknowledge that Africa had been the cradle of all civilisations. Armistead (1848:120-121) makes the point clearly;

With regard to the intellectual capabilities of the African race, it may be observed that Africa was once the nursery of science and literature, and it was from thence that they were disseminated among the Greeks and Romans. Solon, Plato, Pythagoras, and others of the master spirits of the ancient Greeks, performed pilgrimages into Africa in search of knowledge ... Africa once had her churches, her colleges, and repositories of learning and of science.

C. F. Volney (1890:15) makes a similar statement;

There [in Ethiopia] a people, now forgotten, discovered, while others were yet barbarians, the elements of the arts and sciences. A race of men now rejected from society for their sable skin and frizzled hair, founded on the study of the laws of nature, those civil and religious systems which still govern the universe.

Had Darwin had the benefit of modern genetic research findings he would have realised that as a species we are all of African heritage; we all share, in some small part, a common genetic make-up; we all come from the same roots.

When humans first ventured out of Africa some 60,000 years ago, they left genetic footprints still visible today … These great migrations eventually led the descendants of a small group of Africans to occupy even the farthest reaches of the earth. Our species is an African one; Africa is where we first evolved, and where we have spent the majority of our time on Earth. The earliest fossils of recognisably Homo Sapiens appear in the fossil record of Omo Kibish in Ethiopia, around 200,000 years ago. (*National Geographic*)

Post abolition Britain accepted by and large (although grudgingly in certain sectors) the notion that enslavery was wrong and yet was quite happy to be amused and entertained by the racial stereotype of the 'negro' minstrel. Many white performers would 'black up', using burnt cork or shoe polish, to represent a caricature of a black person. In British folk tradition there are Folk dances, Morris dances, and Mummer's Plays that often include a blackface character. These are rooted in pagan traditions and had

Blackface minstrel c. 1890 *(Library of Congress)*

no overtly intentional racial connotations; the black face was simply a symbolic mask, or convention, that represented the social outsider or the scapegoat. It was not until the interface between Christianity and pagan religions that the black mask, or face, became equated to something bad or evil rather than just the 'outsider'; the curse of Ham. Literary figures such as Othello, in Shakespeare's play of the same name, had always been played by white actors in blackface. This was a matter of artistic necessity as there were no black actors available in Britain to play such roles at that time, the precedent had not yet been established. Not until the black American actor Ira Aldridge, nicknamed the African Roscius, arrived in Britain in 1824 did a black person first play Othello. However, his first appearance in the role at the Covent Garden Theatre in London gained a mixed review[3].

Although some scholars may have attributed the blackface with representing evil, in the case of *Othello* it is actually the white character of Iago who is the villain. It is true that Othello himself is the scapegoat and the social outsider in the play, although in the review it is clear that it is Aldridge who is being singled out as the outsider, and not necessarily the character he was playing. Much is made of his physical appearance, having 'an oily and expressive mulatto tint'. Fortunately Aldridge persevered and spent most of his working life in Britain, touring in many plays, in some of which he appeared whiteface to take on the title roles in *King Lear*, and *Richard III*. Between 1723 and 1823 the 'Black Act' in Britain made it a punishable offence to blacken one's face with intent to commit the offence of poaching. It was not until the blackface minstrels arrived on the scene in Britain in the 1840s that we witness the portrayal of blackness for the entertainment of a white audience, and subsequent racial stereotyping (Strausbaugh, 2007). The blackface minstrels burlesqued the language and distorted the image of the enslaved African. One of the earlier white actors who exploited the blackface role was the American Thomas D Rice. In 1828 he popularised the comic song *Jump Jim Crow* and portrayed this character as a nimble buffoon but prone to laziness and untrustworthiness. This caricature reinforced the racist perception of the enslaved African as not being fit for integration. However, *Jim Crow* became a very popular entertainment and Rice was very often mobbed when he performed.

Jim Crow c. 1833 *(Library of Congress)*

In 1833, at a performance of Shakespeare's *Richard III* at the Bowery in New York, he was mobbed by an enthusiastic audience[4]. Strausbaugh likens Rice to the 'Elvis' of his day, with blackface minstrelsy as the 'rock & roll', such was the impact of the genre (Strausbaugh 2007). Certainly the music was very different from the prevalent sentimental ballads and concert music. *Jim Crow* had a catchy repetitive tune that, once heard, it was difficult to get out of your mind. The song of *Jim Crow* arrived in Britain before Rice himself. In December 1833, after a performance of *King Lear* in a Liverpool theatre, was presented;

> An admired and popular American Nigger Song, called "JIM CROW", in character, by Mr. Benwell. (*Liverpool Standard and General Commercial Advertiser*, 6 December 1833)

There is no mention of Mr. Benwell appearing blackface but looking at contemporary images of such shows we can assume that in all probability he did. By the summer 1836, Rice was appearing on the London stage of the Royal Surrey Theatre to great acclaim. He performed as the character Bone Squash Diabolo, and presented a farce entitled *The Virginian Mummy*, as well as singing *Jim Crow*[5]. It is interesting to note in which part of the theatre Rice was so well received, the gallery, especially in respect of the comments made by Nowrojee and Merwanjee above. Rice then went on to tour Europe, before returning to Britain and then back to America. His popularity spawned many imitators, and blackface minstrelsy became a highly popular entertainment during the Victorian period. At the Millstone Concert Hall in Bolton there appeared on the same programme a Mr. Mason ('negro singer') and 'the Far West negro minstrels'[6].

By mid-century many minstrel groups and individuals travelled across the Atlantic to appear in Britain. Initially, many of these were blackface white actors. But as time passed genuine African-American performers, or Ethiopian Singers as they often billed themselves, began to appear on the British stage. At first the British public was unsure how to react to them. Having been so used to seeing the caricature of the enslaved African, when presented with real black people performing with virtuosity it was confused. In one case, a 'negro minstrel company' was not initially well received by the audience and only when they left the stage and covered their faces with burnt cork were they accepted. The public's perception of the 'negro' was so skewed that they found it difficult to separate caricature from reality. Such minstrel groups perpetuated this caricature because they presented themselves in ways in which the white audience wanted to see them. Sheet music was produced so that in many homes popular 'negro' music was being played and enjoyed. Across Britain there were many minstrel societies set up where members would sing and play the latest 'hits'. It is an anomaly that the 'negro' was being ridiculed and celebrated at one and the same time. It is also interesting that the anti-slavery novel *Uncle Tom's Cabin* made its appearance during this period. Written by Harriet Beecher Stowe, it was published in America in book form in 1852. It was an immediate best seller, although it had its pro-slavery critics. When it appeared in Britain in May, the first edition sold 200,000 copies and within a few years there were over one million copies in circulation. The *Morning Advertiser* of 17 May gave it an extensive review;

An English edition of these heart-thrilling narratives of the horrors of the slave trade will doubtless prove a considerable incentive to the efforts of the benevolent in this country to procure its complete suppression, and at the same time they will serve to give a more correct and more general idea of the subject to the public than is commonly possessed ... in "Uncle Tom's Cabin" he will find an ample store of negro life sketches, abounding in scenes, situations, and dialogues of the loftiest order of interest, we leave this admirable book to work its mission of benevolence among the benevolent of this country.

Public readings were given, songs published, and by October 1852 the *Uncle Tom's Cabin Almanack* was being advertised as an 'abolitionist memento'. By December, stage performances were being advertised, as here in Astley's Amphitheatre, the kernel of the modern circus;

ASTLEY'S ROYAL AMPHITHEATRE

Proprietor and Manager Mr W. Batty

The greatest novelty of the season is Uncle Tom's Cabin. In consequence of the crowds unable to obtain admission nightly. The Grand Spectacle of Uncle Tom's Cabin will be repeated till further notice.

On TUESDAY, Dec. 21, and following Three Nights, the Entertainments will commence with the highly popular Dramatic Spectacle of UNCLE TOM'S CABIN.

(Sun (London), 21 December 1852)

One can only assume that the performers playing the enslaved characters were blackface white actors. And, to me, it seems incongruous that the serious novel that Beecher Stowe intended should be reduced to a 'Grand Spectacle'. Although it may have been the greatest anti-slavery novel of its time it also perpetuated the caricature of the enslaved African American in the minds of many of the British public, so accustomed had they become to being entertained by blackface minstrels. I am ashamed to say that this cultural perception continued as a form of entertainment on television in Britain as *The Black and White Minstrel Show* right through until 1978, and still continues today.

The concept of the 'Exotic Other' was also a big draw for circuses of the time. Just as many white actor-musicians appeared as blackface minstrels, so too did white circus performers appear in a variety of ethnic disguises. Many of Cooke's circus posters from the period, held in the Cryer Collection of the Wakefield Library in Britain, offer us entertainments such as the *Jumpers of Pekin*, the *Arab Boy*, the *Hindoo Somerset* [somersault] *Springer*, the *Sioux Indian, Jim Crow on Horseback*, and the *Idols of Mexico*. All of these acts were presented by Anglo-Saxon white artistes in make-up and appropriate costumes. This raises an interesting question. Were these performances on a par with blackface minstrelsy? Blackface performers *deliberately* set out to burlesque enslaved African-Americans through parody and ridicule. The circus performances

Jim Crow not Ducrow, on Horseback

Jim Crow on Horseback c. 1840 *(Library of Congress)*

mentioned above were either equestrian or acrobatic acts. The focus of the performance was the skill being demonstrated, with the exception of maybe *Jim Crow on Horseback*, with its direct links to blackface minstrelsy.

Although they might be deemed guilty in our modern understanding of cultural appropriation, I do not feel that, at that time, there was any deliberate attempt to mock or belittle any of the cultures they chose to represent. However, the use of non-white people as figures of entertainment was, and still is, harmful. These circus performances did cause offense although maybe not quite as pointed as blackface minstrels.

This was an age when Science met Spectacle. Ethnic groups and individuals, the exotic 'Other', were brought to Europe for 'scientific examination'. The strange and the different have long been objects of curiosity. Rather than acknowledge a common humanity it is easier (and sometimes psychologically safer for the spectator) to focus upon difference. In ancient Egypt black Sudanese dwarves were exhibited. During the days of the Roman Empire conquered 'barbarians and savages', those people who were different, non-Roman and therefore uncivilised (Adams, 1975), were paraded through the streets as a spectacle and to reinforce Roman superiority. Perhaps the most infamous case in nineteenth century Britain is that of the 'Hottentot Venus'. Sawtche (Sarah) Bartmann was born in the East Cape area of modern South Africa. She was enslaved as a child and then bought by a Dutch naval doctor who brought her to England in 1810. She was humiliatingly and degradingly exhibited naked throughout the country and men and women of all persuasions paid money to gape at her and to touch her – and much worse; being 'exotic' was equated with being sexually available. Her particular physical anatomy, steatopygia and macronymphy, were the subject of scientific debate. It is interesting to note that the nonmedical, and humiliating, term 'hottentot apron' is still used today for the condition of elongated labia. It was clear to doctors and scientists that she was an example of the black race's inferiority.

She died in Paris in 1815, at the early age of twenty-six. Her humiliation continued after her death, as she was dissected and her remains were displayed for many years, until 1975. It was only in 2002 that her remains were returned to South Africa and interred near the place of her birth.

The scientific fields of Ethnography and Anthropology really developed in the 1840s, both in the USA and in Europe. For these scientists there were two main modes of operation – study 'in the field' or having subjects brought to them for observation and examination. With expanding British colonisation, it was much cheaper to have 'human collections' brought to England. And so we see the rise of 'human zoos', a family group or a tribal group displayed for scientific study and popular entertainment. Ethnographic scenes were created and were promoted as to amuse, inform, and educate, such as the Japanese Village created in London in 1885. Some of these groups could be displayed in many venues; the science laboratory, a zoological park, at a world fair, in the music hall, or at a circus.

Colonel Harrison and his Pygmies. Late C19th Postcard (*Author's collection*)

... a visit to the zoological gardens, to the circus or to a 'negro village', was not just a chance to witness the diversity of humanity, it was an opportunity for the visitor to understand not only the Other's place in the world, but also his own (Barthe & Coutancier, 1995 cited Blanchard et al 2008:24)

Human zoos actually said little about the 'exotic' subjects on exhibition. They became little more than a pastiche of how the white European colonisers thought the 'inferior' races should be portrayed. These degrading exhibitions fed the public's need to clarify its own identity; the Self vs the Other. Growing imperial expansion established two broad racial worlds; the world of the ruling colonisers and the world of the subjugated natives. Commercial exploitation of these 'exotic' groups was rife. Many were trundled from one venue to another with the minimum of care and thought. Many suffered illness or died through exposure to diseases from which they had no immunity. But there were some who were treated well, with humanity. Some had 'contracts' of sorts and were paid enough for them to be able to send money home. This raises an interesting question. Could it be that in some cases these so called 'savages' were cleverly exploiting the white society by providing what that society thought it needed? As a colleague of mine commented;

Africans arrived with their own humanity but held it back to provide the roles the British public wanted. (Williams, 2019)

Whilst Williams is talking specifically about people from Africa his comments could equally well apply to other racial groups put to exhibition; indigenous people from Java, Polynesia, Egypt, Australasia, and North America to name but a few. When Buffalo Bill (William F. Cody) brought his Wild West Show to Britain in 1887, native American performers were central to the show. They provided a narrative for how superior white Anglo-Saxon America had 'tamed' the wild-west and subjugated the natives. But with Cody's shows there was a difference. Firstly, these native Americans were not passive exhibits to be gaped at, they were an active part of the shows and could display the physical skills

Folk Show. Carl Hagenbeck Circus. Late C19th Postcard *(Author's collection)*

of horsemanship that were so prized in their society. In their encampment that accompanied the Wild-West show they could withdraw from view if they so wished into their tepees. Secondly, all of the native performers were contracted and paid; they were there because they chose to be. After a European tour in 1890, there had been incidents that resulted in a ban by the U. S. Secretary of the Interior on all native Americans performing in Wild-West shows. Native American performers went on to argue for the ban to be lifted to allow them to still work for Cody and to be financially independent. Black Heart, from the Lakota Sioux tribe and a veteran performer with Cody, made the case that;

> If Indian wants to work at any place and earn money, he wants to do so; white man got privilege to do same – any kind of work he wants … When this show is ready to go again, I want to go with it (Maddra, 2006;79)

Cody eventually managed to get the ban overturned and many native Americans toured with his 1891-1892 Wild-West Show to Europe. But this was moving towards the close of the Victorian era.

In spite of 'human zoos' masquerading as ethnological study, degrading blackface entertainers, and an endemic post abolition racism, there had been a variety of ethnic performers throughout the nineteenth century in the British circus. Initially beginning with an influx of European performers, the circus was a repository for all that was strange and wonderful and the ring was a democratic place (Assael, 2005). The 'Exotic Other' was here for all to see. Performance skill became the benchmark by which an individual was judged, not by the colour of skin, nationality or race. One was *del circo* first, then everything else after. And it is within this context that we now examine individual performers of non-white heritage who rose to fame during the Victorian period. Some of these arrived in Britain with no circus background; some came from a line of circus families; and yet others were born in Britain. Skin tones ranged from the light tawny to the deepest black. Nationalities ranged

Native Americans as part of Buff Bill's Wild West show c. 1886 *(Library of Congress)*

from the western native American to the people of Japan. It mattered little, because the circus can be perceived as one family; diverse and accepting, and it allows individuals to achieve on merit rather than race, belief, or nationality. As David Konyot, himself a descendent of two Jewish circus families, wrote (2020);

> I have always stressed that around an average Circus Tent you will find a mixture of ethnicities, religions, creeds, beliefs and more importantly, none of that matters, we are the last bastion of the philosophy 'You are what you do', our time in front of an audience defines us, everything else is just practising or waiting for the next show … that unity of purpose to please the public is what binds us, inspires us and makes us what we are. We Are Circus.

We do not know if this sentiment was shared by minority performers in the past as their thoughts on the matter were rarely, if ever, written down. Instances of racism did occur, as we shall see. However, much of this was institutional and underpinned by the social ideologies of the time. In the chapters that follow I set out to explore how, in the face of this, notable minority individuals achieved success.

Trade card advertising Buck's Stoves and Ranges. Late C19th *(Author's collection)*

Notes

1. *Minutes from the Abolitionist Committee*, May 22 1787, British Library Add 21254 (152f)

2. *Runaway notice for Harriet Jacobs.* Published the *American Beacon* 4 July 1835. Available online at; https://www.pbs.org/wgbh/aia/part4/4h1541b.html

3. *Sun (London)* 11 April 1833

4. *Public Ledger and Daily Advertiser* 19 January 1833

5. *Morning Advertiser* 29 July 1836 and 2 August 1836

6. *Bolton Chronicle* 28 September 1844

Joseph Hillier. Image from *The Squib* 30 July 1842 *(Author's collection)*

CHAPTER 2
THE WILD COSSACK RIDER
– JOSEPH HILLIER

On the morning of 8 June 1841, Astley's Amphitheatre was destroyed by fire. Nothing new one might think, fires in wooden built theatres were a common occurrence at this time. However, the destruction of Astley's had a consequence that would give two ethnic performers, of differing backgrounds, the opportunity to achieve fame and fortune.

> Astley's Amphitheatre, the scene of the glories of old Philip Astley, and of the more recent triumphs of Ducrow, is now a heap of ruins. Shortly after four o'clock this morning (Tuesday) a tremendous fire broke out at the back of the Theatre, and in less than three hours the whole of the premises, with the exception of the front towards the Westminster Bridge Road, was totally destroyed. The fire is supposed to have had its origin in the stable facing Stangate Street, and to have arisen from some defect in the gas pipes but on this subject it is impossible at present to obtain any accurate information.

> Three of Mr Ducrow's valuable horses have perished in the flames, and an unfortunate donkey, which was in the stables at the time, has also fallen a sacrifice. We are sorry to add, that this calamitous fire has not been unattended with loss of human life. One of Mr Ducrow's female servants was suffocated in the flames and the body, dreadfully burned, was this morning dug out of the ruins. (*Freeman's Journal* 8 June 1841)

The cause of the fire remained a mystery for some time, but at the inquest into the death of the servant, Elizabeth Briton, it was found that the fire was caused accidentally but that the theatre's fireman had been negligent and should have seen the fire earlier on his rounds before it had managed to take hold of the largely wooden building. The fire probably started under the stage and it was suggested that paper from fireworks used during the performance had fallen through cracks in the stage boards and lain smouldering on the wooden joists before later igniting. Whatever the cause the experience deeply disturbed Ducrow and he fell into a deep depression, as reported in *The Bradford Observer* of 12 August 1841:

> Ducrow, who had been for so many years a popular favourite and a nonpareil in his own peculiar way, is so seriously affected by his recent loss, as to be under restraint. The aberration of mind is too marked to be mistaken.

His condition worsened and he died in January 1842. Ducrow had been a flamboyant figure in life and continued to be so in death. In spite of the loss of his amphitheatre, Ducrow died a significantly wealthy man. His estate was valued at 50,000 pounds sterling, equivalent today to approximately two-and-a-quarter million pounds. But his legacy was far more. In Ducrow's company was a young man named Joseph Hillier of a non-white ethnicity. Ducrow must have held Hillier in high regard, for in his Will he left him the princely sum of 300 pounds sterling[1], more than any other individual bequest to a non-family member. With this money Hillier made a down payment of 270 pounds sterling (the residue of the bequest after tax) to Ducrow's widow to buy Ducrow's stud of horses, which comprised of seventeen horses and seven ponies. The total cost of the stud was 700 pounds sterling, and Hillier agreed to pay quarterly instalments of 25 pounds sterling until the balance had been paid. In this way the name of Ducrow continued and Hillier became the sole equestrian director of his own company.

Hillier is a shadowy character and little, if anything, is known about his early years. Ducrow 'discovered' him when he took his circus to Milan in 1820 and brought him back to England. Whether Hillier was already working in the circus or whether he was 'sold' to Ducrow is not known. Exactly how old Hillier was at the time is uncertain. The three extant records[2] referring to Hillier's date of birth differ widely and give us a time frame anywhere between 1779 and 1819! Young children were often 'apprenticed' to circus owners but I suspect that Hillier could not have been any younger than four or five years old when taken on by Ducrow.

Hillier was born in Italy and throughout his career he was often billed as the 'Italian Rider', as here in the *Bristol Times and Mirror* of 2 April 1842;

> Signor Hillier, the Italian Rider, will give his popular and characteristic delineation, on the backs of several horses, as THE RUSSIAN DESPATCH BEARER, wherein he will execute some extraordinary Feats of Equitation (peculiar to himself), at the same time Riding, Conducting, and Managing a Troop of Fleet Steeds.

In a later Insolvency Court case Hillier was also referred to as being born in Italy[3]. His swarthy complexion and black hair gave rise to comments about him working so hard that he was 'black in the face' and at least one nineteenth century writer referred to him as a 'nigger' (Blackburn 1880), although this was often a generic term used to describe anyone who was non-white.

A descendent of Hillier provided the information that his father was possibly a south Asian seaman, and that he was illegitimate. An illustration in *The Squib* of 30 July 1842 shows a dark faced Hillier performing the act known as *The Courier of St Petersburg*. Although there are no extant photographs of Hillier that we know of, there is one of his son by a second marriage, William Angelo Hillier. Joseph Hillier married a Lucy Butfoy and a photograph of her shows her to be distinctly European looking. The photograph of William Hillier clearly shows a young man with swarthy features, so maybe he took after his father rather than his mother. The photograph of William Hillier's three daughters also show that two of them have the features as their father. So it is highly possible that Joseph Hillier was the product of an Indian father and an Italian mother. Information is very difficult to come by; early Italian genealogical records are notoriously difficult to access. Initial research has shown no Italian baptism records for a 'Joseph Hillier'. Ducrow probably anglicised the name; Joseph from Giuseppe – but Hillier? We return to the children of Hillier's second marriage for a clue. Several of them had Italian middle names and the first born in 1862 was named Garibaldi Butfoy Hillier, after his mother's family name. The second born in 1864 was named Joseph (even more confusing!) Menotte Hillier, presumably after his father's family name. If so, then searching for a Giuseppe Menotte (and variants) produced a possible candidate; Giuseppe Manetti born in 1813 to a Maria Collini[4.] Now, to me, it is a bit of a coincidence that the Italian word for hill should be *Collina*. Is it possible that Ducrow used this as the basis for naming Giuseppe as Joseph Hillier? Purely a theory at present.

(Left) William Angelo Hillier *(Reproduced with permission of David Tonkin)*
(Right) Daughters of William Angelo Hillier *(Reproduced with permission of David Tonkin)*

Hillier first appeared in England in Ducrow's production of *Cortez, or the Conquest of Mexico* at Covent Garden on 5 November 1823 (Davies, 2017). By 1827 he was performing solo in Ducrow's company at the Arena, on York Street in Manchester;

> In the course of the evening, and, for the first time here, a new comic Extravaganza, on a single horse, by Mr. Hillier called THE APE OF BRAZIL (*Manchester Courier and Lancashire General Advertiser* 3 March 1827)

and, on 4 August 1829 this description of his *Cossack Riding* act was given in the *Weekly Dramatic Register*.

> [Hillier] rode with a most extraordinary power of retaining his hold on the horse, he went at full gallop, tumbling, reeling, under and over, and all about the animal, yet never coming to the ground, with really frightful celerity and cleverness.

In 1834 he married for the first time, to an Elizabeth Reekie. She is listed on the 1841 British Census returns[5] as an equestrian and appeared in many of Ducrow's shows.

> Mr. and Madame Ducrow contribute, conjointly with Signor and Mrs. Hillier, some agreeable equestrian exercises, which are executed with extraordinary neatness and precision (*Globe* 21 May 1841)

She would soon be performing as a solo artiste, taking on some of the central roles in dramatic equestrian pieces, as here in Bristol at *Ducrow's National Olympic Arena of Arts*;

> CATHARINE OF RUSSIA. This splendid scene will terminate with a Cotillion and Waltz in which each horse will dance a Pas Seuel. Catharine of Russia ….. Mrs. Hillier (*Bristol Mercury* 2 April 1842)

And in Liverpool at the Royal Amphitheatre;

MAZEPPA, or THE WILD HORSE … Olinska …….. Mrs. Hillier. The SCENES of the CIRCLE will introduce the unequalled Performances of the following Native and Foreign Artists; Signor Hillier, the Great Italian Rider … (*Liverpool Mail* 3 June 1843)

She was clearly an accomplished horsewoman and actress in her own right. Joseph and Elizabeth had three children together; Joseph (very confusing), Grace, and Robert William. Grace from a very early age was also performing and there is a record in the *Bibliothèque Nationale de France*[6] confirming this:

> Grace Hillier, ageé de 6 ans ½, Ecuyère au Cirque Nationale de Paris [Grace Hillier, aged 6 ½ years, equestrienne at the Cirque Nationale of Paris. *Author's translation*]

By 1836 Hillier was well established with Ducrow, not only as an accomplished performer but also as the equestrian director. In his displays of horsemanship he was able to combine his wild Cossack style riding with more traditional British figures. Here, in an item from *The Iris* of 15 November 1836 is a description of his act *The British Fox Hunter*:

> After throwing himself off the horse and afterwards running by its side with the speed of a deer, he would bound on the saddle in an instant, down again in a moment, and planks being placed during the time he was going round [the ring], probably 5 feet high, the horse and its late rider leapt side by side over two or three obstructions placed near together, several times repeating this most astonishing feat of activity.

In early 1843 he was appearing in Liverpool, where he was involved in a court case over licensing infringements when he presented an act called *The Horseman of the Rialto*. By the June the company was in Hull. He then embarked on a European tour, to Hamburg, Paris, and Vienna. At that time he listed his property to the value of 1,200 pounds sterling. But all did not go well. It was a financial disaster. His stud of horses, costumes, and properties were sold by auction in Hamburg in 1843 to satisfy his creditors.

Signor Hillier ... has lately been induced to visit the Continent with the stud and principal exhibitants of the arena. They embarked some weeks since for Hamburgh [sic] impressed with the idea, from the late proprietor's [Ducrow] success in the Continental cities, that a similar result would attend the prestige of his name. It is to be regretted that the reverse has been the result. The company opened at the Circus Gymnasticus [erected in 1808 on the Prater in Vienna], and after having performed for some weeks with considerable loss each night of representation, Signor Hillier as compelled to close his arena, from the liabilities incurred during his stay there, to announce for sale the stud of horses, dresses, theatrical appointments, &c., to satisfy his creditors. This is a lamentable issue to the exertions and deservings of Signor Hillier, whose industry and honourable conduct since his connection with the equestrian profession, has merited the commendation of all those who appreciate artistical [sic] talent and private worth. (*The Era* 3 September 1843)

By 1845 he was back in London in the Insolvent Debtors Court. It appeared that the agreed quarterly payments to Ducrow's widow had not been paid and that he had lost most of his financial reserves. Even his mother-in-law made a claim upon his furniture in lieu of rent paid on a house in London. Stating that he was illiterate, he blamed the failings on those he had entrusted with his book keeping. The case was adjourned but he was acquitted at a later hearing. After this Hillier almost disappears from the press. He obviously continued with the circus to some success because he is mentioned in a short item in *The Era* of 30 January 1848:

Le Petit Ducrow, the adopted son of that 'Genius of the Ring', the late Andrew Ducrow, with Hillier and a small equestrian company in the Mauritius, drawing immense houses

This is the last mention in the media of Hillier performing with the circus. In 1849, the *Bombay Times*[7] records the arrival of the Hillier family in India. In 1859, his wife died of dysentery and he remarried in 1862. On the marriage record his profession was given as 'Riding Master'[8] and he continued working as such, teaching equitation, for the Nizam of Hyderabad, a fabulously wealthy Indian Prince, until his death from cholera in 1876[9].

Notes

1. *England & Wales, Prerogative Court of Canterbury Wills 1384-1858.*
   Online at https://www.ancestry.co.uk/interactive/5111/40
   611_309656-00537?pid=340250&backurl=https://search.
   ancestry.co.uk/cgi-bin/sse.dll?indiv%3D1%26dbid%3D5
   111%26h%3D340250%26tid%3D%26pid%3D%26useP-
   UB%3Dtrue%26_phsrc%3DAnq216%26_phstart%3Dsuc-
   cessSource&treeid=&personid=&hintid=&usePUB=true&_
   phsrc=Anq216&_phstart=successSource&usePUBJs=true&_
   ga=2.210490333.951192050.1591020761-8519783.1584367827

2. *1841 UK Census.* Online at https://www.ancestry.co.uk/
   interactive/8978/SRYHO107_1057_1058-0240?

(ii) *British India Office Marriages.* Online at https://search.findmypast.co.uk/
   record?id=BL%2FBIND%2F005137624%2F00041&paren-
   tid=BL%2FBIND%2FM%2F102743%2F1

(iii) *British India Office Deaths & Burials.* Online at https://
   search.findmypast.co.uk/record?id=BL%2F-
   BIND%2F005137636%2F00131&parentid=BL%2F-
   BIND%2FD%2F338634

3. *Morning Advertiser* 22 January 1845

4. *Italy Birth & Baptisms* 1806-1900, https://www.findmypast.co.uk/
   transcript?idR_677341955

5. *1841 Census.* Online at https://www.ancestry.co.uk/interac-
   tive/8978/SRYHO107_1057_1058-0240?pid=1017380
   1&backurl=https://search.ancestry.co.uk/cgi-bin/sse.
   dll?indiv%3D1%26dbid%3D8978%26h%3D10173801%
   26tid%3D%26pid%3D%26usePUB%3Dtrue%26_phs-
   rc%3Dsbc1441%26_phstart%3DsuccessSource&tree-

id=&personid=&hintid=&usePUB=true&_phs-
rc=sbc1441&_phstart=successSource&usePUB-
Js=true&_ga=2.186831786.301302419.1581328281-
1986502099.1539097385

6. Wild N. & Remy T., Le Cirque, *Iconographie. Catalogues de la bibliothèque de l'opera*, p.107, Bibliothèque Nationale de France

7. *Bombay Times* entry of arrivals 1849; https://search.fibis.org/frontis/bin/aps_detail.php?id=2384345

8. *British India Office Marriages*. Online at https://search.findmypast.co.uk/record?id=BL%2FBIND%2F005137624%2F00041&paren-tid=BL%2FBIND%2FM%2F102743%2F1

9. *British India Office Deaths & Burials*. Online at https://search.findmypast.co.uk/record?id=BL%2F-BIND%2F005137636%2F00131&parentid=BL%2F-BIND%2FD%2F338634

CHAPTER 3
A TRUE GENTLEMAN OF COLOUR – PABLO FANQUE

The death of Andrew Ducrow opened the door for another 'gentleman of colour' who performed under the name of Pablo Fanque. This was not his given name, he was born William Darby in the St Andrew's Workhouse in Norwich, in the east of England. To be placed in a Workhouse was a clear sign of destitution and such institutions were set up to provide shelter for those who could not support themselves. The record of his birth on 30 March 1810 gives, 'William son of John & Mary Darby late Stamp'[1], where the word 'late' refers to his mother's maiden name. This date is now generally accepted as the correct date of his birth, even though the inscription on his gravestone indicates a birth year of 1796. John and Mary Stamp did have a son named William who was born in 1796, but he died in 1797[2]. It was often the case that parents who had lost a child very early went on to have further children with the same given name. But what of William's heritage?

We know that William, referred to by his performing name of Fanque after he had joined the circus, was mentioned as a 'gentleman of colour' in some newspapers, and the photograph we have of him with his second wife shows a distinctly dark skinned individual. William had a little known sister, Frances Stamp Darby, who was also 'of colour', as recorded in this newspaper passage;

> Thursday se'nnight an inquest was held … on view of the body of a still-born bastard male child. It appears in evidence that the mother of the child, Frances Stamp Darby (a woman of colour), being in

the seventh month of her pregnancy, quarrelled with an Irishwoman named Hannant, a disgraceful scene of fighting and violence followed, and Hannant being the more powerful woman of the two, succeeded in throwing Darby backwards and then fell on her. Darby was taken home and there fainted; a premature labour followed in the course of a few days, and Darby was delivered of a still-born male child. (*Norfolk Chronicle* 4 June 1831)

Her baptism record[3] shows that they shared the same parents.

William's father was born in Norwich in 1766 but whether his grandfather was born in Norwich or not has not yet been established. One source[4] suggests that his great grandfather was born in St Kitts in the Caribbean and arrived in Norfolk as a sailor and settled there. What we can say is that William was at least a second generation black Briton.

As is the case with many of William's station details of his early life are unknown and it is unclear how he came to be with the circus. From the early nineteenth century, young boys could be 'apprenticed' from the age of ten years old. Britain was in the grip of a post-Napoleonic economic depression during his early years and many families had to look for Poor Relief, the system by which impoverished families looked to their Parish for support, as they were unable to keep themselves. William and his family were in the Norwich St. Andrews Workhouse during his early years, and there is always the possibility that the Guardians of the Workhouse placed him as an apprentice to a visiting circus – in this case *William Batty's Circus*. Batty would later become the owner of Astley's Amphitheatre. However, the *Guardians of Poor Court minute books 1813-1833 for Norwich* (Davies, 2017:28) hold no records of such an apprenticeship so it is quite possible that this was a private arrangement between John Darby and William Batty. Such arrangements was not uncommon during the nineteenth century, for both boys and girls. William, as Pablo Fanque, himself was to take on apprentices later in his career;

We understand there was no truth in the statement which appeared in our last paper with respect to the alleged sale of a boy to Monsieur Pablo Fanque. The lad was regularly indentured [apprenticed], and his father, so far from receiving a sum of money, was very glad that his son should be afforded so good an opportunity of earning a profitable livelihood. Monsieur Fanque, we are quite sure, from his character, would be incapable of taking part in any unworthy transaction. (*Cork Examiner* 3 January 1851)

It had earlier been reported that the boy had been sold to Fanque for the princely sum of two shillings. Money was however often given to parents as a bond for the apprentice and this lead to stories of children being sold to the circus, although stories of children being 'kidnapped' by circuses still abounded. Whether by apprenticeship, sale, or some other means William ended up with *Batty's Circus*. Although the exact dates are not known, it is commonly thought that his first appearance was with *Batty's Circus* in Norwich in 1821, appearing as 'Young Darby'[5]. This is, however, all secondary evidence and no primary record of *Batty's Circus* visiting Norwich at this time, or of a 'young Darby 'performing has come to light. Batty, like other circus proprietors was not shy of seeking publicity and relished any mention in the local press. I find it strange, therefore, that the first mention of Batty in Norwich appears in the *Norfolk Chronicle* of 14 April 1827, when a report on the Tomblands Fair (Castle Meadow) mentions;

… a more than usual number of travelling establishments … the most conspicuous of these was Mr Batty's troop of equestrians from Paris.

Certainly, during the period 1821 to 1827 many circuses are mentioned in the press; those of Powell, Adams, Ducrow, West, Woolford and Valentini, Davis, Saunders, Cooke, Bridges, Ryan, Antonio, and Samwell all get noted. But Batty is notably absent until 1827. In 1829 he is reported as performing at the Pantheon in Ranelagh Gardens in Norwich. Clearly he had been in France for some of that time and there is a tantalising hint in the *Sun (London)* of 19 December 1823 that mentions an un-named troupe of equestrians at a fête in Paris. Could this perhaps have been Batty? If so, then he spent several years abroad. Perhaps the young William Darby was with him learning his trade?

At what point William Darby took the name Pablo Fanque is also a mystery. During the 1820s, the name Pablo was very much in the news, especially in the person of Colonel Pablo Chapalangara, who was a Spanish revolutionary guerrilla leader against the French, who had invaded Spain in support of the monarchy. It is not impossible that Darby (or maybe Batty), looking for a more exotic name to match his looks, should choose Pablo. But Fanque? It has been suggested that Fanque was a contraction or even misspelling of the word 'fantastique' but fantastique has never appeared in the media in connection with Pablo. The first recording of Pablo Fanque working with William Batty was given in the *Leicester Chronicle* of 30 November 1833, where one could witness; 'PABLO FANQUE'S SURPRISING EVOLUTIONS On the Corde Floxo'

The Corde Floxo, or sometimes also referred to as the Corde Volante, or Corde Crescent, was a U shaped loop of rope on which the performer would have presented acrobatic feats whilst the rope was swinging. It is more commonly known today as a Cloud Swing. Although Fanque became later known as an equestrian, this type of performance would have been representative of the training he would have received as an apprentice. It would have given him a grounding in the physical skills and proprioception critical for his trick riding. In his 1871 obituary it was stated that;

> Pablo was trained in a good though severe school, that of the late Mr. Batty, of Astley's circus, and he never forgot the rough but practical lessons he there received (*Leeds Times* 13 May 1871)

The life of a young acrobat would have been tough and physical and, to our modern eyes, somewhat cruel. Low (1895) give a detailed account of how Victorian child acrobats were trained, an example of which is given below;

> Stories of little boys having their spines broken at the age of two (to make them supple!), of little, writhing, creatures condemned to stand for hours daily with one leg strapped up, and of a multitude of other horrors, were impressed upon my youthful mind …

Fanque would first have learned vaulting, leaping, and acrobatics, and it was for this that he became well known. By February 1834, Batty's circus was in Southampton where, among the many 'Olympic Exploits ', was;

> PABLO FANQUE, the American Voltigeur [an acrobat, in circus terms] and Flying Mercury, will make his first appearance here and exhibit his Performances on the CORDE VOLANTE, upon which he is not surpassed by any Performer in Gymnastic Exercises (*Hampshire Advertiser* 15 February 1834)

American? Perhaps this was an allusion to his colour, the Slavery Abolition Act had only been passed in the previous year. The following week, in the same newspaper, was a more descriptive account of his act, with particular reference to his colour; the first direct reference seen.

> The Entertainments will commence with FEATS OF LEAPING, by Pablo Fanque, the man of colour, the loftiest jumper in England, who will take a number of surprising leaps without the assistance of any elastic apparatus – first, over a garter 12ft. high – second, through a hoop 2ft. 6ins. In diameter – third, through cross hoops – fourth, through a balloon 2ft. 9ins. In diameter – fifth, through two balloons – sixth, through a military drum 4ft. 6ins. long – seventh, will take a surprising leap over 10 horses – eighth, will leap through a hoop of real steel daggers – and lastly, will take an unparalleled leap over A POST CHAISE [a closed four wheel coach] LENGTHWAYS! (*Hampshire Advertiser* 22 February 1834)

William Darby, known as Pablo Fanque. Image originally published in the *Worlds Fair* 22 March 1913 *(Reproduced with permission of the National Fairground and Circus Archive)*

As well as opening the show, he made a later appearance on the Corde Volante. He certainly was an adept performer and well received by the public.

It is interesting to note that in the above advertisement he was reported as *the* man of colour. By using the definite article, William Batty's advertising elevated Fanque to a position of some importance; he was more than just *a* man of colour, grouped with all the others of his skin colour. Using *the* added emphasis to his colour. Within the context of the time, a tall dark skinned man with an exotic sounding name was the embodiment of the 'Exotic Other'. But Fanque did not perform in ethnic 'costume' and neither did he parody his ethnicity. It was his skill that was applauded and he proved that he was an accomplished performer because of that skill and not the colour of his skin. Throughout his career there is no evidence to suggest that Fanque was prejudiced against in any way because of his ethnicity. Some years after his death, the Rev. Thomas Horne, chaplain of the Showman's Guild, wrote of Fanque, 'The camaraderie of the Ring has but one test, ability'[6]. A lack of evidence does not necessarily mean that there is no evidence and I am sure that Fanque did come across instances of prejudice in his life but it would seem, from all accounts, that he was a thoroughly respected member of society. There is one documented incident, and that is found in the autobiography of his friend, the renowned clown William Wallett. He wrote;

> For a few days I amused myself with Pablo Fanque fishing in the Isis. Pablo was a very expert angler and would usually catch as many fish as five or six of us within sight of him put together. This suggested a curious device. You must know that Pablo is a coloured man. One of the Oxonians, with more love for angling than skill, thought there must be something captivating in the complexion of Pablo. He resolved to try. One morning, going down to the river an hour or two earlier than usual, we were astonished to find the experimental philosophic

angler with his face blacked after the most approved style of the Christy Minstrels. (Wallett, 1890:73)

Angling was considered a 'peaceful' and 'respectable' social pursuit and men (women were not encouraged) fished in canals, rivers, and ponds (Locker, 2014). However, I think the above instance perhaps reflects a degree of ignorance on the part of the Oxonian rather than a calculated racial slur in assuming the cause and effect of having a dark skin.

We think of Fanque as being primarily an equestrian; certainly most current accounts of his life make reference to that aspect. However, it was for Leaping, Vaulting, the Corde Volante, and the Slack Rope that he became famous during the earlier part of his career.

The first mention of him as an equestrian appeared in the *Manchester Times* of 31 March 1838, where he was referred to as 'Mr. Pablo Fanque – the Great African Equestrian' (another nod to his ethnicity). On the same programme, with *Batty's Circus* in Manchester, we find;

Master Pablo, the Infant of Prodigy, only six years old, will go through his dating Evolutions on the Tight Rope.

This Master Pablo had first been mentioned in the press when *Batty's Circus* had been in Bath during November 1837. Who was this child? It is thought that he was William Banham Darby, born in Norwich in 1828, the illegitimate child of Fanque and a Maria Banham. There is no recorded marriage for Fanque and Maria Banham. In December, Master Pablo was referred to as being 'the offspring of African parents'[7] and later as the 'gem of Africa'[8]. Both comments clearly referring to his ethnicity, although there is no record that Maria Banham was a woman of colour. Master Pablo was an accomplished tight rope artist, and one can imagine that he learned much from his father. They frequently appeared on the same programme, as here in Leeds;

WONDERFUL LEAPS of Pablo Fanque.

> The apparent ease with which he rises to an amazing height and passes over distant objects has universally gained for him the appellation of "The Loftiest Leaper in the World". Without the aid of a springboard, he will jump over a Garter Fourteen Feet from the ground, through a Hoop of Daggers two and a half feet in diameter, Two Hoops across, through a Hoop of Real Fire, and over 10 horses, &c., &c. … Master PABLO FANQUE, the Youngest Performer in the World; whose Precious Talents have obtained for him the Appellation of The Gem of Africa, the Wonder of the World, will go through some Pleasing Feats on the Tight Rope. (*Leeds Times* 2 June 1838)

But on 3 December 1838, when Batty's circus was in Edinburgh, the *Caledonian Mercury* recorded that 'Master Pablo Fanque will appear in an act of horsemanship'. Clearly something else that he had learned from his father. Fanque had trained first as an acrobat before progressing to equestrianism; his son likewise.

If one reads the common history of Pablo Fanque it would be easy to assume that he spent all of his early career with *William Batty's Circus*, travelling the length and breadth of the United Kingdom; from Southampton to Edinburgh and over to Ireland. This is not so. In June and July of 1836, Fanque appeared with *Ryan's Circus* in Birmingham, the advertising claiming that Mr. Ryan had engaged the 'loftiest jumper' in the world at considerable expense. Fanque gave his exhibition of Leaping as described above in the *Hampshire Advertiser* 1834. Was it the lure of money that took Fanque to *Ryan's Circus*? We will never know.

Fanque returned to *Batty's Circus* for the December/January season In Dublin, where he appeared on the billing alongside Pablo Paddington. He also spent a few months working for Andrew Ducrow, the future owner of Astley's. In March 1839 he was in Birmingham and then from April through to September he appeared at Astley's in London, under Ducrow's management, in a rather strange act;

... to be followed by an Extraordinary Gymnastic Scenic Ballet of Action, for the purpose of bringing forward the Extraordinary Phenomenon Pablo Fanque, to be called Jumping Jean of the Jungle; or, the African Lion Hunter (*Bells New Weekly Messenger* 14 April 1839)

A further news report two week later gives us a little more detail;

... the extraordinary performances of PABLO FANQUE, in which he will introduce the Wild Chase of the Living Zebra on a Colossal Dromedary and beautiful Peru [sic] (*The Era* 28 April 1839)

In this instance I think we see an example of Fanque's ethnicity being exploited purely for entertainment purposes. Ducrow was playing on Fanque's colour and stereotypically portraying him as being 'of the jungle' and in taking the part of a wild savage chasing down exotic animals. One assumes that he was costumed according to his role, thereby reinforcing the popular perception of the 'black savage'. In a later programme in the July, he was billed as 'the Flying Indian' reverting back to his performances on the Slack Rope. It is difficult to assess how Fanque may have felt about these performances as 'Jean of the Jungle'; whether he was comfortable or not with how Ducrow wanted him to portray his ethnicity according to the whims of the performances. Earlier, in 1837, he had appeared with Batty in Manchester on the same programme as the melodrama that went by the name of *Obi; or Three Fingered Jack*. This drama was taken from the 1800 novella by William Earle[9] which is about an escaped Jamaican slave who sets out to avenge his family and people. Although Obi was an historical figure, his role was often demonised in pre-abolition Britain. In one instance the Public Authorities withdrew the performance when it was realised that 'Jack' was a robber (*Morning Post* 10 February 1826). In *Batty's Circus* it was presented as a piece of horsemanship by a Mr. Mackintosh. Given that Obi is a Jamaican, it is clear that Mr. Mackintosh would have performed in blackface. How did this make Fanque feel? Would he have been offended by a blackface performer taking a character he could have naturally played himself? Or maybe, in 1837, Fanque was not yet an accomplished enough rider for

Batty to use him in the role. My own feeling is that for Fanque this 1839 Ducrow season was an experiment that was short lived, even if lucrative in pay, and by January 1840 he was back with *Batty's Circus* presenting acts of Leaping and on the Slack Rope. He was clearly famous for these as in Leicester he was billed as 'that old favourite'. He was also now back working with his son;

> Pablo Fanque, the Indian performer, whose leaping we have before
> mentioned, has surprised us this week on the slack rope ... his son too
> is a very excellent performer on the tight-rope, as well as a capital rider
> (*Cambridge Chronicle and Journal* 11 July 1840)

There is also a hint that Fanque's wife, Susannah, may also have been performing with Batty as an equestrienne. In September the company was in Southampton and in the bill for the programme a list of female equestrians was given amongst which the name Fanque appears. I suspect that she had been with the company for some time, as she gave birth to another of Fanque's sons, named Lionel, in 1836. She was not the mother of the Master Pablo we have so far seen performing with *Batty's Circus*.

By this time it is likely that years of leaping and vaulting were taking its toll on Fanque's body. In October 1840 he makes his appearance as the 'Director of the Circle'[10]. In effect, he became the ringmaster. From this point on, while with Batty, he continues as either a 'Riding Master', teaching equitation to the public outside of the shows, or as the 'Conductor of the Circle' in the arena. In the spring of 1841 the company was in Dublin and this brings us to that moment when Astley's was destroyed by fire and the subsequent death of Ducrow that provided such an important opportunity for Joseph Hillier.

When Astley's caught fire, *Batty's Circus* and Fanque were in Dublin. It is frequently written that Batty immediately returned to London with a view to taking on the lease of the Amphitheatre and rebuilding it, leaving Fanque in charge of the circus in Dublin. This is not quite the case. It is true that Batty had designs on the Amphitheatre but in the July he moved his circus to Oxford, where both Fanque and his son appeared. Batty himself was on the programme. Wallett (1870:74) goes on to say;

> It was my last night at the circus, and also that of Pablo, who left Batty to start an establishment of his own … After leaving Oxford, I went to Wakefield, Yorkshire to join Pablo Fanque, who had erected a fine circus in Wood Street.

Wallett was indeed in Oxford with Fanque, but from July through to November we find Fanque and son performing at the Royal Amphitheatre on Great Charlotte Street in Liverpool. They were performing under the management of a Mr. Egerton, who held the lease of the Amphitheatre, so clearly they had parted company with Batty by this time. Batty moved his operations to London and initiated the lavish rebuilding of Astley's, temporarily continuing his circus at the Baths on nearby Westminster Road;

> Already the necessary measures are in progress for the erection of a new building on the same spot … And in the meantime the Baths in the Westminster Road have been tastefully fitted up by Mr. Batty, and opened with the most unequivocal success. (*Cambridge Independent Press* 1 January 1842)

Wallett did not go to Wakefield on leaving Batty to join Fanque. Newspapers show that between September and December he was performing in Leicester and Nottingham[11]. Fanque was clearly planning a move to create his own circus, after all, he had much experience and a good fan base around the country. The first report of his new venture came in the January of 1842;

> THE NEW CIRCUS – Notwithstanding the badness of the times, Mr. Pablo Fanque, an equestrian formerly belonging to Mr. Batty's establishment, has had the courage to venture upon erecting a circus

in Newton-street, Warrington. Monday last was his opening night [3 January], and it is with considerable pleasure we have to report that the house was crowded to the ceiling, and that there could not have been much less than one thousand persons present. The amusements offered to their notice comprised the usual scenes in the circle; the principal performers being Pablo Fanque, his son, a child stated in the bills to be only nine years old, and Master Bell, a youth of very considerable promise. (*Manchester Times* 8 January 1842)

Also on the programme were a Mr. Meeranardo, a strongman, some other artists under the name of the 'Wrestlers of Persia' (in all probability white performers in ethnic costume), and the clowns, Bell and Fuller. No mention of a Wallett at all. At this time he was touring his own *Wallet's Royal Circus*, moving from Nottingham in December 1841 (*Nottingham Journal* 31 December 1841) on to Hull by early February 1842 (*Hull Advertiser* 11 February 1842).

It was a busy first year of operation for Fanque. Beginning in Warrington he also appeared in Chester, Wrexham, Liverpool, and Huddersfield. For every place he visited he had newspaper coverage hailing his company; and he made sure that his audiences were well accommodated;

> MR. PABLO FANQUE respectfully informs the Inhabitants of Preston and Vicinity, that the Circus has been fitted up with every attention to comfort, having been thoroughly lined – particularly the Boxes, every crevice being stopped, to prevent draughts, and fitted up with taste; in short, every care has been taken to render the place as comfortable as possible, the Proprietor having spared neither pains nor expense to ensure him patronage and support. (*Preston Chronicle* 23 May 1842)

Fanque had a full programme, including feats of Leaping and Horsemanship by himself, and his son, the young Pablo Fanque, performed a comic equestrian number as well as a routine on the tight rope. Occasionally their colour was still referenced, although not as much as in former times, perhaps their ethnicity was becoming less of a novelty as there were now other minority performers around. The young Pablo was still billed as the 'Gem of Africa' and Fanque sometimes was billed as the 'Great African Rider'. It seems that in order to establish himself as a legitimate circus proprietor, Fanque deliberately set out to make himself an accepted part of society. He frequently made charitable donations to a variety of organisations. In Chester he gave money to the sporting Race Fund. In Bradford he donated money to the Oddfellows' Widows and Orphans Fund. Charitable donations were a regular occurrence and it could be argued that Fanque was attempting to 'buy' his way into social acceptance. Did he feel the need to do so because of his ethnicity, his humble background, or was he simply just a generous and philanthropic person? On the other hand these actions may have just been public relations exploits. We shall never know. His generosity extended beyond financial giving. In 1846 the following took place in Leeds;

> Yesterday a scene took place in King Charles' Croft, which is beyond description. Mr. Pablo Fanque … distributed a quantity of bread and cheese, and several barrels of ale, to those who liked to partake of his generosity (*Leeds Times* 1 August 1846)

It was a riotous event and drew a large crowd of onlookers as well as participants. Generous on the part of Fanque admittedly, but also a very good advertising ploy that created much attention. Fanque was not alone in this. Circus cannot function without an audience so all circus owners would employ all means available to attract a crowd. This might be parades, 'give aways', or other stunts, such as the incident in which a Mr Brown, performing with *Cooke's Circus* in Leeds in 1850, for a wager had himself packed into a small basket and then sent by rail at luggage price to Bradford (some ten miles distant) at half past two o'clock in the afternoon, to return to Leeds for the half past six o'clock show. He made it back in time for the performance (Stewart, 2012).

Fanque even became a member of the Order of Ancient Shepherds. This was a 'secret' fraternal society affiliated to the Freemasons. The Loyal Order of Ancient Shepherds was founded in Ashton under Lyne in 1826, and was one of many 'Friendly Societies' in the early nineteenth century. Before the advent of the Welfare State system, Friendly Societies were often the only way impoverished people could receive financial assistance in times of illness or injury. By the late 1800s there were approximately 27,000 such Societies registered in Britain. The 'Shepherds' Society was largely responsible for providing relief and support for bereaved families, and for the promotion of peace and goodwill towards the human race. By becoming a member of such an institution Fanque was establishing himself as a quintessential Englishman. It is interesting to note that news reports from this period of his career now begin to refer to him as a 'gentleman' rather than simply 'a man'.

Within a couple of years, Fanque had grown his small company into quite a large outfit. In July 1844 he was in Leeds with a company of around forty persons, including female performers (Mrs Fanque is also listed), and infant actors. La Petite Pablo (possibly Master Pablo in female attire as it was not unheard of for young boys to perform as young women) presented *The Equestrian Prodigy's Feats of Equitation*, and there was a large stud of horses on display. In the programme were a variety of equine acts, including 'Santeurs [possibly centaurs], Elastic Negroes; Chinese, Russian, Polish, Turkish, Asiatic, English, Swedish, and Tartar entrees'[12]. Also in this report Fanque is at pains to give us a full itinerary of his circus to date. At least one is missing from this list. In the Cryer Collection of the Wakefield Library there is a poster from May 1843[13], advertising *Pablo Fanque's Celebrated Equestrian Company* 'on the ground opposite the Woodman Inn, Wood Street, Wakefield'. This seems to be the first time that Fanque visited the town and it was still a relatively small company compared with the above and makes no mention of Mr. Wallett. You may remember that in his autobiography he claimed to have left Oxford in 1841 to join Fanque's circus in Wakefield. In fact the first reporting of Wallett being with Fanque was in the *Leeds Times* of 16 August 1845. Maybe at the time of writing his autobiography in 1870 his notes were lost or were confused in his memory.

Fanque continued to tour mainly in the north of England, from Liverpool in the west to Hull in the east. But he did make one excursion to London. In February 1847, the *Illustrated London News* announced that Fanque would make his first appearance in London, at Astley's Royal Amphitheatre, under the management of William Batty. This was not exactly true. Fanque had made his very first performance in London as early as 1834. On 16 September he presented on Croydon Lawn, as part of a Grand Scottish Fete, a tight rope performance[14]. He had also appeared at Astley's in 1839, when Ducrow was in charge. Be that as it may but nobody seems to have noted that. Fanque was an enormous success as a solo equestrian, an 'artiste of colour', and his act was reported effusively, although here slightly edited for brevity;

> The gem of the evening was … Mr. Pablo Fanque on his tutored steed. This performance transcends everything that has hitherto been exhibited in the way of horsemanship. It is perfectly unique. A beautiful jet black thorough-bred horse [by name Beda], bridled and saddled after the ordinary fashion, is introduced into the arena. The orchestra plays a slow air, and the steed prances around the circle, keeping time to the air. The music quickens, and the horse quickens his movements, keeping time to the music with his fore feet … the rider guiding him, and swaying backwards and forwards as the horse moves, even as if they were one … Words cannot do justice to this unique, and wonderful, and most elegant performance. It is impossible to describe the indescribable (*Sun (London)* 9 March 1847).

It was a short visit to Astley's before returning north again. The press coverage he received only bolstered his popularity and the illustration in the *Illustrated London News* of him performing on his mare Beda has become the widely seen iconic image of Pablo Fanque. Davies (2017:69) maintains that Fanque first appeared with Beda in 1849 but a news report in the *Bolton Chronicle* of 13 March 1847 clearly indicates that the horse was the property of Fanque.

Pablo Fanque performing at Astley's. *Illustrated London News* 20 March 1847
(Author's collection)

His triumphs continued until 1848. It was to be a troubled year. To begin with, an apprentice going by the name of Pablo Fanque Junior ran away from his circus. Fanque placed an advertisement in the local Leeds press advising anyone employing this youth would be prosecuted. Who was this youth? The newspaper said that he also went by the name of Master Burkham. Fanque's son, Master Pablo (William Darby Banham) was beyond apprenticeship and famous in his own right. I think it is highly unlikely to have been him. So was there another boy of colour being trained up and to continue the name of Pablo Fanque? By now William Darby Banham would have been eighteen years old and Fanque's other son Lionel, by his wife Susannah Marlow, would have been around twelve years. Lionel did become a circus performer and in the 1901 Census returns he is listed as 'Lionel Pablo' (one of his daughters is listed as a 'female jester'). So there is a possibility that the absconder could have been Lionel. It certainly was not William junior (Master Pablo) because on the 18 March he was performing at King Charles' Croft in Leeds when;

FATAL ACCIDENT AT LEEDS – Leeds, March 19th – (By Electric Telegraph) – Between nine and ten o'clock last night, a spacious temporary building constructed as a circus for the equestrian company of Mr. Pablo Fanque, in consequence of it being over-crowded, for the benefit of Wallett, the clown, fell in with a tremendous crash, seriously injuring several persons, and killing the wife of the proprietor and manager. It appears that the gallery fell in, crushing the pay-place, in which Mrs. Fanque and Mrs. Wallett were seated, and burying them in the ruins. The corpse of the former has been removed and the latter lady was dragged from the ruin in so injured a condition that it is very uncertain whether she can recover (*Morning Post* 20 March 1848).

The inquest into the accident and his wife's death was held on the 20 March. There, Fanque stated that his son was performing on the tight-rope at the time when the collapse occurred. A full account of the inquest was given in the *Leeds Times* of 25 March. Susannah Darby (Fanque) was buried on the 22 March in Woodhouse cemetery Leeds. It was reported that several thousands of people turned out to watch the funeral procession.

Undaunted, or so it seems, Fanque moved his circus on to Sheffield and then across the Pennines to his favourite stamping ground of Lancashire, appearing at the Knott Mill Fair in Manchester, and then Oldham. Given that his wife Susannah had only recently and tragically died, it is quite surprising to find the following marriage announcement;

Yesterday week [19 May], at Rotherham, Mr. Pablo Fanque, to Miss Corke[r], of the Bull and Oak, Cattle Market, Sheffield (*Leeds Times* 27 May 1848)

Had Fanque had very small children who needed a mother, this quick remarriage might be explained. But William was eighteen and Lionel at least twelve. Was she pregnant with Fanque's child? There is no record of this. How long had he known her? Again, this is unknown but it has been suggested that she may have been an equestrian performer with Fanque's circus. Whatever the circumstances, they stayed together and their three children were born in 1854, 1855, and 1857. It is interesting to note that the third child Caroline died in her second year but was interred in the grave of Fanque's former wife, Susannah.

The 1850s was a period of expensive expansion for Fanque. He borrowed heavily and was able to establish two companies. He extended his coverage of the British Isles by taking his circus to Dublin, Glasgow, and Edinburgh. But this expansion became financially problematic for Fanque. In April 1858, Mr. Nelson, a clown who had been engaged by Fanque, brought an action against Fanque for the non-payment of wages[15]. The court hearing showed that there had been irregularities in book keeping and the judge found for the plaintiff Nelson. Fanque was ordered to pay 33 pounds sterling and ten shillings remuneration plus legal expenses. Worse was to follow. In the September;

SEIZURE OF PABLO FANQUE'S CIRCUS FOR DEBT - ... when the party of equestrians travelling under the name of Pablo Fanque's Circus were performing at Harrogate ... the performers ... at that time were under a dark cloud of adversity, their stud, and all things belonging to them, being seized under a bill of sale, for debts contracted in another locality; and the company, consisting of parents and children, were a once turned adrift, houseless and homeless, to seek their fortunes as they could (*Bolton Chronicle* 25 September 1858)

Pablo Fanque poster 1848 *(Courtesy of V. Toulmin)*

William Batty had made the seizure against money loaned to Fanque. He had already made a previous seizure in 1854 whilst Fanque was in Worcester, on the understanding that Fanque would pay him back at ten pounds sterling weekly to the sum of about 500 pounds sterling per annum. Accounts had failed to be kept and so it was unclear if this debt had been paid or not. In October 1858, Fanque was in court for bankruptcy[16]. The sum of over 606 pounds sterling was claimed against him and the contents of his circus were put up for auction in Leeds on 11 November[17]. The mare Beda was also put up for auction by order of the court in March 1859[18]. The continuing court hearing in November placed his debts at 2,900 pounds sterling. The case rumbled on until April 1859, when the court finally refused Fanque a certificate of bankruptcy[19]. Throughout this turbulent period, Fanque was able to keep performing at various venues around the country, but things were to take a turn for the worse in Scotland. In March 1860, he was discharged bankruptcy on a composition of 6d (pence) in the pound. This means his creditors could claim 6d for each pound (2.5%) they were owed by Fanque. One might have thought that this would be the end for Fanque, but no. He took to the road again as *Pablo Fanque's Phoenix Circus* and continued to work in the north of England. It seems that Fanque's reputation and good social standing drew him support from northern audiences.

And what of his family during all of this? William junior (the Master Pablo Fanque) was making his own career in the circus and had run away to Australia. There he had been performing as Pablo Fanque. Lionel was a circus performer working under the name of Lionel Pablo. And Elizabeth his wife? Well, we are not sure what happened but on the 1861 Census returns we find a William Darby, equestrian, living with a Sarah Darby[20]. She is listed as his wife. Also with them is their eleven month old daughter Eliza[21]. Fanque never divorced Elizabeth and neither did he marry Sarah. Perhaps Elizabeth had had enough during the bankruptcy hearings or maybe Fanque had an affair with Sarah, who was referred to as being 'formerly attached to his circus'. Whatever it was, Elizabeth and her children were back with Fanque in Stockport by the 1871 Census. And it was there that he would die on the 5 May 1871. Reports of his death were listed in newspapers across the country, as here;

> Mr. Pablo Fanque, the well-known equestrian, died at Stockport, yesterday. He was, as our readers are probably aware, a man of colour … His remains will be interred at Leeds on Sunday next, where he placed a handsome monument over his first wife some years ago (*Birmingham Mail* 6 May 1871).

As with his first wife, thousands of people lined the streets to view the funeral procession and he was laid to rest at the foot of his first wife. Elizabeth and their two sons attended – I wonder how she felt at the arrangements? She went on to remarry and died in Ireland.

Even in death, the newspapers pointed out that he was a person of colour. For all the good that he had done in all of the communities in which he had lived and worked; for all the plaudits that were heaped on him during his life, society still felt it necessary to label him as something different.

The story of Pablo Fanque has often eclipsed the successes of other Victorian circus performers of ethnic backgrounds. We should remember that he was not the only one and all of the others, like Joseph Hillier, should be celebrated just as much.

Notes

1. *William Darby baptism record.* Online at https://www.familysearch.org/ark:/61903/3:1:S3HY-6P7H-VW9?i=28&cc=1824706

2. *William Darby burial record.* Online at https://www.ancestry.co.uk/interactive/61636/48393_b406796-4143497_01014?pid=2582863&backurl=https://search.ancestry.co.uk/cgi-bin/sse.dll?indiv%3D1%26dbid%3D61636%26h%3D2582863%26tid%3D%26pid%3D%26usePUB%3Dtrue%26_phsrc%3Dsbc1310%26_phstart%3DsuccessSource&treeid=&personid=&hintid=&usePUB=true&_phsrc=sbc1310&_phstart=successSource&usePUBJs=true&_ga=2.76671453.91645169.1580288256-1986502099.1539097385

3. *Frances Stamp baptism record.* Online at https://www.ancestry.com/interactive/61636/48393_b406801-4143498_00121?pid=2670085&backurl=https://search.ancestry.com/cgi-bin/sse.dll?indiv%3D1%26dbid%3D61636%26h%3D2670085%26tid%3D%26pid%3D%26usePUB%3Dtrue%26_phsrc%3Dsbc1358%26_phstart%3DsuccessSource&treeid=&personid=&hintid=&usePUB=true&_phsrc=sbc1358&_phstart=successSource&usePUBJs=true&_ga=2.199470382.1005595409.1580731247-1811029445.1539097870

4. Online at https://en.wikipedia.org/wiki/Talk:Pablo_Fanque

5. Online at https://www.chrishobbs.com/sheffield/hendersons.htm

6. Online at https://100greatblackbritons.com/bios/Pablo_Fanque.htm

7. *Yorkshire Gazette* 28 July 1838

8. *Leeds Times* 2 June 1838

9. Online at https://mary shelley.fandom.com/wiki/William_Earle,_Jr._Obi;_or,_The_History_of_Three-Fingered_Jack_(1800_novella)

10. *Hampshire Advertiser* 10 October 1840

11. *Leicester Chronicle* 25 September 1841

12. *Leeds Times* 27 July 1844

13. Online at http://www.twixtaireandcalder.org.uk/

14. Online at http://www.croydon.gov.uk/leisure/parksandopenspaces/parksatoz/lawns/tlhistory

15 . *The Era* 18 April 1858

16. *Leeds Intelligencer* 16 October 1858

17. *Leeds Times* 6 November 1858

18. *Bell's Life in London and Sporting Chronicle* 27 March 1859

19. *Glasgow Herald* 4 June 1859

20. Online at https://www.ancestry.co.uk/interactive/8767/wry-rg9_3320_3323- 0307?pid=10235263&treeid=&person-id=&rc=&usePUB=true&_phsrc=sbc1440&_phstart=successSource

21. *GRO Index Warrington 1860*, 8c/142. Online at https://www.freebmd.org.uk/cgi/search.pl

CHAPTER 4
THE MYSTERY OF CARLOS PABLO PADDINGTON

Another ethnic performer who was a contemporary of Pablo Fanque was Pablo Paddington. In fact his full name was Carlos Pablo Paddington, and the spelling of his name often varied, as was the case with many performers of the period. Like many other performers of the time, this was certainly not his given name but there is no extant record of his age, place of birth, or of the name Pablo Paddington. Like many others, how he became involved in the circus and how long he had been performing before he first appears in records is a mystery yet to be solved. The one thing that we can say is that he was one of the 'artistes of colour'. He is first recorded in 1825, working for *Cooke's Circus*. In the April, he appears in an advertisement for *Cooke's Olympic Circus* at the Knott Mill Fair in Manchester;

CARLOS PABLO PADDINGTONE

THE FLYING INDIAN

Will make his first appearance in Manchester, on the Corde Volante, and exhibit the most Incredible Evolutions, in a manner never attempted by any other person. (*Manchester Courier and Lancashire General Advertiser* 2 April 1825)

In later appearances that year in Leeds and Wakefield he is billed as 'The Flying African'[1], a clear reference to his perceived ethnic heritage but what exactly that may have been we cannot say for sure. To confuse matters, in 1826 he was performing with Cooke, again at the Knott Mill

Fair, where he was billed as Carlos Pablo Paddingtoni the 'Brazilian Phenomenon'[2]. Then, in 1827, there came an astounding revelation;

TWO FEMALE IMPOSTERS AND COURTSHIP EXTRAORDINARY

A woman now in the York poor-house has given to the master there a strange account of herself and of another female imposter, who formerly travelled with Cooke's equestrian troop. They appeared as men of colour, and in all the feats of the most dextrous horsemanship were not to be surpassed by any others of the company. In addition to this, being dressed in male attire, and having their persons stained black, suspicion of their real sex was readily subdued by an allowance for the difference of personal appearance which opposite climates generally occasion.

The real name of the woman now in the poor-house, is Ellen Lowther, but when with Cooke's company she called herself John Clifford — she is of eastern origin, though born in England; her grandfather, she says, was called Signor Rammapattan; he was brought to England from Bengal, by the late Lord Lowther, and when they arrived in London, his lordship changed his name to Lowther: he afterwards resided in the north of England, was killed by a pitman at Sunderland, when he was 106 years and nine months old. Her father, she says, lives at Tadcaster.

She represents herself as being but 20 years of age, and having commenced her equestrian performances at 5 years old; she has been with the two Cookes 15 years. As might have been expected, this vagabond way of life led to vice and immorality, and the woman (alias John Clifford) was removed to the parish at St. Martin's, Coney-street, in a state of pregnancy, and thence to the work-house, where on the 2d inst. " John" was delivered of a still-born male child. The other woman, who passed for a black man, in the same company, went by the name of Pablo Paddington, and effected the deception so dextrously, as to have deceived even those about her, and by assiduous attentions gained the affections of a Miss King, who also travelled with Mr. Cooke.

The courtship thus commenced was carried on for some time, till scandal whispered in the ears of the unsuspecting fair one, that her favourite Pablo was too much a man of the world, possessing more of female acquaintance than was consistent with his solemn promises and plighted vows. A lover's quarrel was the consequence: and slighted attachment led to some estrangement of the lady's affections. Misfortunes, however, often overtake the faithless, and the fair are sometimes, in those cases, too ready to forgive. This was the case with the parties in question. Pablo had his arm broken soon after, and pity again called forth the tender affections of Miss King, who, during her lover's illness, attended him with peculiar care. How the impostor rewarded her kindness, or whether she ever found out the cheat, we know not — but the whole carries with it such an air of romance and of a novel story, that we cannot but think the detail will be amusing to some of our readers. (*York Herald* 13 January 1827)

The story was published widely throughout Britain and caused some controversy. How true was it? Certain facts can be corroborated. There was a Miss King performing with *Cooke's Circus* at this time and, as we have seen, Pablo Paddington was a person of colour. Beyond that the facts are difficult to ascertain. None of the advertising or posters for *Cooke's Circus* from the period mention a John Clifford. But she may have been working as a member of the ensemble and therefore not credited. Ellen mentions that her father lives in Tadcaster, Yorkshire. The name Lowther is common to Yorkshire but there are no specific records relating to Tadcaster, and neither can I find a birth record for an Ellen Lowther around the time she indicates. Of course, a lack of evidence does not necessarily mean that her account is not true, and there seems to be no reason why Ellen Lowther should have invented this story. However, there is speculation that this may have been an attempt to damage Paddington's reputation or even that he may have been a white performer in blackface, although there is currently no direct evidence of either of these suggestions.

The account does raise further questions. If Pablo Paddington was female did Cooke know about this and happily present him as a man? Or was he, too, fooled by the deception? Why did Paddington feel the need to perform as a man? There was more opportunity for a man to perform on the Corde Volante than a woman, and in early circus advertising we certainly find this discipline to be male dominated. It may have been a question of his own gender identity, especially when we take into consideration the alleged relationship between Pablo and Miss King. Trans gender identities and gender fluidity is not a modern occurrence by any means. It is perfectly plausible that Pablo lived and loved as a man. However, what effect this exposé had on Pablo's relationship with Miss King, and with his employer Cooke, is not recorded but it is interesting to note that Pablo Paddington is never associated with *Cooke's Circus* or with Miss King after this time. The next time we find Pablo in the news he is working with *Adam's Circus* at the Royal Hibernian Circus in Dublin;

CARLOS PABLO PADDINGTONII [sic] the Aerial Phenomenon (*Dublin Evening Post* 3 October 1829)

Later that season, Paddington is also recorded as performing an act upon the 'Single Horse'[3]. Like other gymnastic artistes of the time, he has expanded into equestrian performances. The controversy of 1827 appears not to have daunted Paddington and did not put a halt to his career. It may have actually helped it because many, knowing of the story, might have gone to view this 'unusual' performer. We can only assume that Mr. Adams was aware of Paddington's situation and was quite happy for the billing to allude that he was a man;

PABLO PADDINGTON, the Siamese Aeronaut, will take his flight on the Corde Crescent, exhibiting peculiar and elegant Devices, by a rapid circulation equal to the power of complicated machinery. (*Leeds Patriot and Yorkshire Advertiser* 17 July 1830)

Wakefield Summer Fair.

COOKE'S

New Olympic Circus, Wood-Street,
WAKEFIELD,

Will open

This Present MONDAY, 4th JULY, 1825

When he will have the Honor to introduce his large Company of

37 Performers,

AND NUMEROUS STUD OF

TWENTY HORSES,

Unequalled for Symmetry, Beauty, & Docility, forming the
LARGEST ESTABLISHMENT IN THE KINGDOM.

MON. CLINE

Will appear on the

TIGHT ROPE,

AND WILL INTRODUCE HIS EXCELLENT PAS SUEL IN WOODEN SHOES,

This Gentleman is unequivocally the best Performer in Great Britain.—His Aerial Figure, combined with the precision of his different and difficult FEATS, render Mons. C's. Performances pleasing and interesting, when other Performers of the same Nature have caused only Astonishment and Terror.

HERCULEAN FEATS OF STRENGTH,
AND PRECISION OF EQUILIBRIUM,
Forming a routine of difficult and astonishing specimens of

BALANCING,

BY

SIGNOR SPELTERINI,
(FROM MADRID.)

The heavy weights this Gentleman sustains on different parts of his body, causes a surprise that can only be exceeded by the wonder occasioned by the finished, minute, and particular manner in which he preserves the equilibrium of lighter substances; the whole is without parallel.

Equestrian Exercises,
BY

MISS KING,

Who will, in Addition to several graceful and pleasing Performances, introduce the SIX
DIVISIONS OF THE

Broad Sword Exercise.

Carlos Pablo Paddington,
THE

Flying African,

His First Appearance, will introduce his astonishing Evolutions on the

CORDE VOLANTE.

MR. WOOLFORD,
(His first Appearance in Wakefield,)

WILL RIDE HIS EXTRAORDINARY ACT WITHOUT

Saddle or Bridle,

Accomplishing several of the most arduous Feats with Garters, Hoops, Skipping Rope, &c. and conclude with the novel performance, perfectly unique, on

TWO WILD HORSES.

Clown, Mr. PRITCHARD.

In the course of the performance will be represented the

GRAND REVIEW,
AND

Bonaparte's Address to his Army
PREVIOUS TO THE

BATTLE OF WATERLOO,

Taken from the Grand historical Military Melo Drama, patronised by his Grace the Duke of Wellington, and most of the Generals engaged in that momentous struggle, and performed upwards of 170 Nights at the Amphitheatre, Westminster Bridge, London.

Bonaparte, Mr. BROTHERTON—General Grouchy, Mr. COOKE—Marshall Ney, Mr. CLARKE, General Frimont, Mr. BENGEERMAN,

Cuirassiers, Dragoons, Body Guards and Staff by the whole of the Company.

THE WHOLE TO CONCLUDE WITH THE LAUGHABLE EXTRAVAGANZA OF

MR. BUTTON'S

Disastrous Journey to Brentford.

ADMISSION.—BOXES, 3s.—PIT, 2s.—GALLERY, 1s.—STANDING PLACES, 6d
A Change of Performance on Tuesday.

R. NICHOLS, TYPOGRAPHER, WAKEFIELD.

Poster for Cooke's Circus featuring Carlos Pablo Paddington 1825 (*Reproduced with permission of Wakefield Council Libraries Photographic Collection*)

This particular insert is interesting in that it gives us a further indication of his skin tone. He is variously referred to as 'Indian', 'African', and here as 'Siamese' which might imply that he had a lighter skin tone. The other possibility is of course that he was of mixed heritage, just as Pablo Fanque had been.

It seems that Paddington was quite prepared to move from one company to another on a fairly regular basis. Throughout 1834 we can find him working with *Samwell's Circus* where he appeared on the Corde Volante and also as an equestrian. We can get an idea of his act from the following later description;

> Signor PABLO PADDINGTON will, for the first time here, perform his pleasing Act on the single horse, concluding with riding on his head on a pewter pint pot: the horse at three quarters speed (*Staffordshire Advertiser* 27 October 1838)

In 1836 we know that he replaced Pablo Fanque in *Batty's Circus* and then stayed with Batty into 1837, working on the same bill as Pablo Fanque, where he presented his 'act of horsemanship'[4]. In 1838 he was back with *Samwell's Circus* but then he seems to disappear from circus bills until September 1839, when he reappears with *Ryan's Circus* in Bristol. Here;

> PABLO PADDINGTON, the Man of Colour, will display his surprising Evolutions on the CORD VOLANTE, and will conclude his Feats in a Brilliant Display of Fire Works (*Gloucestershire Chronicle* 5 September 1840)

He was certainly going for the visual effects! In this billing, a direct reference is made to his non-white ethnicity, drawing attention to his exoticism. A week later[5], still with Ryan in Bristol, Paddington was one of the main attractions, appearing no less than three times on the same programme; twice being referred to as a 'man of colour'. He first presented Slack Rope Vaulting, then came his equestrian act, followed later by his work on the Corde Volante. By the October he was billed as the 'celebrated Man of Colour'[6], when he appeared on the Flying Rope, yet another term for the Corde Volante. It seems that Pablo Paddington remained with *Ryan's Circus* throughout 1841 and there is an interesting item that appeared in a Nottingham newspaper referring to a road collision that confirms this. A local resident was returning home one evening with friends in a light cart when;

> A horse and gig approached, which was running at a tremendous rate, and in consequence of the darkness of the night, a collision took place. Several persons were slightly injured ... The gig contained Signor Bernaskino ... Pablo Paddington, and Pablo somebody else [sic], all belonging to Ryan's Circus. On perceiving what had happened, the riders [sic] were desirous of making a speedy exit, each individual leaving his name. But not so; two constables were brought to the spot (*Nottingham Review and General Advertiser for the Midland Counties* 15 October 1841)

The upshot of this incident was that Signor Bernaskino and the other two were placed in confinement until the next morning. One is to hope that they had no performance that evening. It is interesting to note that there was another Pablo belonging to *Ryan's Circus*. This was not Pablo Fanque or his son--they were performing in Liverpool at the time. Who this other Pablo was is a mystery and no mention of another Pablo is made in connection with *Ryan's Circus* during this period. He may have been one of the juvenile performers, who were rarely mentioned by name, or he may have been a locally employed non-performer.

Yet another change of employer came in 1842, where he was performing with *Wallett's Circus* in Huddersfield as the 'Flying Man'[7]. This is the same Wallett the clown who was a friend of Pablo Fanque. Paddington also performed as part of the equestrian troupe. He must have stayed with Wallett until around August because by then Wallett became insolvent and had spent a short time in the Debtor's Prison[8]. Bail was accepted and the next month he went to work for the circus of

Price and Powell?. What became of Pablo Paddington is not known. He disappears from all newspaper reviews after this time. What happened to him during the ensuing eight year gap? Did he go abroad to work? There are no records or newspaper reports to suggest that he did. Was he ill or injured? Did he just take a break? Despite this mysterious gap in his media presence he is next discovered performing in Cork, Ireland in the December of 1850;

> On last evening, Mr. Paddington, a native of this city [Cork], made his debut on the slack rope, and was received with loud applause. His performance on the slack rope is most wonderful, and worthy of a visit (*Southern Reporter and Cork Commercial Courier* 31 December 1850).

It would appear that, from a newspaper report a few days later this Mr. Paddington was performing with *Pablo Fanque's Circus Royal*. For his benefit night a description of his act is given;

> Being for the Benefit of Mr. PADDINGTON. Corkonian, and First Slack Rope Vaulter in the World [in this context First means best]. First appearance of Mr. Paddington as MILOA THE ATHLETE, upon the Slack Rope, in which character he will perform several incredible feats of strength. First and only appearance of Mr. Paddington in a Daring Act of Horsemanship. First and only Night of Mr. Paddington ascending and descending to the top of the Circus, while standing on his head, on the top of a Balloon, surrounded with Fire Works (*Cork Constitution* 4 January 1851)

Now this entry poses some questions. Firstly, the name Pablo seems to have been dropped so was there another Mr. Paddington performing with Fanque? We know from previous descriptions of his work that Paddington was an accomplished performer on the Slack Rope, that he performed an equestrian act, and that he had worked with Fire Works before. This would suggest that they are one and the same person. The name Pablo may have been dropped simply because he was working for Pablo Fanque and they wanted to avoid a confusion of names. Secondly, both reports state that Paddington was a native of Cork. If this is correct, and it is another Mr. Paddington, then there should be birth/ baptism records showing a male Paddington birth in Cork. If we assume that Pablo Paddington and Ellen Lowther were of a similar age then a time frame of 1800 – 1810 would seem appropriate. Unfortunately, no such records can currently be found on a variety of genealogical data bases to substantiate this, although recent research by Conrad Bryan of the Association of Mixed Race Irish (AMRI) suggests that he may have been born Joseph Paddington[10]. If the statement of being a native of Cork *is* accurate then the implications are that *Mr.* Paddington was not born there. Pablo Paddington may have been, as a female and under another name. Of course, the statement could all have been advertising hype put out by Pablo Fanque to favour his audience! We will never know for certain.

Pablo Paddington is next mentioned by name in 1853. He was recorded performing in the Royal Pavilion Gardens in North Woolwich as 'Pablo Paddington – the Great Slack Rope Vaulter' in *The Times*[11]. In July he was in the Zoological Gardens in Bristol[12], and in the December he was back at the Royal Amphitheatre in Dublin, performing as 'The Flying Man'[13]. All of these venues were not connected with a specific circus proprietor and it seems very much as if Paddington was now freelancing, getting work where he could rather than staying with a particular circus for any length of time. One gets the feeling that his career was gradually winding down. In January 1854 he was back in Dublin[14], and in the July he made a return visit to the Zoological Gardens in Bristol[15]. The final reference that I have been able to find for Pablo Paddington was in an advertisement placed by his agent, Mr. Clarke;

> TO PROPRIETORS OF PLEASURE GARDENS and COMMIT-
> TEES OF FETES, GALAS &c. – After Monday next, the 19th of May
> … PABLO PADDINGTON, the renowned Slackrope Vaulter …
> OPEN for ENGAGEMENTS either for long or short duration (*The
> Era* 18 May 1856)

Did Pablo Paddington's career end there? Certainly he disappears from advertising and reviews from this point on. The circus had developed rapidly from when he began working. Circus was no longer just about horses, important as they still were. A new and younger generation of performers was arriving on the scene with an increasing variety of acts on offer. Adding to the growing number of circuses in operation bigger and brasher circuses were now arriving from the United States. As an artiste of colour, he had made his mark. As his career was coming to a close, however, another artiste was born—one who would become internationally renowned.

Notes

1. *Leeds Intelligencer* 9 June 1825 and Circus Poster for Cooke's Circus in Wakefield 4 July 1825. File 2235/08 Cryer Collection.

2. *Manchester Courier and Lancashire General Advertiser* 25 March 1826

3. *Dublin Evening Packet and Correspondent* 21 November 1829

4. *Warder and Dublin Weekly* Mail 21 January 1837

5. *Bristol Mercury* 12 September 1840

6. *Gloucestershire Chronicle* 17 October 1840

7. *Leeds Mercury* 26 February 1842

8. *Morning Post* 19 August 1842

9. *West Kent Guardian* 17 September 1842

10. *Pablo and George Paddington.* No date. On the AMRI website; https://mixedmuseum.org.uk/amri-exhibition/pablo-and-george-paddington/

11. *The Times* May 30 1853

13. *Bristol Mercury* 16 July 1853

14. *Freeman's Journal* 27 December 1853

15. *The Era* 1 January 1854

16. *Bristol Mercury* 15 July 1854

Passport photograph of Olga Woodson (née Brown) c. 1919 *(Reproduced with permission of David G. Marks)*

CHAPTER 5
THE BLACK VENUS– MISS LA LA

In 1858, around the time that Pablo Paddington's career was coming to a close, a mixed race child was born who would become internationally famous for her amazing feats of strength. She was Anna Albertine Olga Brown, later to become famous as Miss La La. She was born in Stettin-Bredow on 2 April 1858[1]. Stettin was a major Prussian port and became fully part of the German Empire in 1871, after the Franco-Prussian war. After World War II the city was ceded to Poland and it is now known as Szczecin. Anna's parents were William Brown and Marie Christine Borchardt, and in an Affidavit attached to a 1919 United States passport application[2] she states that her parents were both American and that her father was born in Philadelphia. She considered herself to be an American citizen, by both parentage and later by marriage, although there is no record of her ever visiting the country. The ethnicity of her mother is unknown, although Desbonnet (1911:350) writes that her mother was white and her father black. The statement that her father was black seems to be supported by at least one genealogist[3], 'William (Wilhelm) was of African descent'. How did such a man of colour come to be in Stettin at this time? One theory is that as Stettin was a port, he could have been a discharged seaman. This is a possibility, as there are records of seamen being discharged in Stettin after completing their terms of service on board ship, although none for a William Brown at this period. Another more plausible theory is that he was an entertainer of some sort. Desbonnet (1911:350) records that Olga, as Anna became more widely known, began her circus career at the age of nine years. A letter written by Legation Official John W. Garrett, attached to the 1919 passport application (referenced [2] above) corroborates this;

> Mrs. Woodson [nee Brown], according to her statements … resided in Stettin until she was nine years of age, when she began travelling with a circus as a trapeze performer, following that profession for nearly forty years.

David G. Marks, a genealogist and former editor of *Die Pommerschen Leute* (Pommeranian People) quarterly magazine, commented to me that he makes the assumption that Marie Christine Borchardt was born in Germany, probably Stettin. This assumption is based on the fact that her children, grandchildren and great grandchildren all remained and married in Germany. As Olga had several siblings born earlier in Stettin from 1847, it appears that her parents had been there for some time before she was born. What they were doing is not recorded but there is a logic in suggesting that they were in the entertainment business and that Olga followed this; just as Olga's daughter Rose became a Dancer in later years.

Olga, in her own words, toured mainly in Europe throughout her career. We know little of her early performing years but by 1878 she was certainly performing at the Cirque Fernando in Paris. She was immortalised by the artist Edgar Degas, himself of mixed heritage on his mother's side, in a series of sketches entitled *Miss La La at the Cirque Fernando*. Degas was fascinated by Miss La La (Olga's performing name at that time) and he completed around twenty sketches of her performing over a period of several days during the January of 1879. Most of Degas's subjects were women, and mainly 'working' women;

> He did countless studies of cabaret singers, mouths so wide open that one can peer down the song-filled tunnels of their throats; prostitutes in black stockings and garters, waving their legs at prospective clients

in the whorehouse parlour; sturdy laundresses yawning with fatigue as they lift irons as a heavy as a gymnast's weights or lug huge sacks of linen that put a becoming tension in their backs (Richardson, 2002)

In her paper for *The Art* Bulletin, Brown (2007) gives a detailed analysis of Degas's attitudes towards race and sexuality as embodies in his study of Miss La La. She suggests that;

Although explicit sexuality is not featured in Degas's painting. I contend that desire is present nonetheless.

In the same paper she goes on to say;

The circus in particular was a hybrid space where class, gender, and race could intersect in performance, where the sexuality associated with working-class women and with darker races could come together … all of which could been enjoyed voyeuristically without endangering the detached observer's own socially prescribed sense of privilege and masculinity.

Miss La La's muscularity and strength were undeniable. In Degas's painting, one of which can be seen at the National Gallery in London, Miss La La is captured being hauled into the air holding on to the rope only with her teeth. Desbonnet (1911:350), a nineteenth century champion of physical culture, comments specifically upon her physical build;

Elle avait des bras superbes, vraimant extraordinaire pour une femme, à tel point que, quand je la vis pour la première fois … je fus jaloux de ces biceps. Et ils y avais de quoi! Elle avait en effet 38.5cms de bras tout en muscles et d'un modelé incompatable.

[She had superb arms, really extraordinary for a woman, so much so that when I saw her for the first time … I was jealous of these biceps. And they were something! She had in effect 38.5cms of muscular arms and an incomparable shape. *Author's translation*].

According to her description in the later passport applications she stood around five feet and one inch tall (155 centimetres), her eyes were dark, and her face was oval with a scar above the right eye. Her complexion was described as 'coloured', although an attached letter is more specific in saying that she was of 'negro blood'.

But her performances of feats of strength were not to everyone's taste. When it was rumoured that Miss La La was to visit England the following appeared, here given in full to illustrate the depth of feeling;

> A RIDICULOUS PERFORMANCE. A new performance is promised from Paris. We are told that a "lady" there rejoicing in the name of "Lala, the black Venus", winds up her performance in the Cirque Fernando by being suspended from a trapeze – head downwards of course – with a man hanging round her waist, and a cannon weighing 300 kilos hanging from her mouth, the piece of ordnance being fired off. We are assured there is no mistake about the weight of the cannon, as it has been duly tried and guaranteed. Now we care not if there is a mistake or not. We simply hope that Miss Lala will remain in Paris, or go wheresoever she chooses, so that England is not honoured by her attentions. No sensible person cares to witness such disgusting and altogether idiotic scenes. We have plenty of them enacted at the present moment, and Heaven forbid that any addition should be made to their number. A taste which hankers for exhibitions in which the elements of utter uselessness and great danger are combined is indeed vitiated and depraved, and it is pitiful to find so many pandering to it. And at the risk of being considered ungallant, we only wish that "Lala [sic], the black Venus", and all her compeers in the "sensational" line, possessed more sense than to imperil their limbs and lives for the gratification of morbid people who seem to revel in aught that may sooner or later lead to a frightful accident, and perhaps fatal results *(Portsmouth Evening News* 10 January 1879)

The writer of this piece clearly has an axe to grind. I suggest that it was a man who was misogynistic to say the least. The use of language is used in a demeaning way, not to mention full of racist overtones.

The label of the 'black Venus' alludes to a sexuality and refers back to the exhibition of the 'Hottentot Venus' earlier in the century[4]. The article also displays that endemic xenophobia found in Britain of the period, particularly in the smaller towns and cities which had much more parochial views. Had this article been in a national newspaper rather than a provincial one, it could have been argued that this was an elaborate marketing ploy to encourage people to visit Miss La La's performances when she arrived in Britain. But Miss La La had previously been briefly mentioned in the British press the year before[5], when she was referred to as one of the stars of the Cirque Fernando, 'a Negress, Miss Lala, the black Venus', without any vitriol or comment.

Whatever feelings may have been voiced against her, Miss La La made her debut in Britain at the Gaiety Theatre in February 1879. Much was made of her colour and a completely fabricated exotic history was 'puffed' by the manager, Mr. Edward Garcia;

> the African Princess, attended by her courtiers … the programme states that "La La formerly reigned supreme over a vast dominion, but her chiefs, having tendered their allegiance to our sovereign, Queen Victoria, La La's power over her people was no longer recognised; her palace was burnt to the ground by a ruthless mob, La La taken prisoner, and for some time treated as a slave by a firm of West Indian merchants, who acquired possession of her, but eventually was set at liberty, obtaining a small position in a travelling Cirque in the south of France, the Manager of which speedily discovered that intrepid courage and indomitable strength were two great combined essentials in La La; he paid a little attention to her education, and the result is that La La is now in a position to defy the world (*The Era* 23 February 1879)

A significant achievement for a girl born of Afro-American parentage in Germany! This advertising traded upon her 'otherness' and 'exoticism' but also deferred to an Anglo-Saxon supremacy, in that La La's chiefs 'sold out' to the British. It would be interesting to know how La La herself felt about how she was being portrayed. She appeared at the

Westminster Aquarium in early March 1879, where she performed with other acrobats from the Cirque Fernando, known as the *Troupe Kaira*. It is necessary here to give a full account of her act, as detailed in the press to understand the full extent of her physical powers that astounded audiences in France:

Sensation appears to be the order of the day, and of the night, too, at this pleasant and popular resort … During the past week an additional attraction has been introduced in the person of a dusky lady known as La La, whose feats of strength fairly eclipse anything and everything of the kind that has gone before. She does all that her muscular rivals have done, and a great deal more. She has, we believe, already astonished all Paris, and we have little doubt that her fame in London will rapidly spread. La La, as we have hinted, is a representative of a dark-skinned race, but in the matter of strength she is prepared to assert her superiority of the boastful people who will have it that all the virtues are associated with a light complexion. La La commences her duties by mounting to a framework suspended above the stage, and from there she hangs head downwards. A boy, a young woman, and a man now take it in turn to test the strength of her jaw. By means of a rope and pulley, which she holds in her mouth, they raise themselves to her elevation. They subsequently, upon a bar supported in a similar fashion, go through a number of those tricks generally to be found in the repertory of gymnast and acrobats, La La, apparently, being altogether indifferent as to whether one or two persons are upon the bar, going through the familiar evolutions. The man of the party is presently hauled aloft, and being taken by the teeth of the Amazon, is turned into a kind of human teetotum [a kind of spinning top], to be whirled round with an amount of rapidity which, we should say, was conducive to a shocking attack of giddiness. Then La La, still hanging by her legs, supports three men … one by her teeth and the other two by her hands and arms. Her great feat, and that which should undoubtedly prove the sensation, comes at the end of her share of the entertainment. Six men strain their muscles to lift to her a cannon of no mean dimensions. This also she supports by her teeth alone, never leaving her hold even when, the match being applied, the gun is fired and gives a tremendous report. La La is evidently a very modest young lady, and she takes the compliments that are heaped upon her in the way of hearty plaudits with becoming reserve, and bows her acknowledgements in style which seems to indicate that her tasks, although apparently difficult, and in reality difficult to ordinary mortals, are to her matters of the greatest ease and simplicity (*The Era* 16 March 1879)

There is a very different tone to this piece. It is more of a genuine review that applauds La La's performance rather than decrying it. There is a veiled reference to those who propound the racial superiority of the white race, but in this instance the reviewer raises La La above that. Neither does he demean her as a woman. The latter part refers to her modesty and reserve at her accomplishments. True, he does use the term 'Amazon', and in this it sets up a tension between the exotic and the intimidating. La La was severally referred to in the press as 'the black Venus', 'the dusky lady', 'the African Princess', and 'the Venus of the Tropics'. All of these terms infer an exoticism and sensuality. Juxtaposed against this we have other descriptions of her, such as 'la mulâtresse-canon'[6] (literally translated from the French as 'mulatto cannon woman', alluding to her skin colour) that infer that she,

is a formidable, rather intimidating, and ultimately castrating "cannon-woman," an Amazon" with "miraculous," phenomenal strength who puts mere "hulking" white men in the shade by comparison, or else spins them into dizzy "human teetotums" as she "takes them" with her teeth. (Brown, 2007)

She was to be both desired and feared at one and the same time; for the repressed Victorian male she could be a fantasy of the bedroom tempered with the fear of an overbearing nanny or governess.

By 1880, La La was back in Paris at the Hippodrome[7]. Now she had teamed up with an Austrian girl who performed under the name Kaira. Sometimes they appeared as *Olga and Kaira*, at other times *Kara and Olga*; it seems to have been an equal partnership. It will be remembered that it was the Kaira troupe who performed with La La at the Cirque Fernando, so we can assume that Kaira was a member of that original troupe. Kaira's real name was Theophila Szterker, and often referred to as 'Kaira the White' (Kaira la Blanche). Desbonnet (1911:352) records that Kaira was;

> une femme également superbe et qui faisait un numéro de voltige remarquable

> [a beautiful woman and who made a remarkable aerobatic number. *Author's translation*]

They regularly performed at the Hippodrome through the early years of the 1880s, in a daring aerial act;

> Mlles Olga et Kaira sont encore plus étonnantes. Olga se pend par les pieds a plus de vingt mètres du sol et tend les mains a Kaira, qui, de quinze mètres de distance, s'élance dans le vide, et vient se pendre aux mains de sa compagne. Et cela si gracieusement qu'on n'a pas peur. (*Le Rappel* 10 July 1883)[8]

> [Miss Olga and Kaira are even more amazing. Olga hangs herself by the feet more than twenty meters from the ground and offers her hands to Kaira, who, fifteen meters away, jumps into the void, and comes to hang herself by the hands of her companion. And this so gracefully done that one is not afraid. *Author's translation*]

They went on to develop an aerial act which they called *Les deux Papillons* (The two Butterflies), and it was this act with which Olga returned to Britain in late 1883. They made their debut at the Westminster Aquarium in London, appearing as 'the black and white butterflies'. The Westminster Aquarium had been opened in 1876 as an aquarium but soon fell in to financial difficulties. Within a few years the managers had turned to a more profitable venture offering dangerous and sensational circus and variety acts. Olga and Kaira were just one such act. The *Morning Post* 16 October 1883 gave them quite a lot of coverage;

1880 poster for Miss La La and the Kaira Troupe *(Author's collection)*

A daring gymnastic exhibition, furnished by two female performers, Olga and Kaira, the one being an African and the other a Circassian. At any rate Kaira, whatever her birthplace, is fair-skinned and no-one would care to question Olga's Ethiopian descent … 'These beautifully formed female representative types of opposite climes' – to quote from the programme –'after many years' practice as amateurs, reached such perfection both of grace and skill that they have been persuaded to appear in public' … A number of tricks, not particularly novel, are first performed on the double trapeze, and these are followed by some singularly well-executed feats on the flying trapeze. Kaira, then, after walking on a wire without balance [presumably without a balance pole], leaps head downwards and forwards, a distance of 30 feet, into Olga's hands, and subsequently performed a genuinely sensational feat by leaping from a suspended vaulting board, turning a forward somersault, and being caught be her companion … The entertainment culminated in a headlong dive by 'the fair Circassian' from the high dome in to the net below.

The use of language in this report is again interesting and reflects the underlying social attitude towards race and colour, even if not deliberately meant by the writer of the piece. Kaira is described as both 'fair-skinned' and 'the fair Circassian'; this having a feeling of being praiseworthy and superior. Olga is merely described as being 'African' and of 'Ethiopian descent'. It is Kaira who does the dare-devil tricks. Olga appears to be relegated to a subsidiary of the act, taking part in some relatively simple tricks on the double trapeze before becoming nothing more than the 'catcher' to Kaira. This attitude was echoed by a similar report in the *Dundee Advertiser* of the next day, 17 October. In this they were reported as 'the Black and White Butterflies', and they were understood to be 'natives, the one of Circassia [alluding to her Caucasian ethnicity or perhaps her homeland in the region of North Caucasus] and the other of *some part of Africa* [Author italics], are sufficiently remarkable of their kind, although that kind doubtless will not commend itself to all tastes'.

Miss Kaira and Olga. *La Culture Physique* 15 March 1910

They went on to appear at the Canterbury Theatre of Varieties in December as 'Kairo [sic] and Olga the Black and White Butterflys'[9]. The poster is interesting to view. Olga is presented in side-on silhouette only, we see no physical details, thereby emphasising her 'blackness'. Kairo is presented half-turned towards the viewer and in full detail, emphasis being on her fairness and beauty. Another oddity of this poster is that Olga is drawn black on a white background under the black legend 'Kairo', and Kairo is drawn on a black background under the white legend 'Olga'. Was this an accidental design error or did the artist relate the names to the figures? Olga sounds more Circassian and Kairo has the more 'exotic' sound to it, therefore more likely to be 'black'.

Their stay in Britain was brief and they returned to Paris but even there, when reported in the British press, there were still overtones of racial discrimination in the language used. *The Stage* of 8 August 1884 made reference to 'One of them is a woman of colour, and the other as fair as a lilly [sic]'"

In their visit to Britain there is no mention of the cannon act that Olga had become famous for in earlier years. But by 1887, Olga is appearing at the Cirque d'Hiver in Paris. This time her partner is named Fatima in a pantomime piece entitled *La Lutte*. Lutte can be translated as a struggle, or sometimes wrestling. Olga's and Fatima's act takes place in the eighth scene. It is billed as;

> Entrée de saltimbanques. Luttes à main plate entre Olga ('Hercule féminin) et Fatma [sic] (la jolie Athlète) - Exercices de force et jeu du canon par Mlle Olga (*L'Orchestre; revue quotidienne des théâtres* 1 April 1885)

> [Entry of the acrobats. Flat hand fights between Olga (female Hercules) and Fatma (the pretty Athlete) - exercises of strength and cannon act by Miss Olga. *Author's translation*]

Again, the use of language is very descriptive and alludes to Olga's evident muscularity juxtaposed against the implied femininity of Fatima. Was this Fatima actually her partner Kaira? Certainly they worked together until 1888, when Kaira had a tragic and fatal accident whilst performing near Dusseldorf in Germany. On 21 June, during her final dive, she crashed to the ground and suffered for several days before passing away. With Kaira's death it would seem that Olga's performing career would take a new direction.

In 1887, whilst Olga was performing at the Cirque d'Hiver, across at the Cirque Fernando an American contortionist was making his debut. His name was Emanuel Woodson, although he performed under the name Manuel Woodson. He was of Afro-American heritage and was born in St. Louis, Missouri in 1859. He left the USA sometime after 14 April 1884[11] and became renowned as a 'quick' contortionist, preferring simple and effective figures done with fluid rapidity rather than more complicated 'close bending' which has to be executed slowly. A lavish perfectionist, used to the high life, he recounted in an interview for *The Sketch* in 1893[12] that it was his manager who encouraged him to get married in order to curb his lifestyle.

He married Olga "Miss Lu Lu" Brown on 11 October 1888 in Heligoland[13]. The year after his marriage he was appearing at the Canterbury Theatre of Varieties in London, but no mention is made of Olga.

In fact, Olga seems to disappear from performing reviews after her marriage.

That they were in Britain in 1894 is certain because Woodson was performing at *Hengler's Circus* on Argylle Street, with *Circus Wulff*[14]. While on this stop of their tour, their daughter, Rose Eddie Woodson, was born on 3 March and baptised on 22 March 1894 at All Souls church in St. Marylebone, London[15].

By the age of sixteen, in 1910, Rose was performing a dance act with dogs[16]. After this time records of Olga's life become a little confusing. Several different academics offer theories as to what happened next to her. Toulmin (2018) writes that she became part of a performing troupe named *The Three Keziahs*, which toured with Woodson. Laryea (2019) cites an article in *The New York Age*[17] of 21 November 1915 that claims that Woodson and Olga went on to have two more daughters and that the three children went on to perform as *The Three Keziahs*. I have yet to find any other reference to any daughters beyond Rose Eddie. The first mention of the Keziahs comes in a French newspaper of 3 March 1896, where both Woodson and the trio make their debut at the Nouveau

Cirque[18]. Here the Keziahs are called 'trois jeunes at jolies femmes' (three young and pretty women). The troupe made its first appearance in the British press in November 1896 at the Palace of Varieties in Manchester;

> The Keziahs are three demoiselles who cleverly and expeditiously distinguished themselves as upright ladder performers. The young ladies, who wear particularly bright costumes, appear on the ladders as benders, equilibrists, trapezists, and pendants. Their pyramid work is very effective and very skilful (*Music Hall and Theatre Review* 27 November 1896)

Now this review does not say that Olga is not one of the Keziahs, but it does refer to them as 'young ladies', and the French term 'demoiselles' also has implications of girls. Olga would have been thirty-eight years old at this time and had a two year old child of her own. Of course, this would not have prevented her from having gone back to performing, but I believe that she may well have trained the group, rather than performing in it.

Woodson does not appear on the same bill as the Keziahs again until July 1897 at the Empire Palace in Portsmouth[19]. The make-up of the Keziah troupe performing at the Blackpool Tower Circus the following year is given in small news insert in 1898;

FRENCH CYCLISTS ON THE FOOTPATH

> The Paris cyclists El Dorado, Manuel Woodson, Heline Keziah, and Ethel Keziah, performers at the Blackpool Tower, were charged at Kirkham, yesterday, with riding bicycles on the footpath. They pleaded ignorance of the law. The case was dismissed on payment of costs (*Yorkshire Evening Post* 14 July 1898)

So we have two names of the Keziahs but, unfortunately to date, it has not been able to confirm if these were daughters of Olga and Woodson. Was Olga, herself, the third Keziah?

We do not know, although the author believes it might have been Rose. I strongly suspect that these girls had been 'brought in' by Woodson, and maybe Olga, to create a performance troupe. My reasoning behind this is that in *The Era* of 28 October 1893, Woodson advertises for an;

> Apprentice, a Girl, Fifteen Years old, pretty and slender, but well made, to learn a Gymnastical Act, with Respectable Family.

It is quite possible that Heline or Ethel may have responded to this advertisement.

In March 1899, *The Three Keziahs* set out for Australia with Woodson[20]. Although no mention is made of Olga by name circumstantial evidence suggests she made the trip as well. In a later passport application, Olga mentions that she had toured widely, including Australia and New Zealand, so there is no reason to doubt this. They toured throughout Australia, the Keziahs with their 'silver ladder act' and Woodson with his contortionism. From Australia they moved on to New Zealand. It is while they were in Auckland that a Maude Woodson joined the company as a contortionist[21], perhaps another apprentice? The troupe plus Woodson were back in Britain between 1900 and 1902 but after that time all notices for the *Three Keziahs* disappear. Woodson appears to have given up performing and took up the management of the Palais d'Eté Variety Theatre in Brussels, Belgium in 1903[22], where he remained until his death from liver trouble in August 1915[23].

Olga, now a widow, remained with her daughter Rose, who had made a career as a dancer. In her 1911 passport application she was in Warsaw[24], at that time in Russia, where she stated that she was 'sojourning temporarily' and that she was a 'music hall artist'. In 1916 she was in The Hague, the Netherlands, applying again for an American passport. This appears to have been rejected, as a letter attached to the Application states;

The applicants have no family ties or business connections with the United States and apparently no desire to proceed there. In view of the fact that their [Olga and Rose] interests seem to lie chiefly in Belgium I do not recommend that a passport be issued to them as their residence there would not come into any of the categories approved of by the Department's regulations on residence of American citizens abroad.[25]

The final date that we can assign to Olga and Rose is in 1919, when she made her final application in Brussels for an American passport[26]. This again was recommended for rejection by the Legation. There are no American immigration records for either Olga or Rose, and neither do they appear on any American databases, apart from the Passport Applications described. What happened to them after 1919 is presently unknown.

Physically small she may have been, but Olga Brown was a larger than life character who, fortunately for us today, was immortalised in that moment of performance by Edgar Degas.

Notes

1. https://familysearch.org/pal:/MM9.1.1/N6CB-886

2. *1919 USA Passport application under her married name of Wood-son.* Online at https://www.myheritage.com/research/re-cord-10720-1899655/olga-woodson-in-united-states-pass-port-applications?s=118043382

3. https://www.genealogyfreelancers.com/project-1270/Archive-Re-search-Genealogy-Research/Husband-and-Wife-in-Bredow. html#

4. Refer to Chapter 1

5. *The Era* 22 December 1878

6. *The Era* 2 February 1879

7. *Hippodrome poster for Kira & Olga* 1880. Online at https://gallica.bnf. fr/ark:/12148/btv1b9004252z.r=Kaira?rk=42918;4

8. *Le Rappel* 10 July 1883. Online at https://gallica.bnf.fr/ark:/12148/ bpt6k75403638/f3.item.r=Olga%20et%20Kaira.zoom

9. *Poster held at the British Library.* Online at https://www.bl.uk/collec-tion-items/poster-advertising-kairo-and-olga-the-black-and-white-butterflys

10. *Le Cri du Peuple* 5 July 1888. Online at https://gallica.bnf.fr/ ark:/12148/bpt6k4683554n/f4.image.r=Kaira?rk=729617;2

11. USA passport application dated 14 April 1884. Online at https:// www.ancestry.com/family-tree/person/tree/151653980/ person/162010828589/facts

12. *The Sketch* 3 January 1893

13. Heligoland is a group of islands off the north-west coat of Germany. Originally belonging to Denmark, between 1807 and 1890 they were governed by Britain. In 1890 they became part of Germany.

14. *The Referee* 14 January 1894

15.   https://www.ancestry.co.uk/interactive/1558/31280_19920 5-00285?pid=5521939&backurl=https://search.ancestry.co.uk/cgi-bin/sse.dll?indiv%3D1%26dbid%3D1558 %26h%3D5521939%26tid%3D%26pid%3D%26useP-UB%3Dtrue%26_phsrc%3Dsbc1638%26_phstart%3D-successSource&treeid=&personid=&hintid=&useP-UB=true&_phsrc=sbc1638&_phstart=successSource&use-PUBJs=true&_ga=2.226519641.532646855.1582214018-1986502099.1539097385

16. *La Culture physique: revue bi-mensuelle illustrée* p173. Online at https://gallica.bnf.fr/ark:/12148/bpt6k54226414/f17.image. r=Manuel%20Woodson?rk=21459;2

17. I have been unable to access this article to corroborate the citation.

18. *La Presse* 3 March 1896. Online at https://gallica.bnf.fr/ark:/12148/ bpt6k548004p/f4.item.r=Manuel%20Woodson.zoom

19. *Music Hall and Theatre Review* 23 July 1897

20. *Clare's Weekly* (Perth WA) 4 March 1899. Online at https://trove.nla. gov.au/newspaper/article/14209908?searchTerm=Three%20 Keziahs&searchLimits

21. *The Era* 21 October 1899

22. *La Culture physique: revue bi-mensuelle illustrée* p173. Online at https://gallica.bnf.fr/ark:/12148/bpt6k54226414/f17.image. r=Manuel%20Woodson?rk=21459;2

23. *Reports of Deaths of American Citizens Abroad 1835 – 1974.* Online at https://www.ancestry.com/interactive/1616/31070_1709 60-00187/191701?backurl=https://www.ancestry.com/family-tree/person/tree/151653980/person/162010828589/facts/ citation/622013711039/edit/record

24. US passport application 1911. Online at https://www.myheritage. com/research/record-10720-56843/olga-woodson-in-united-states-passport-applications?s=118043382

25. Letter attached to US passport application 1916/1917. Online at https://www.myheritage.com/research/record-10720-1210895/olga-woodson-in-united-states-passport-applications?s=118043382

26. US passport application 1919. Online at https://www.myheritage. com/research/record-10720-1899655/olga-woodson-in-united-states-passport-applications?s=118043382

Leona Dare. Carte de Visite c. 1875 *(Author's collection)*

CHAPTER 6
QUEEN OF THE ANTILLES
– LEONA DARE

Iron Jaw performances by female artists were not uncommon during the Victorian period. In fact, Miss La La was only one of several women at this time to take to the air suspended only be her teeth! One of her contemporaries, another woman of mixed heritage, performed under the name of Leona Dare.

Her given name was Susan Adeline Stuart (sometimes also written as Stewart). Her death certificate[1] gives a year of birth as 1858 (although this may in fact have been a few years earlier in 1854, as a descendent of hers claims) and her parents as Andrew J. Stewart and Anna Meiza. An article in the *Freeland Tribune* of 29 March 1900[2] gives a fully detailed description of her life in her own words.

> My father, Andrew Jackson Stuart, was a Scotchman by descent, born in Georgia. He served in the Mexican war and afterwards settled in Iuka, Miss. He brought back from that war not only the rank of colonel but my mother, who was a Mexican. When the war of the Rebellion broke out I was a little girl and the last I saw of my father he rode away to join a cavalry regiment. He never came back, having been killed in battle. The Federal army, coming to the vicinity of our home, my mother, with my two brothers and myself 'refugeed' as we call it, into Indiana. At the close of the war my mother went South to see if she could find any remains of our property, and I have never seen her since. She had left us in the care of neighbours, who turned us over to the postmaster, who promptly farmed us out.

We know that Susan had two brothers; Meredith Leonard Stuart and John Stuart, as one of Meredith's great grand-nephew confirmed in a genealogical report[3]. Meredith was born 10 October 1858 in Iuka[4], with the father given as Andrew J Stewart, so that part of her account does confirm that they shared the same father. This being so, then there is every reason to accept her other facts given – within reason.

In an obituary in *The New York Times*[5] her father is promoted to the rank of General, and her mother apparently killed at the Alamo massacre. We clearly have to question the sources of this obituary. The battle of the Alamo took place in 1836, at least twenty years before Susan was born and she herself stated that at the end of the [civil] war her mother returned south. This would have taken place around 1865/6 and accords with Susan's claim that she started to work in a circus at around ten years old. However, a lengthy article in *The Arkansas Gazette* of 1912[6] entitled *What became of the 'Child of the Alamo', Lost during Sherman's Match to the Sea?* offers a little more sense.

It would seem, according to this account, that it was the grandmother of Leona Dare who was killed at the Alamo, leaving her newly born daughter Annie Meiza in the care of soldiers. The child was sent to Cuba to be educated and then returned to America at the age of about thirteen. It was here that she met Andrew J. Stuart, Leona Dare's father. There is no historical evidence to support her claims and there is an element of romantic mythology surrounding her parents and her early years, perhaps built around stories she may have read of the Alamo. This may have been her own invention or created by an agent wanting to create a more 'exotic' image for her. Groneman (2019) recounts the authenticated story of the 'Baby of the Alamo', Angelina Dickinson and he have never heard of the story of Leona's 'Child of the Alamo'[6]. In an email to the author 28 February 2020, Groneman writes; 'I can say without hesitation that I've never heard that story before. I'm guessing that it is Victorian era flim-flam'

There are other instances in her life when fact and fiction appear to have become so intertwined that it is difficult to know where one starts and the other ends without any primary evidence.

Here, in 1902, a colourful newspaper story places her somewhere in Michigan;

> The big omnibus collided with a cage that contained two powerful lions and Miss Leona Dare, their tamer. It was hurled across the street and turned over ... Miss Dare was stunned by the shock and her body was thrown out into the street. One of the lions sprang over the girl, and the other stopped couchant by her side. His eyes were glaring with rage and his mane fairly bristled as he began to roar and gnash his teeth ... A black horse, with an Indian on his back, shot through the street with the speed of an arrow ... The trained animal, going at the top of his speed, stopped for a second at the side of the lions. The accomplished horseman, with a quick movement, leaned over and picked the girl up from under the nose of the astonished lion (*Muskegon Daily Chronicle* 30 June 1902)

The "Indian on horseback" was Chief Harry Edge, who opposed the 1887 Dawes Act[7] and the article gave details of his many exploits. An evocative drawing showing him galloping toward the lions as they stand over the recumbent Leona Dare accompanies the article.

But did it ever happen? I have found no other reference to Leona Dare being a lion tamer, and in the few years leading up to the 1887 Act, Dare is recorded as performing throughout Europe. A possible copycat act or another part of the romancing of Leona Dare?

Whatever the mystery of her upbringing, she was spotted by two gymnast brothers, Thomas and Stuart Hall, and trained as a trapeze and tightrope artist.

It has been suggested that her first engagements may have been under the name of 'Mademoiselle Zoe' in a theatre in New Orleans in 1865, although reviews for this artiste do not specifically mention aerial work. In a later court hearing (see [15]), Thomas Hall said that she had gone to New Orleans in 1869 to look for work. The two brothers performed as the 'Dare Brothers'. When Susan married Thomas Hall in 1871, she took the name *Leona Dare* as her stage name. It would be under this name that she would enter fame.

Susan Adeline "Leona Dare" Stuart Hall began her early performing career in the United States and a report from Indianopolis, quoted in several British newspapers gives us an idea of her act;

> Many of our readers remember Miss Leona Dare, who resided in this city last fall and winter ... She went away from here last Spring and has been West since, thrilling people there with performances on a trapeze suspended to a balloon which was rising ... Leona, in circus clothes, dangling down from the trapeze bar, holding in her teeth a strap which encircled the wait of Tommy Hall [her husband] ... Just as soon as they left the earth Leona commences spinning Hall round until it made us giddy (*Henley Adviser* 17 August 1872)

The act continued with a doubles trapeze between Dare and Hall at a height of over three hundred feet. There are clear similarities between Dare and Miss La La, although the latter confined her acts to the stage. She continued to tour throughout the United States during the first half of the decade, appearing in such places as New York[8] and Boston[9].

Interestingly and perplexingly, a report was given in January of 1876[10] that a young performer by the name of Leona Dare had fallen from a trapeze in a performance in New Orleans, dying of her injuries. As Dare was performing in Boston the following May, either this was a misreporting of her death or there was another performer using the

The rescue of Leona Dare by Chief Harry Edge. Illustration published in the *Muskegon Daily Chronicle* 30 June 1902

same name. This might also have a bearing on the 'lion-tamer' incident previously mentioned.

In any event, by the autumn of 1876, Dare had made her entrance into Europe and was appearing at the famous Parisian theatre – the Folies Bergèr.

> She is in fact creating quite a *furore* in Paris, and the admirers of the beautiful Americaine [sic] may be counted by the thousands. Her performance is too complicated to be described here; but I may mention that she executes the rare feat of holding a man in mid-air with her teeth, she meanwhile hanging by the legs from a trapeze, and without using her arms in any way to support her (*Yorkshire Post and Leeds Intelligencer* 30 November 1876)

An interesting performance for a woman who was supposedly reported dead! Leona Dare took the Parisian audiences by storm and, it has to be remembered, before Miss La La made her mark at the Cirque Fernando a little while later. Dare continued to perform in Paris and Vienna before making a move to England. There, at the end of October 1878, she made her first appearance at the Oxford Music Hall in London, England;

> Miss Leona Dare made her *debut* at the Oxford on Monday last. She is assisted by a male representative of her profession. Avoiding the conventional mode of being raised to the high trapeze from the ground by others, or reaching it by means of a ladder, Leona Dare, with a leather or gutta-percha strap attached to a pulley rope, placed between her teeth hoists herself up from the floor to the roof of the building, where she goes through most astonishing and graceful performances. Her most wonderful feat, however, is – after having traversed nearly the whole length of the hall on a long trapeze to another fixed on the stage – her seizing her male companion [not her husband], by means of a strap affixed to his waist belt, between her teeth … performing a variety of evolutions with him in that position … All these performances are effected without the protection of a net, but we are assured that there

is not the slightest ground for apprehension (*Western Times* 7 October 1878)

We are fortunate in that some of her aerial equipment, notably the mouth piece that she used, is on display in the North West Museum of Arts and Culture in Spokane, Washington[11]. Although an accomplished performer on the trapeze, this 'iron-jaw' act would be her signature performance. She was one of a growing number of female performers who were confounding the prevalent, and largely patriarchal, opinion that female bodies were inferior to male bodies by becoming one of the leading names in a male dominated circus discipline. Her performances were not to everyone's taste, as we see in the following review (written by a man no doubt!);

> A fine woman is Leona Dare; but I say no more about her, because that sort of performance – woman, however graceful, dangling in the air by her feet and with a button in her mouth, sustaining a man, whom she twirls round like a whipping-top, till he loses the shape on a man, and looks like a bell – is almost too painful (*The Entr'Acte* 2 November 1878)

Although she may have initially perfected the 'spinning-man' routine with her husband Thomas, the two separated around 1875 and performed apart. The Dare Brothers, Thomas and John, were performing at the Royal Aquarium in London in the November of 1877[12], the year before Leona Dare hit England. Thomas and John continued working throughout Britain with their 'laughable gymnastic performance'[13], before travelling to Spain and Portugal in the autumn of 1879[14].

In May 1879, Leona Dare was again in the British newspapers[15], this time for a different reason.

Thomas Hall brought a court action against his wife and Mr. Jennings, the manager of the Oxford, to recover possession of aerial equipment used by Leona Dare in her performances. Dare did not attend the hearing as she was performing in Europe, possibly Vienna at the time. She gave her evidence by written deposition. Hall claimed that he had made the apparatus specifically for his wife. He had gone to the Oxford and confronted her and demanded the return of his property. She refused, claiming that she used it in her professional work with his knowledge and consent. The matter was debated in court and the jury decided that consent had not been given and accordingly the judge ordered that the aerial apparatus be returned to Hall or 100 pounds sterling be paid to him in default of it being returned. The case was covered in many newspapers (for the public, it made titillating and diverting reading from Britain's involvement in the Zulu Wars) but it was never recorded if Leona Dare returned the equipment or paid off Hall.

As she continued to perform her routine, I suspect that it was more effective for her to pay the money, and presumably she was still actually using the equipment while she was abroad in Europe. Why Hall should have waited so long before attempting to recover the material can only be guessed. Was it the case that Leona Dare, Thomas' protégé and estranged wife, was becoming so well known that there was an element of jealousy and 'sour-grapes' in his action?

Certainly she was in Vienna in the spring of 1880 performing with *Circus Renz*, which was a well-respected German circus of the time with permanent circus buildings in Berlin, Hamburg, Bremen, Breslau, and Vienna. Dare was, if nothing else, a socialite and enjoyed the high life. Not long after her arrival in Austria she caused something of a scandal while attending a dinner in her honour at Pappenberg's, a fashionable restaurant in Vienna. Members of the elite and several high ranking Court dignitaries attended, and the Crown Prince was scandalised at the behaviour that was reported to him. The 'scandal' was covered widely in the British press, although actual details were scant. It appeared that the gentlemen present 'drank to the health of the well-known tight-rope dancer' (*Globe* 17 January 1880). Two of the offenders, one a Prince and the other a Count, promptly left the Court. Dare certainly cut an attractive figure. With long dark hair swept back, and piercing black eyes, her Hispanic heritage was quite evident. She was called, at various times, the 'Queen of the Antilles'[16] or the 'Queen of Madrid', reflecting her appearance. However, her skin was quite light – it was described as being creamy – and as such, much more acceptable within an Anglo-Saxon society than skin with more pronounced pigmentation.

Both Leona Dare and Miss La La performed under the banner of being American citizens but La La was darker skinned and therefore lower in the pecking order of the Victorian constructed racial hierarchy. Advertising imagery for Leona Dare seemed to emphasise her 'whiteness' and portrayed her as a former day heroic 'Wonder-woman', often appearing under the billowing Stars and Stripes of America[17]. The lighter skinned Leona Dare was deemed an incredible performer in spite of her mixed heritage. Conversely, advertising for La La emphasised her 'blackness' and exoticism. The darker skinned La La was seen as an incredible performer because of her 'otherness', despite being of mixed heritage like Dare. Due to an accident while performing in Hamburg in June 1880, she was forced into a temporary retirement, although some reports felt the situation might be permanent.

> Leona Dare, the bold trapeze performer, has met with a serious accident, by which she will probably for a long time, if not altogether, be incapacitated from again appearing in her *tours de force*, all her teeth being injured (*The Era* 27 June 1880)

It appears that the trapeze swung back into her face causing her teeth break. Another report gave a less than sympathetic response to her injuries;

> Leona Dare has given her dentist a big order, and it is more than probable she will never resume those of her duties in which the jaw played a prominent a part; at least, it will be with somebody else's teeth if she does (*London and Provincial Entr'acte* 10 July 1880)

While recovering from her injuries in Vienna she managed to court controversy once again. Being separated (estranged) from her husband Thomas Hall she considered herself to be not married. Susan met a young Count by the name of Ernest Grunebaum and in a whirlwind romance, they got married in June 1880. Dare was now a bigamist! During the Victorian era divorce was both difficult and expensive to come by. For a woman there was also the stigma attached of being a divorcee. Although the Matrimonial Causes Act (UK) of 1857 permitted men to file for divorce simply on the grounds of adultery, women had to provide further evidence of incest, bestiality or bigamy. For many couples whose marriage had disintegrated it was easier and cheaper just to part, and should either remarry declare themselves as 'single'. This was a relatively common situation at this time, although if discovered it could attract a custodial sentence. Susan and Ernest returned to Chicago, where she intended to have dental work carried out, and there she presented herself as the Countess Grunebaum. She managed to obtain an official divorce from Hall *in absentia* and then legally remarried Grunebaum on 15 November 1880[18]. Ernest's father attempted to have the marriage declared null and void[19] in 1882, as Ernest was a minor at the time, but the case failed. The Count and his newly-minted Countess had not been married long before their extravagant lifestyle caught up with them. Dare was still recovering and had not returned to performing as yet. Without income, the couple had to declare themselves bankrupt[20], and the bailiffs seized 2,000 pounds sterling worth of jewellery (approximately 135,000 pounds sterling today). Leona Dare certainly liked a lavish living. The two later separated. Grunebaum moved to South Africa, where he later died, disowned by his father.

By this time, however, Leona Dare's dental re-fit had been completed, and she returned to performing in the spring of 1882. February saw her back with *Circus Renz* in Berlin, the company with which she had had her accident. That May, she was back in Paris at the Hippodrome.

I believe that the accident may have affected her confidence because while performing in Spain in 1884 she was involved in a fatal accident;

Lately, at the Princess's Theatre, Valencia, Spain, Leona Dare, the American acrobat, was suspended from the roof of the theatre by her feet, and held in her teeth the ropes of a trapeze-bar on which a male acrobat, known as M. George, was performing. During the act Miss Dare was seized with a nervous fit and dropped the trapeze. M. George and the apparatus dropped whirling to the floor. The audience were horror stricken. Every one rushed for the doors, and a panic ensued, in which many people were crushed and otherwise injured. Miss Dare clung to the roof, screaming hysterically. She was rescued with difficulty after the excitement had somewhat subsided and is now confined to her bed from exhaustion following the shock. M. George has since, by cable, been reported dead, and Miss Dare in a precarious condition (*London and Provincial Entr'acte* 13 December 1884)

One might expect that, with this fatal accident happening under her watch, Dare would give up the performing life. She was clearly very shaken by what had happened and took some time to recover, not appearing in a single press notice for the next several years.

However, after what must have been a difficult two years, she made a tremendous comeback in 1886 with perhaps her most astounding feat. It was obviously something that she had planned for a long time and, given that there were now several other 'iron-jaw' acts on the circuit, she needed something spectacular to regain her public renown. She was hauled to the roof of a theatre by her teeth every night in her old act, but Leona had planned a new exploit that would test the bounds of credibility.

At the Parc Leopold [in Brussels, Belgium] on the 11th inst. Leona Dare actually performed the bold and difficult feat of holding on by her teeth to a sling suspended from the car of a balloon as it rose in the air … and it was only when Leona Dare could no longer be distinguished except with the aid of glasses that she drew herself up to the trapeze and entered the car by a trap-door in the bottom … It appears that Leona has been contemplating this Dare-ing [awful pun!] feat for three years but was prevented by indisposition from carrying it out (*The Era* 17 July 1886)

The Ascent of Leona Dare from a Balloon at the Crystal Palace. *The Illustrated Police News* 16 June 1888 *(Author's collection)*

Perhaps she had been planning this act before the fatal accident in Spain but, this time, she had heeded cautionary advice and attached herself to the balloon's car by a safety rope. A second news report[21] suggests that the balloon rose to the impressive height of 1,500 metres (about 5,000 feet). Certainly, she must have regained her nerve somewhat.

For this exploit, she had teamed up with a Signor Spelterini, who was a well-known balloonist, or aeronaut as they were called then. She would continue to work with him over the next few years. The next recorded instance of her performing her 'ascending balloon' feat was at the Vienna Flower Festival in July of the next year.

Astounding audiences across Europe in cities such as Berlin, Vienna, Budapest, Moscow, and Brussels, she arrived back in England for the Whitsun holiday celebrations at the Crystal Palace.

Here it was widely advertised that she would perform her 'new and startling open air Balloon Ascent'[22]. No more details than this were initially given but, the first performances being presented, the British press wanted to know more. She was interviewed by journalists and details of how such an act could be executed were given in her own words;

> Miss Leona Dare has been obliging enough to explain how the feat is accomplished. A trapeze is attached to the bottom of the basket suspended from the balloon, and "to the cross-bar an iron hook is fixed, which has an india-rubber mouthpiece at one end [see note [12]]. This, Miss Dare proceeds, "I take into my mouth; the balloon is started, and I ascend, hanging below it with my arms and legs, and, in fact, my while body perfectly free except that I hold the mouthpiece between my teeth" ... How long do your teeth stand the terrible strain? ... "For a quarter of an hour or twenty minutes I can do it without any special fatigue. Sometimes we are over 3000 metres high by that time; at all events I am out of sight of the spectators below. When I begin to get tired I catch the bar, sit on it, and give the captain ... a sign. A

ladder is handed to me and I get into the basket through a trap-door in the bottom of it … Through gradual and continual training the teeth, jaws, and muscles of the neck get very strong indeed, and as soon as I begin to feel the fatigue I leave off, for, falling from a height of, say, three thousand metres, I could not get up and resume work after the interruption" (*Daily Gazette for Middlesbrough* 21 May 1888)

The authorities insisted that Dare should have a safety rope attached to her as she had before, as a condition of allowing her to perform her feat. This she did, but on one occasion while performing in Leicester that August, she was seen casting off the rope and continuing her performances[23].

The dangers of a fatal fall were often compounded by the weather conditions. The following month, still in Leicester, strong winds made controlling the balloon very difficult and Dare managed to complete her performance but returned to earth visibly shaken.

Her performances were not without their critics, and drew comment throughout her stay in England. A letter to the *London Evening Standard*[24] complained that it was 'a deliberate courting of a hideous catastrophe', and another article in the *Yorkshire Post*[25] forcefully made the point that 'Any such performances … are contrary to good morals, debasing, retrograde, uncivilised, and ought to be denounced and discontinued'. Strong words indeed, but they did not deter the intrepid Leona.

Dare and Spelterini returned to the continent for at least one more exploit together that year. In November a balloon ascent was made in Antwerp, Belgium but there was consternation when it seemed to disappear and nothing was heard from them for several days. Eventually word reached that they had landed safely near Turnhout, some fifty kilometres away from their starting point. After this she and Spelterini appear to have parted company for a while.

Throughout the early part of 1889, Dare appears on the bills for the Folies Bergèr in Paris once again. Ballooning was obviously still a passion for her. That May she was trying to arrange a series of balloon and trapeze performances at the Eiffel Tower, although it is unclear if this actually took place.

One event that did happen was the following month as part of the Paris Flower Festival. A captive balloon ascent was made in the Bois de Boulogne[26]. This was not a free flight, as she had made previously with Spelterini, as the balloon was tethered and could only reach a certain height, but still impressive for the Parisian audience. It is not certain if Spelterini was actually the pilot of this ascent but we do know that they were together again in the October of 1889.

Buiu (2007) relates that the Dare and Spelterini had been performing together in Moscow, where they were attacked during their balloon's descent by fanatical mob of Russian peasants. Surviving this ordeal they arrived in Romania where, between October 8 and October 22, they made three ascents with Dare performing on the trapeze, in the Cismigiu Gardens in Bucharest. After this time, the records reveal one more performance by Dare and Spelterini at Porte Maillot in Paris in 1890, in which Dare broke her leg in a fall (Tait 2005:46).

What happened to her after this is not certain. Spelterini took his ballooning exploits to Switzerland but Dare did not go with him. She disappears from all press commentary during the 1890s, apart from occasional retrospective comments about her career.

During the early 1900s a trapeze artist called Leona Dare does make an appearance in Britain, though it remains unclear if the performer was actually Susan Stuart. This "Leona Dare" performed at many of the chain of Empire theatres owned by Edward Moss and Oswald Stoll, including the well-known Leicester Square Empire, the Glasgow

Empire, and many others around the country. In 1903, she was at the Empire in Edinburgh;

> The trapeze act of Leona Dare, who seems to be a form of feminine Sandow[27], was also one that met with approval. Hanging by the heels from a trapeze, she supports a young lady who sings prettily who plays a violin solo in a position of difficulty, and finally, still hanging head downwards, holds up from the ground a piano and the young lady seated at it for a sufficiency of time to enable the pianist to sing a song. The 'lift' was said to amount to 600 pounds (*The Scotsman* 23 June 1903)

This type of act was well within Susan Stuart's repertoire, but by this time she would have been in her forties and had had several injuries that would have ended most acrobats' careers. Was she still able to continually punish her body by repeated performances of this kind—especially as much of the work consisted of one or two night stands before travelling on to the next venue?

The last mention of Leona Dare in the British press was in March, 1906[28], where she is described as giving a 'remarkably clever musical trapeze act' at the London Hippodrome. But the central question remains – was this Susan Stuart an impersonator? Could it have even been the same impersonator as the one previously? At this point we simply do not know. What we do know is that Susan 'Leona Dare' Stuart eventually retired to live with a niece in Spokane, Washington. Exactly when she arrived back in America is unsure, but there is an immigration record for a Leona Dare arriving at Ellis Island in 1909[29], which could easily be her.

She lived out the rest of her life in Spokane and died there in June, 1922. Her death was briefly mentioned in the British press;

> The beautiful Leona Dare, who was the idol of the Oxford nearly forty years ago, recently died in New York [sic] alone and forgotten at the

age of 67. How frequently do the dazzling beauties of bygone days end their lives in such sad surroundings (*The Stage* 15 June 1922)

A brief obituary for a woman who had defied Victorian perceptions of gender and ethnicity. Leona Dare had wowed audiences across America and Europe during the second half of the nineteenth century and should be celebrated along with all the other ethnic minority performers of the era who achieved so many incredible successes.

Notes

1. Washington, Death Certificates 1907 – 1960. Online at https://www.myheritage.com/research/record-30019-146524/leona-dare-in-washington-death-certificates?s=118043382

2. She was interviewed by an old friend Townsend Percy and she gave a detailed account of her life. The full article can be read online at; https://www.newspapers.com/image/465086116/?terms=leona%2Bdare

3. Ancestry Message Board submitted by Chris Fox 4 March 2006. Online at; https://www.ancestry.com/boards/thread.aspx?mv=-flat&m=1883&p=localities.northam.usa.states.newyork.counties.richmond

4. Birth record available online at; https://www.myheritage.com/research/record-40001-1597022434/meredith-leonard-charley-stewart-in-familysearch-family-tree?s=118043382

5. *The New York Times* May 25 1922. Online at; https://timesmachine.nytimes.com/timesmachine/1922/05/25/107057487.pdf

6. The full and informative article can be read online at; file:///C:/Users/Steve/Pictures/LD%20true%20story%201912%20untitled.pdf

7. The Dawes Act, or Indian General Allotment Act, of January 1887 was signed in by President Grover Cleveland and gave powers to divide Indian reservation land into separate tracts of land for individual tribal members.

8. *The Era* 25 April 1875

9. *The Era* 7 May 1876

10. *Sheffield Independent* 3 January 1876

11. The items can also be viewed online at; https://www2.northwest-museum.org/museum/detail-leona-dares-aeronaut-mouth-piece-and-case-33334.htm

12. *Illustrated Sporting and Dramatic News* 11 November 1877

13. *The Era* 20 April 1879

14. *The Era* 14 September 1879

15. A detailed account of the hearing can be found in the Morning Post 29 May 1879.

16. The Antilles was the general name given to the group of islands in the Caribbean with the exception of Bahama.

17. Posters held at the BNF. Online at; https://gallica.bnf.fr/ark:/12148/btv1b9015601m.r=Leona%20Dare?rk=21459;2 ; https://gallica.bnf.fr/ark:/12148/btv1b53198986f.r=Leona%20Dare?rk=21459;2

18. *The New York Times* 26 November 1880

19. *Le Galoise* 18 September 1882. Online at; https://gallica.bnf.fr/ark:/12148/bpt6k524365g/f3.image.r=leona%20dare'leona%20dare'?rk=901292;0

20. *London and Provincial Entr'acte* 26 February 1881

21. *Officiel-Artiste* 15 July 1886. Online at; https://gallica.bnf.fr/ark:/12148/bpt6k6252840z.r=Mlle%20Leona%20Dare?rk=21459;2

22. *Croydon Advertiser* 12 May 1888.

23. *Sheffield Evening* Telegraph 9 August 1888

24. *London Evening Standard* 1 June 1888

25. *Yorkshire Post* 6 October 1888

26. *Morning Post* 3 June 1889

27. Eugen Sandow (1867 – 1925) was a German (Prussian) body builder and showman. The strong woman Sandwina (Katie Brumbach 1884-1952) took her name when she bested Sandow in a weight lifting contest in 1902.

28. *The Era* 3 March 1906

29. Ellis Island Immigration Records. Online at; https://www.libertyellisfoundation.org/passenger-details/czoxMjoiMTAxNTYwMTcwMTMzIjs=/czo5OiJwYXNzZW5nZXIiOw==

CHAPTER 7

THE GREAT AFRICAN ROPE DANCERS – GEORGE AND JOHN CHRISTOFF

Herr Christoff sounds a very Germanic name but, like many other performers of the era, it was an adopted stage name that hides the real identity. 'Herr' Christoff, the famous tight rope artist of colour, was born George Frederick Christopher. The actual date and place of his birth is unknown; extant records suggest a date of either 1828[1] or 1829[2]. Likewise, his place of birth is given as either South Wales[3] or Middlesex[4]. What we can say for certain is that his baptism took place on 24 July 1831 in Suffolk[5]. His parents were given as Kitt (a shortened name for Christopher) Christopher and Rosina.

It is possible that George was born into a performing family, as there is evidence that Kitt was a performer himself;

> Balancing feats were also exhibited, and in one of these canons illustrations of the sights which delighted our fair-going ancestors, the balancing of a cart-wheel is represented— a trick which might have been witnessed not many years ago in the streets of London, the performer being an elderly negro, said to have been the father of the well-known rope-dancer, George Christoff, who represented the Pompeian performer on the cord-elastique when Mr. Oxenford's version of The Last Days of Pompeii was produced at the Queen's Theatre (Frost 1875:20)

As Kitt died in 1865, this observation of him being a performer is quite plausible and is supported by an advertisement in the *Maidstone Gazette* of 20 December 1842;

ASSEMBLY ROOM, STAR HOTEL ... the extraordinary Performances of Signor CHRISTOFF and Family

This advert tells us two important things. Firstly, that although George Frederick took the stage name of Christoff it is unlikely that he was the 'Signor' mentioned in the newspaper; he would only have been in his early teens. It seems likely that it was Kitt, his father, who was performing with the family, including his not-yet-famous son George. (I say "his son" as Kitt's wife Rosina had died years earlier, in 1838.) The second point of note is that Kitt was using the name Christoff before George placed the 'Herr' in front of it and began his own career.

That Kitt was black has already been alluded to in the above Frost extract. George's ethnicity was also occasionally referred to in the press while he worked under the name Herr Christoff;

> Herr Christoff, an African tight-rope dancer has made his appearance at this Arena of Arts, and the astonishing feats performed nightly have been the wonder of crowded audiences. He is the most daring rope dancer we have ever seen (*The Era* 20 January 1856)

So, where did the family originate?

It is difficult to say without primary evidence, but when Kitt re-married in 1844 to a Rosehannah Gillart[6], he gave his father's profession as 'Mariner'. It would seem quite feasible that Kitt's father, George's grandfather (also confusingly named Kitt), was a black sailor who arrived in Britain from overseas somewhere and settled there. I mentioned a second marriage for Kitt junior, George's father. His wife Rosina (although no marriage certificate has yet been discovered) died in the spring of 1838[7], shortly before the baptism in August of their son John Henry Christopher[8], George's brother. This suggests that she either died in childbirth or shortly afterwards. So, Signor Christoff's performing family of 1842 probably included both George and John.

Signor Christoff on the Cord of Tension. Poster for Pablo Fanque's Circus Royal 1848 *(Reproduced with permission of Leeds Libraries, www.leodis.net)*

Kitt continued to perform with the title of 'Signor'. In 1848 he was appearing with *Pablo Fanque's Circus Royal* on Boar Lane, Leeds where he appeared on the Cord of Tension[9], another name for the tight-rope. A few years later he was working with his younger son John. In 1852 they appeared at the Rosherville Gardens in Ipswich;

P. and C. [Pryke and Coe] have much pleasure in announcing that they engaged the RENOWNED SONS of EUTHYMUS, SIGNOR CHRISTOFF & SON, whose wonderful feats have astonished every beholder. They will appear in their popular entertainment, entitled "A NIGHT WITH RISLEY". Master J. Christoff will, in the course of the evening dance his JUBA PLANTATION DANCE. Master Christoff will go through his wonderful feats on the tight rope. (*Suffolk Chronicle* 10 July 1852)

Juba at Vauxhall Gardens. *Illustrated London News* 5 August 1848 (*Author's collection*)

This is one of the very few occasions where a physical skills based performance is coupled with minstrelsy. Performing a Risley act and a tight rope act falls within the gamut of the 'circus arts' but the Juba Dance, making a direct reference to enslaved people and how the British Anglo-Saxon population perceived them, seems at odds with this.

The dance draws attention to the ethnicity of the Christoffs rather than focusing upon their acrobatic skills. Admittedly, the Juba Dance was quite energetic and athletic. Dickens (1842:36) witnessed such a dance and made wrote this description;

> Single shuffle, double shuffle, cut and cross-cut: snapping his fingers, rolling his eyes, turning in his knees, presenting the backs of his legs in front, spinning about on his toes and heels like nothing but the man's fingers on the tambourine

But was young John Christoff's performance received for its skill and athleticism? Or was it just seen as a quaint and quirky "black man's dance" that served only to reinforce a racial stereotype? Juba Dances, as performed by various African-Americans at this time, were not always well received and press reviews were sometimes full of racist bigotry;

> "Master Juba's" performances may be thus described; - At the end of the first part a monkey-faced mulatto, apparently about twenty years of age, glides onto the stage, attired as a woman, if aught of womankind ever wore such an aspect, and dances a "flash dance", which, exhibited outside a penny show few would stop to look at it. At the conclusion of the second part he enters in the costume of Jenny Lind ... and sings, or, rather screams, what purports to be a parody on the rataplan [a drumming or beating sound] ... at the end of the third part, the same "flash dance" is repeated, not this time in woman's attire, but in a costume, which we should conceive to be that of a New York costermonger. How such disgusting trash has been tolerated so long at the St. James's Theatre we are at a loss to imagine (*Leamington Spa Courier* 31 March 1849)

Why the Christoffs chose, or were requested by the manager, to include such an item in what was otherwise clearly an accomplished acrobatic performance will never be known. One can only hope that John Christoff's performance was better received than the above.

It has been suggested by some that "Signor Christoff and Son" were actually the brothers George and John, taking advantage of their age difference. I do not agree with this.

By this date George was already performing solo as Herr Christoff. In the spring of 1852 he was working with *Cooke's Circus Royal* in Newcastle[10]. Throughout the summer he worked independently at various venues including Manchester, Sheffield, and Leeds before returning to Cooke's circus in Aberdeen for the winter season.

Also, by this time George was a married man. He married Sarah Frazier (who also used the name Eddles) in 1849[11]. Sarah's father, John Frazier, was an equestrian who went on to become the proprietor of the *National Circus* (one of several of this name at this time in Britain) in Greenwich by 1853[12]. George and Sarah went on to have three children; Sarah Rosina (1851)[13], Harriet Hannah (1852)[14], and Frederick Kitt Eddles (1853)[15]. The last child died within a year of birth. It is interesting to note that Frederick was born in the Workhouse – had times become so hard for Sarah, already with two young children, while George was away in Scotland performing with *James Cooke's Circus*? Sarah was discharged from the Workhouse the following year[16], although where she went to we do not know. In 1861 she was living as an unemployed lodger with her eight year old daughter Harriett in Norwich. She was going by the name of Christoff and George was working with *Emidy's Circus* in Norwich at the time of the census.

At some point, it appears that George and Sarah's marriage began to crumble. In 1868, we find a record of George marrying a woman named

Maria (sometimes also Marian or Mary Anne) Maskell[17] who had worked with George as a 'female jester' years prior, in 1862[18]. There is no record of any divorce between George and Sarah, nor any other record of what happened to Sarah in the meantime. Did this new couple marry bigamously? Any extant death records for a Sarah Christopher postdate George's second marriage. However, there are two very interesting entries for 1873 and 1874 that help shine light on this question.

In 1873, a Sarah Christopher is admitted once again to a Workhouse[19]. The next year, there is a corresponding death entry in 1874 in the County Lunatic Asylum in Wandsworth[20]. We could conjecture that this might have been the fate of George's wife. George seems to have been unlucky in his marriages because in 1869 Maria moves on to marry a James Fegan[21] (again, without any trace of divorce papers.) John Christoff appeared alongside William Pablo (William Banham) in *Pablo Fanque's Circus Royal* in Leeds in 1854;

> ENGAGEMENT FOR SIX NIGHTS ONLY of Mr. Wm. PABLO and young Herr CHRISTOFF, the TWO greatest ROPE-DANCERS in the world! … The entertainments, concluding with Laughable Extravaganza, entitled 'JEREMIAH STITCHEM' [an equestrian act], in which Mr. Wm. PABLO will appear (*Leeds Times* 25 March 1854)

It would seem that John was not averse to taking his brother's working title of 'Herr', and there is little doubt that it is John performing here with William Pablo. Around the same time, George also appearing as Herr Christoff was performing with *James Cooke's Circus Royal* in Newcastle upon Tyne. It will be remembered that William Banham was the illegitimate son of Pablo Fanque, who used the performing name of Pablo. Both he and John Christoff travelled to Australia to arrive in the December of that year[22], where William used the name Pablo Fanque and John as Master (sometimes as Herr) Christoff. By January 1855 they were both working together at the aptly named Astley's Amphitheatre in Melbourne. This should not be confused with the amphitheatre of the same name in London, and neither was the Melbourne company an off-shoot of the London one. Initially they worked solo acts, Christoff as an equestrian and Fanque both equestrian and tight rope acts. By February of 1855, they had developed a doubles act;

> Extraordinary and astounding evolutions on the Persian column, by Mr. Pablo Fanque and Master Christoff entitled, LA PERCHE. To attempt to convey an idea of the astounding performance is impossible. It may, however, be necessary to name the following – One of the brothers [sic] supports, in a perpendicular position, a large pole 30 feet in length, on his chest, and he other brother walks up it whilst in that position, and performs feats the most amusing (*The Age, Melbourne* 7 February 1855)[23]

They then went on to work with *Burton's Circus* throughout the year. In May, Christoff continued using the title Herr, as he had done previously with Pablo Fanque's circus. It should be pointed out that John and Pablo were not partners. In fact, John was legally indentured to Banham! Clearly all was not well between them, for the following notice appeared in *The Argus, Melbourne*[24] 16 October of that year;

> To Equestrians, Theatre Managers and Others – Caution – Notice is hereby given that anyone found harbouring or engaging my indentured Apprentice, John Christoff, who has run away from my service, will be prosecuted as the law directs, in such cases made and provided. The said John Christoff is about the age of 18 years, and is a coloured boy. W. Banham [signed]

The sad irony is that William Banham, himself, appears to have run away as an apprentice from Pablo Fanque's circus in Leeds in 1848—a positive step for him, as he went on to achieve the same stature as his father, in being a notable performer and businessman

Whatever the disagreement between the two, they appear to have parted company from this point onwards. Fanque forms his own circus and begins touring in the spring of 1856. Some have suggested that this was the Pablo Fanque senior, from Britain. However, British newspapers of the same period record that Pablo Fanque appearing in person in such places as Manchester and Bolton at this time[25]. John Christoff reappears in the Australian newspapers in July 1856 as a solo performer with *Burton's National Circus*. He stayed with this company for a short while and then disappears from reviews for a year. He emerges again in February 1859[26] with the grandly named *Australian Amphitheatre and Roman Coloseum* [sic], performing on the tight rope and also working as the Conductor of the Circle (in effect, the Ringmaster). Fanque and Christoff did work together again on the same bill with *Burton's Circus* in April 1859, but they were very much solo performers. John Christoff toured extensively in both Australia and New Zealand throughout the rest of his life. He married Elizabeth Barham in 1858 in Tumut, New South Wales, and they had one son, George James Christoff, in 1859. Their descendants are still alive in Australia today. John Christoff died on 17 December, 1872 and was buried in the Necropolis in Sydney[27]. William Pablo Fanque had died from consumption three years earlier, on 9 June 1869[28].

So, while John Christoff was wowing audiences in Australia, what was his brother George achieving back in Britain? John had been appearing at the Astley's Amphitheatre in Melbourne in 1855, but George was appearing himself for a season at the very epicentre of circus – Astley's Royal Amphitheatre in London, under the direction of William Cooke;

HERR CHRISTOFF (l'Empereur des Funambles) on the Tight Rope, with the (until now) unattempted miraculous feat of throwing a Summersault, and alighting on the rope on his feet!! (*Sun (London)* 1 September 1854)

He continued to work with Cooke's circus the following year, appearing in Scotland. In the advertising he challenges 'Europe to produce his equal on the tight rope'[29]. So great were his accomplishments on the tight rope that, in 1858, he was awarded a medal.

PRESENTATION TO HERR CHRISTOFF, THE TIGHT ROPE DANCER. Mr. T. Burton, the proprietor of the Royal Casino, Manchester, assembled a few friends together at Tom Donley's in that town, on Wednesday evening, and presented Herr Christoff with a medal of very elaborate design and workmanship, as a token of esteem, and in consideration of his merits as a tight rope dancer. Many healths were drunk, and conviviality reigned until the small hours of the morning (*The Era* 24 January 1848)

He was back at Astley's later that year, performing to much acclaim and clearly a well-established performer by now. He was billed as 'the most wonderful rope dancer in the world' and as 'a symmetrically formed man, possessing great agility, and a thorough master of his art'[30]. This was one of a few mentions of Christoff's physical appearance, as opposed to his ethnicity. In 1864, he was described as 'jolly and rotund in person'[31] and in 1865 as weighing 'some fifteen or sixteen stone'[32] (210 – 224 pounds weight). That is some weight to be throwing somersaults on a tight rope. There are no known photographs of Christoff, but there is an image that regularly appears on various websites[33] purporting to be that of Pablo Fanque. We know, from a photograph with good provenance that appeared in the *World's Fair* March 22 1913 that Fanque was a tall, thin, lean-faced man. The photograph purporting to be him shows a round faced and quite thick set man. Could this be George Christoff? I like to think so, though further investigation would be needed to say with any authority or conviction.

By January 1856, George Christoff was working with *Ducrow's Circus* in Birmingham. Here he was billed as 'Christoff – the African. The greatest rope dancer in the world'[34]. For some unknown financial reason, Ducrow ran into difficulties. His circus closed in February, not long after George's arrival with the company. Many of Ducrow's horses, equipment, wardrobe, and properties were put up for auction to settle his debts.[35] Ducrow soon left England for an engagement in Copenhagen, Denmark, leaving the company without a proprietor. Herr Christoff appears to have taken up the challenge, joining the likes of Fanque and Hillier in becoming another gentleman of colour to run his own circus;

> Herr Christoff, the celebrated rope dancer, boldly ventured to open this Circus on Monday last, providing a tolerably good company, male and female. The bills of the day made an earnest appeal to the inhabitants of Birmingham for support, and the appeal has been responded to satisfactorily, which will enable the *corps* to be relieved from those difficulties in which they were unfortunately placed consequent on the sudden closing, &c., of Ducrow's establishment (*The Era* 2 March 1856)

Unfortunately, this venture did not work out for him. By April, a few short months after this new chapter began, George is found working in Cheltenham with the *Cirque de L'Imperatrice* under the direction of Madame Newsome[36].

In Cheltenham, he appeared as 'Professor Christoff – The Great African Rope Dancer'. It has been suggested that this Professor was actually Kitt Christopher, George and John's father. The 1851 Census shows Kitt Christopher living in Lambeth and working as a carpenter[37] and his performing days seem to have ended by this time. However, we find *Madame Newsome's Circus* in Worcester and in the programme is 'G. Christoff, the African Rope Dancer' and other named artistes who appeared alongside Professor Christoff in Cheltenham the previous month. I think it is safe to assume that Professor Christoff and G. Christoff were one and the same person. During the summer, Christoff changes company and moves back to working with *Pablo Fanque's Allied Circus*, ending the year in Bristol.

He stayed with Fanque through to the beginning of April 1857 and then he left that outfit to perform with the little known *Sardinian Circus* in Manchester[38]. From there he moved on to the Royal Colosseum – the 'National Place of Cheap Amusements'. Here he is given a hyperbolic billing;

The GREAT CHRISTOFF, the most astounding Performer in the World, who never has had, and probably never will have, a rival at all comparable with him. His thrilling, electrifying, and unparalleled feats upon the Tight Rope have been the theme of admiration and astonishment wherever he has appeared. Christoff the Wonder – the Voltigeur. His lofty bounds, his extraordinary twistings and turnings, so unlike anything ever before attempted by mortal man; in fact his performances altogether are so singular and unequalled, that during its execution Christoff becomes an object of great interest, not only among the audience, but also among his brother artists, who invariably throng the entrance to the circle during his performance (*Northern Daily Times* 30 April 1857)

High praise indeed! Christoff was becoming something of a legend in his art and in May it was announced that at the end of his contract at the Royal Colosseum he would be taking up an engagement at the Tivoli Gardens in Copenhagen. Now, here is a mystery. In early May this notice appeared in the *Gloucester Journal* 2 May 1857;

Herr Christoff, a coloured man, who recently gained some notoriety in Bristol, as a tight rope dancer at the circus, had the misfortune to break his neck during a performance in Manchester last week. The accident followed the turning of a double summersault and, on Christoff being picked up, he was found to be dead.

The story was repeated in the *Gloucester Journal's* sister paper the *Gloucester Chronicle*. But was there any truth in it? There is no other record in any other newspaper of the tragedy and neither can any death entries be found. It is possible that the unrest in India, that would shortly become a full rebellion against British rule, dominated the national press at this particular time and so eclipsed such a relatively minor news item. Christoff's performances in Denmark were reported in *The Era* on 5 July, so clearly he was very much alive. I suspect the reality of the death notice may be one of two things; either it was a slow day for news and a journalist invented the story, or Christoff may have possibly had a fall and knocked himself out, which was then wrongly reported as his death.

Christoff did experience such an accident in which he fell heavily and 'hurt himself severely, but not seriously' a few years later in 1866 while executing a double somersault during a performance[39].

Denmark was not the only European country that Christoff visited in his career. In the July of 1861 he was reported as working with the *Circo de Price* (formerly known as *Price and North's Circus*) in Madrid, Spain[40]. By the September he was in Valencia. The winter season took him on to Portugal in January 1862 and he stayed in the Iberian Peninsula until his return to England was noted in the September[41].

In February 1864, Christoff was performing in Leeds at the Amphitheatre and Concert Hall. Mysteriously we find on the same programme, the 'First appearance of Mrs. Christoff, the Serio Comic Vocalist' (*Leeds Times* Saturday 6 February 1864). Could this be Sarah, his wife? We know that she was in Norwich, with her younger daughter the same time that Christoff was working with *Emidy's Circus* there. But if this is her, then it is surprising that she has never before been mentioned as a performer. She does appear again, in October 1865 in Dublin when Christoff was appearing there with *Quaglieni's Circus*. She was billed as the 'best and most popular characteristic vocalist and danseuse of the day' (*Freeman's Journal* 16 October 1865). At the Metropolitan Music Hall in 1866, this item was described;

> On Monday last Christoff, a performer on the low rope, made his first appearance, and was well received. His feats are bold and very cleverly executed. Few men of his great bulk and weight would like to risk their necks in the positions in which he places himself. Christoff is attended by a lady, in elegant costume, like a Court page, who acts as his jester with a good deal of wit and grace (*The Era* 12 August 1866)

Here there is another reference to his physical build, but more interestingly we have him working alongside a female 'clown' type character. Was this Madame Christoff again? Possibly, because a week later in the *Marylebone Mercury* of 18 August she is specifically named as a 'Serio Comic'. Although this mysterious lady is referred to as a 'jester' and a 'serio comic', it is difficult to work out exactly what her role was. However, in the September we find both Herr and Madame Christoff working together in Portsmouth, and billed as 'Tight rope Artistes' (*Portsmouth Times* 1 September 1866). The two continue to perform on the same bill in London until the end of the year[42], although often separately and never together on the tight rope. A more detailed description of her role is given as such;

> His [Herr Christoff] somersault throwing has been something startling and a novel supplement to his entertainment has been given by Madame Christoff, who has appeared as a kind of Clown, and has filled up the pauses between the tight-rope feats by some clever dances and witty speech and sayings (*The Era* 20 January 1867)

But this still does not fully explain who this female was. The *Norfolk Chronicle* of 23 March describes her as his 'attractive wife', although whether this was actually his wife Sarah or another female is not clear. A letter written by Edward C Fanque, the son of Pablo Fanque, appeared in *The Era* of 24 September 1913 gives us the best indication as to who she may have been;

> Mrs. Ada Maskell's death recalls to me that it is over fifty years since I first met her, viz; about 1862. She was then playing Female Jester to George "Herr" Christoff's tight-rope act. I afterwards met her again in 1869 when she and her husband (Fabian, Clown and Posturer) …

This now begin to make some sense. We know that George Christoff married a Mary Ann Maskell in 1868 and that by 1869 she had left him to marry a James Fegan, who went by the stage name of Monsieur Fabian. Later in her career, Mary Ann took on the persona of Ada Maskell, after the equestrienne Ada Isaacs Menken, who died in August 1868, hence Fanque's memory being of an Ada rather than Mary Ann.

Mary Anne Maskell *(Reproduced with permission of Alison Young)*

Christoff and his female partner continued working together on and off over the next two years in a variety of venues around the country. Occasionally she appears in her own right on a programme different from Herr Christoff but more often than not they were together on the same bill. She seems to have appeared in several different guises; Madmlle Silvia, Mdmlle Silvid, Madame Christoff, and Madame Silvain. She was variously billed as a 'serio-comic', 'a characteristic', and 'the only female clown in the world'[43]. The two of them received great plaudits in September 1868 while performing at the Winchester theatre in London;

Herr Christoff may be called the chief and particular star now shining in the Winchester hemisphere. His performance is exceedingly clever of its kind, and, in the course of the entertainment, he sets himself some uncommonly difficult problems to solve. One of them is whether a full-grown man, with no firmer footing than that afforded by a vibrating rope, can turn a back somersault and alight safely on his feet. This extremely difficult exploit Herr Christoff performs and it is not surprising that several attempts have ordinarily to be made before a perfect success is achieved. The artist enters heart and soul into his work, and, according to announcements, is the only person who has ever attempted this back somersault on the tight-rope … Herr

Christoff is accompanied by Madame Silvain, who, in the programme, enjoys the proud distinction of being "the only Female Clown". This lady does not affect the ordinary habiliments of the noble order (as one of her sex once did at the Strand Theatre), but appears in a remarkably becoming costume of the modern burlesque pattern. Madame's manner is pleasantly free from any offensive and obtrusive vulgarity. She, in fact, acts as a kind of philosophical "chorus", and gives a somewhat familiar definition of what a good woman ought to be ... Madame's assistance in this entertainment is invaluable, and Herr Christoff is very fortunate in possessing such a colleague (*The Era* 20 September 1868)

Could the costume referred to look something like the one she was wearing in the photograph? It is difficult for us today to imagine how a 'philosophical chorus' would work against a tight-rope act, but it seems to have been very popular.

After they were married in the November of 1868, they both went to work with *Ginnett's Circus* in Ireland, where Christoff appeared as 'the Great African Rope Dancer'[44]. Madame Christoff (now legally his wife) appeared with the same company, but on her own account as the 'female clown'. In early January 1869 they were still with the same company, but the 8th seems to have been her last appearance and after that date there is no record of Christoff and his wife ever again appearing together. Perhaps she had simply had enough of giving the 'familiar definition of what a good woman ought to be'! She moved on and married again, but Herr Christoff kept going.

The break-up with his wife appears not to have affected his performances unduly. Throughout the rest of 1869 he appeared in a variety of cities round the country; Liverpool, where he was billed as 'the African Blondin'[45], Bristol, Dundee, Leeds, and Sheffield. But as the new decade began so his appearances became fewer. Apart from a short engagement in Hull in the May, 1870 saw an autumn season in Liverpool, Dublin, and Glasgow. He was no longer the great star that he had once been and he was taking work in all kinds of situations. January 1872 was something of a definitive moment for him. He was appearing in a dramatic presentation of *The Last Days of Pompeii* at the Queen's Theatre in London. His role was as an entertainer at the 'Great Banquet of Pompeii'. But all did not go well, during the fourth act;

> At this conjuncture a performance was intended to come off which proved simply impossible even to "the famous Christoff". A tight rope had been stretched across the back of the stage, just where not one of the guests could possibly have seen anyone upon it, instead of at the front, where there was plenty of room and everybody before and behind the footlights might have assisted at the spectacle. When M. Christoff mounted the rope it became apparent that he had no room. His pole caught in the pillars, and when he turned a somersault, very cleverly backwards, it again struck, and he came down very awkwardly on the rope. A second attempt, without the pole, proved equally ineffectual. In front the whole arrangements were as bad as they could possibly be, and to his own mortification no doubt, but we are quite sure with the sympathy of the audience, he was compelled to retire (*Globe* 10 January 1872).

One might imagine that, for such an experienced performer as Christoff, this was a highly embarrassing situation. It also reflects his fall in status; from the star of many shows in the past to a cameo role in a dramatic spectacle, with little consideration for the requirements of his act. I think this was something of a humiliation for him and for the rest of that year he makes only a brief appearance at the Rotunda Gardens in Dublin[46], and there only on the low rope. He did manage to 'headline' once more the following year in November, with *Swallow's Circus* in Bolton, but after that he made appearances at an assortment of different venues with a range of clientele. He worked in Variety Halls[47] and at open air events such as the Coronation Day in Plymouth[48]. In 1875, there seems to have been a dearth of work for he does not appear in any billings at all. The following year he is reduced to appearing in such venues as the Casino Temperance Music Hall in Liverpool and for the Catholic Total Abstinence League in Fazackerley, where he gave 'an exhibition on the tight rope'[49]. However, he was still determined to perform. This advertisement appeared in *The Era* 18 November 1877;

> HERR CHRISTOFF, the Great Tight-Rope Artiste, who has appeared before all the Crowned Heads of Europe. A few vacant dates for Circuses, Theatre, and Concert Halls. No objection to go abroad. New posters.

How effective this advertisement was I do not know, but there is no record of him leaving Britain after that and he does not appear in the newspapers again until 1879. During the summer months he made a brief appearance in Buckingham, followed by two months in Diss, Norfolk, where he was billed as 'the German Blondin'[50]. And that is the final time that he was recorded as performing upon the tight rope. By this time, he was around fifty years old—not an old age, but for a man who punished his body night after night performing backwards somersaults for decades, perhaps this was enough.

In February 1880, Edward Jenkins, a Member of Parliament, set out a Bill before the House of Commons for the 'prevention at exhibitions and public amusements of acrobatic feats dangerous to life' (*The Era* 15 February 1880). It was officially titled the *Acrobats and Gymnasts Bill* and many in the profession met together on the 29th February to discuss it. This was reported at length in *The Era* 7 March 1880 and full details were given as to any amendments to the Bill that arose from the meeting. Over one hundred professional acrobats and gymnasts were present, including Christoff. With his wealth of experience it is hardly surprising that he should be there. Jenkins eventually withdrew the Bill on 15 March[51], stating that;

> As a large number of persons have been thrown out of employment by the introduction of the Bill, arrangements have been made to render it of such a character as will prevent its interfering with ordinary and legitimate acrobatic performances. Bill withdrawn.

But this would be Christoff's last contribution to the world of the circus. On 18 June 1881, *The Era* carried this short notice, tucked away at the foot of a page;

> Died, on Tuesday last, June the 13th, of consumption, at the Lambeth Infirmary, George Christopher(renowned tight-rope artist), of all the principal Continental Cirques, Variety Halls, and Circuses in the United Kingdom), known as George Christoff, aged about fifty five years.

A brief obituary really for a man of colour who, at the peak of his career, had drawn vast crowds and entertained them with his daring backward somersaults on the tight rope. It had been an illustrious and eventful life. He had worked with many of the great circus proprietors of the age; Cooke, Newsome, Emidy, Fanque, Sanger, Quaglieni, Swallow, and Price. But it was a sad ending, the Lambeth Infirmary in reality was the District Workhouse Infirmary. He had been registered there as a patient at the time of the 1881 Census[52]. He gave his profession as 'Tight Rope Dancer Performer'. For two generations the Christoff family had made an impact in the world of the circus, across both hemispheres.

Notes

1. *1881 Census returns for George Christopher.* Online at; https://www.ancestry.co.uk/interactive/7572/LNDRG11_598_600-0533?pid=20694710&backurl=https://search.ancestry.co.uk/cgi-bin/sse.dll?indiv%3D1%26dbid%3D7572%26h%3D20694710%26tid%3D%26pid%3D%26usePUB%3Dtrue%26_phsrc%3Dsbc1733%26_phstart%3DsuccessSource&treeid=&personid=&hintid=&usePUB=true&_phsrc=sbc1733&_phstart=successSource&usePUBJs=true&_ga=2.83355221.2106881672.1583594180-1986502099.1539097385

2. *1851 Census returns for George Christopher.* Online at; https://www.ancestry.co.uk/interactive/8860/SSXHO107_1644_1645-0414?pid=1800530&backurl=https://search.ancestry.co.uk/cgi-bin/sse.dll?indiv%3D1%26dbid%3D8860%26h%3D1800530%26tid%3D%26pid%3D%26usePUB%3Dtrue%26_phsrc%3Dsbc1792%26_phstart%3DsuccessSource&treeid=&personid=&hintid=&usePUB=true&_phsrc=sbc1792&_phstart=successSource&usePUBJs=true&_ga=2.20438139.2106881672.1583594180-1986502099.1539097385

3. *1881 Census returns* ibid. 1

4. *1851 Census returns* ibid. 2

5. *England Select Births and Christenings 1538-1975.* Online at; https://www.familysearch.org/ark:/61903/1:1:N1LF-MQ1

6. *Marriage record.* Online at; https://www.ancestry.co.uk/interactive/1623/31280_195096-00077/2395976?backurl=https://www.ancestry.co.uk/family-tree/person/tree/39068595/person/210173562199/facts/citation/720391119486/edit/record

7. *England and Wales Death Registration Index.* Online at; https://www. familysearch.org/search/record/results?count=20&query=%2Bgivenname%3ARosina~%20%2Bsurname%3AChristopher~%20%2Bdeath_place%3ALondon~%20%2Bdeath_year%3A1837-1839~%20 %2Bspouse_givenname%3AKitt~%20 %2Brecord_country%3AEngland

8. *Baptismal record.* Online at; https://search.ancestry.co.uk/cgi-bin/ sse.dll?indiv=1&dbid=1558&h=3665404&tid=&pid=&usePUB=true&_phsrc=sbc1784&_phstart=successSource

9. Leodis archive of theatre and circus posters. Online at; http://www. leodis.net/playbills/enlarge.asp?ri=2003318_34867495

10. *Newcastle Courant* 9 April 1852

11. *London, England, Church of England Marriages and Banns* 1754 – 1932. Online at; https://www.ancestry.co.uk/interactive/1623/31280 _197828-00024?pid=1053316355&treeid=&personid=&usePUB=true&_phsrc=sbc1724&_phstart=successSource

12. *Kentish Mercury* 22 January 1853

13. *England, Select Births and Christenings 1538-1975.* Online at; https:// www.ancestry.co.uk/family-tree/person/tree/27893850/ person/222155742670/facts

14. *England and Wales Civil Registration Birth Index* 1837-1915. Online at; https://www.ancestry.co.uk/interactive/8912/ ONS_B18524AH-0662/37513738?backurl=https:// www.ancestry.co.uk/family-tree/person/tree/27893850/ person/222155745596/facts

15. *London, England, Church of England Births and Baptisms 1813-1917.* Online at; https://www.ancestry.co.uk/ interactive/1558/31451_212639-00208/6852162

16. *London, England, Poor Law and Guardian Records* 1738-1926. Online at; https://www.ancestry.co.uk/interactive/1557/31436_19 0052-00907/6554118?backurl=https://www.ancestry.co.uk/ family-tree/person/tree/27893850/person/222155739584/ facts

17. *London, England, Church of England Marriages and Banns 1754 – 1932.* Online at; https://www.ancestry.co.uk/interactive/1623/471 88_263021009500_3013-00100?pid=21983576&treeid=&per-sonid=&rc=&usePUB=true&_phsrc=sbc1802&_phstart=suc-cessSource

18. *The Era* 24 September 1913

19. *London, England, Workhouse Admission and Discharge Register 1764-1930*; Online at; https://www.ancestry.co.uk/in-teractive/60391/31436_190821-00361?pid=6877766&b ackurl=https://search.ancestry.co.uk/cgi-bin/sse.dll?d-bid%3D60391%26h%3D6877766%26indiv%3Dtry%26o_ vc%3DRecord:OtherRecord%26rhSource%3D7619&tree-id=&personid=&hintid=&usePUB=true&usePUB-Js=true&_ga=2.25142137.2106881672.1583594180-1986502099.1539097385

20. *London, England, Church of England Deaths and Burials 1813-2003.* Online at; https://www.ancestry.co.uk/interactive/1559/31 280_196246-00386?pid=8654001&backurl=https://search. ancestry.co.uk/cgi-bin/sse.dll?indiv%3D1%26dbid%3D15 59%26h%3D8654001%26tid%3D%26pid%3D%26useP-UB%3Dtrue%26_phsrc%3Dsbc1811%26_phstart%3Dsuc-cessSource&treeid=&personid=&hintid=&usePUB=true&_ phsrc=sbc1811&_phstart=successSource&usePUBJs=true

21. There is an interesting article entitled Fascinating Ada that covers much of Mankell's life. Online at; https://musichallalice.word-press.com/2018/10/11/fascinating-ada/

22. *Victoria, Australia, Assisted and Unassisted Passenger Lists 1839-1923.* Online at; https://www.ancestry.co.uk/family-tree/person/tree/39068595/person/19320863389/facts

23. National Library of Australia Trove newspaper archive. Online at; https://trove.nla.gov.au/newspaper/article/154848924?searchTerm=Christoff&searchLimits=l-decade=185|||l-year=1855

24. National Library of Australia Trove newspaper archive. Online at; https://trove.nla.gov.au/newspaper/article/4820953?-searchTerm=%22john%20christoff%22&searchLimits=exactPhrase=john+christoff|||anyWords|||notWords|||requestHandler|||dateFrom|||dateTo|||sortby

25. *Bolton Chronicle* 8 March 1856

26. National Library of Australia Trove newspaper archive. Online at; https://trove.nla.gov.au/newspaper/article/105997293?searchTerm=Christoff&searchLimits=l-decade=185|||l-year=1859|||l-month=2

27. National Library of Australia Trove newspaper archive. Online at; https://trove.nla.gov.au/newspaper/article/13314234?-searchTerm=%22john%20christoff%22&searchLimits=exactPhrase=john+christoff|||anyWords|||notWords|||requestHandler|||dateFrom|||dateTo|||sortby

28. National Library of Australia Trove newspaper archive. Available online at; https://trove.nla.gov.au/newspaper/article/13191583?searchTerm=Pablo%20Fanque&searchLimits=l-decade=186|||l-year=1869

29. *Dundee, Perth and Cupar Advertiser* 27 March 1855

30. *Morning Advertiser* 6 April 1858

31. *Newcastle Daily Chronicle* 5 January 1864

32. *Brighton Gazette* 23 November 1865

33. Many websites relating to Pablo Fanque carry this image. The origin seems to be that which appears on the Wikipedia site; https://www.bing.com/search?q=Pablo+Fanque&cvid=e-92f591a79124cce91d1e8a76468d268&FORM=ANNTA1&P-C=U531

34. *Birmingham Journal* 23 January 1856

35. *The Era* 17 February 1856

36. *Cheltenham Looker-On* 26 April 1856

37. *1851 England Census.* Online at; https://www.ancestry.co.uk/interactive/8860/SRYHO107_1570_1570-0451/16547338

38. *Manchester Times* 11 April 1857

39. *The Era* 11 February 1866

40. *The Era* 21 July 1861

41. *The Era* 28 September 1862

42. *Morning Advertiser* 22 December 1866

43. *Yorkshire Post* 29 June 1867

44. *Cork Examiner* 5 December 1868

45. *Liverpool Mercury* 3 May 1869

46. *Freeman's Journal* 4 June 1872

47. *Bolton Evening News* 4 February 1874

48. *Western Daily Mercury* 27 June 1874

49. *Liverpool Daily Post* 4 July 1876

50. *Diss Express* 4 July 1879

51. *House of Commons Sittings. HC Deb 15 March 1880 vol251 c1018.* Online at; [BILL 60.] WITHDRAWAL OF BILL. (Hansard, 15 March 1880) (parliament.uk)

52. *1881 England Census.* Online at; https://www.ancestry.co.uk/interactive/7572/LNDRG11_598_600-0533?pid=20694710 &backurl=https://search.ancestry.co.uk/cgi-bin/sse.dll?d-bid%3D7572%26h%3D20694710%26indiv%3Dtry%26o_vc%3DRecord:OtherRecord%26rhSource%3D1623&tree-id=&personid=&hintid=&usePUB=true&usePUBJs=true&_ga=2.92254554.1336073117.1584629123-8519783.1584367827

The Indian Jugglers. Watercolour by James Green c. 1814. Private collection, whereabouts undisclosed

CHAPTER 8
THE REAL CHIEF OF INDIAN JUGGLERS – RAMO SAMEE

Visit a circus today and you will probably see a juggler. In fact, juggling seems to be all around us these days; on the streets, in schools and clubs, in universities, in parks, in gardens, and even in the board room. The ability to manipulate objects in time and space has fascinated people for centuries.

When you think of a juggler today you probably think of an individual, who by repeated practice and skill, can keep several objects in motion simultaneously; balls, clubs, and rings to the more extreme fire torches, knives, and even chain saws! But juggling as we recognise it is only a relatively modern discipline. Wall (2019) gives us an etymological timeline for the word 'to juggle'. The derivation of the word has its roots in the Latin *joculare*, meaning to laugh or to jest. The *Oxford English Dictionary* defines juggling as 'to amuse or entertain people with jesting, buffoonery and tricks', a much broader interpretation than we have today. This wider understanding of 'juggling' was commonplace until around 1897, when an artiste named Paul Cinquevalli gave performances of pure object manipulation and balance with no illusions or tricks[1].

Earlier in the nineteenth century, the concept of a 'juggler' embraced more than just manipulating objects through the air. It included sleight of hand, conjuring, tricks of balance, and the tricks of the *jadoowallah*, known by many today as 'fakir work'. This includes sword swallowing, eating and blowing fire, walking on fire or glass, and lying on a bed of nails. The term 'fakir work' is derived from the Fakirs, who were Hindu ascetic mendicants[2], and who were famed for their abilities to achieve a state of self-denial through extreme practices. But there were other itinerant individuals and groups who were able to perform such feats for entertainment – and of course money. Since the East India Company gained a foothold in India during the 1750s, street performing 'Indian Jugglers' were well known to the British. They marvelled at their exploits;

> The whole tribe of Slight-of-hand Men in Europe are mere bunglers when compared with the Jugglers of India; their deceptions are so admirably executed, and some of their performances of such a strange nature, that the ignorant and superstitious natives, believing as they do all the enchantments described in such books as *The Arabian Nights Entertainments*, may well ascribe to them necromantic powers (*Hereford Journal* 22 November 1809)

High praise for the Indian Jugglers, but tinged with British xenophobic patronisation. Of course the 'natives' were ignorant and superstitious. How could they be anything other – they were not British. There was an ever present tension between the dominant British social structure and the Indian underclass. The fascination with the exotic was juxtaposed with racial bigotry, underpinned as it was with a sense of imperial superiority. Yet there was the desire to bring these entertainers to Britain to present them to the public, to be exploited for profitable gain. The writer of the above piece continues to recount one such attempt to procure a performer.

> I once saw it [swallowing a sword] performed before several gentleman, among whom was the surgeon of an Indiaman [a ship that sailed between Britain and India], then at anchor in Madras Roads, he was very sceptical on the subject … he desired the man to repeat the operation, and when at length all his doubts were removed, he made the Pabdarum a proposal, to go with him to Europe, in consideration of which he would give him one thousand pagodas[3] on the spot (400l. sterling)

[pounds sterling], a like sum on his arrival in England, with his expenses there, and other advantages … but his cast [sic] was an insuperable barrier to him going on board a ship, to the great mortification and disappointment of the Doctor.

Although in the above instance the performer was not tempted to up sticks and move to England, many others did. There was already a sizeable population of Indians in Britain during the nineteenth century. Some had arrived as servants, some were medical practitioners, some were teachers, and there were many street performers (Banerjee, 2011).

Among the performers that did take the long voyage was a juggler who became famous throughout Britain, known as Ramo Samee, although this may well have been a version of the name Ramaswamy. Zubrzycki (2017) describes how Samee was 'discovered' by a ship's Captain named Campbell and subsequently persuaded to go with him to England. In 1813 a group of Indian Jugglers arrived in England and gave a performance before the Prince Regent;

Three or four Indian Jugglers lately arrived in this country from Madras, and had the honour of performing before the Prince Regent, and several of his Ministers. Since that time they have played a most successful game. Their house in Piccadilly is beset from morning to night with carriages of the Nobility and Gentry, and it is supposed that they do not take less than 150l. [pounds sterling] per day [such a sum, unbelievably, is equivalent to about 7,000 pounds sterling per day in 2021!⁴]. Their legerdemain with the cups and balls is very ordinary, and below our own mountebanks; but the play with the hollow brass balls is truly curious – and one of them actually plunges a sword, thirty inches in length, down his throat, to the delight of Ladies who have not *delicate nerves* [sic] (*Bristol Mirror* 24 July 1813)

Indian Jugglers were clearly a great attraction and people would pay good money to witness the 'exotic' gentlemen from the East.

Indian Jugglers. Liebig Trade Card, late C19th *(Author's collection)*

They were also a lucrative source of income for their promoter, which makes me wonder just how much of that 150 pounds sterling they actually received for themselves. Zubrzycki intimates that Samee was among the group, though he is never mentioned by name in the playbills. The first specific reference to an *individual* 'Indian Juggler' appears in the *Cheltenham Chronicle* 20 February 1817, when a Kia Khan Khruse was billed as 'The Chief of the Indian Jugglers'. However, this artiste was perhaps a solo performer, for the following report makes no mention of others;

> The following Nouvelle and Extraordinary Feats of Agility and Deception have been exhibited before several branches of the Royal Families of England, and other Countries, and KIA KHAN KHRUSE and has been honoured with their warmest approbation ... Incredible Agility of the Human Body ... KIA KHAN KHRUSE will go through his Proteau [sic] Transformations, exhibiting the most surprising Evolutions, Serpentine Posturing, &c., ever beheld – with a Glass of Wine on his forehead, and a Tumbler of Water on his chin, he will pass through a Hoop many different ways, without disconcerting the position of the Glasses; and Walk on his Hands with his Foot in his

Mouth! LEGERDEMAIN EXPLODED, *in a Variety of Juggling* with swords, rings, balls, knives, handkerchiefs, ladders, money, &c. He will extract from an egg, which has been previously examined by the company, the Figure of a Child!!! – A small Ball will be turned into a Toad; also Barley changed into Wheat; - three Shillings into a Horse's Foot … He will lift a Bottle of Water by a Straw, and make Half a Crown pass from one Cup to another, at ten yards distance. He will fire a Pistol, charged with twelve Pins, at a Pack of Cards, thrown up, and lodge the pins in the identical card which had been drawn and returned to the pack by one of the company. And again (though it has been said he was killed in performing this astonishing trick), he will catch in his hand a marked Bullet, added to the powder-loading of the pistol, which anyone may fire at him. His performance will conclude with having AN IMMENSE STONE OF 700 WEIGHT! [784 pounds or 355 Kilos] Broken into pieces on hid Breast, by large sledge hammers, with great ease to himself, and without deception (*Hampshire Chronicle* 29 June 1818)

So we have a combination of contortionism, modern 'toss' juggling, feats of strength, and illusions all performed by one man. This encapsulates how the many Indian Jugglers performed at this time. Though in this instance, there is no mention of swallowing a sword that was also a common 'juggling' discipline performed at the time. Perhaps this was not Kia Khan's forte.

This "Kia Kahn" continued to perform in Britain for several years, often billed as the Chief of Indian Jugglers, which is laughable because, in fact… he was not Indian at all!

His real name was Juan Antonio and he had been born in Portugal, not India. He would be one of many who took on the guise of an "Indian" Juggler during the nineteenth century. A false report of Khan's death during a bullet catching trick is given in an advertisement in the *Hampshire Chronicle* of 29 June 1818;

And again (though it has been said he was killed in performing this astonishing trick), he will catch in his hand a marked bullet ...

Interestingly there was a previous report in December 1817 that gave details of the death of an Indian Juggler in an attempt to catch a bullet in his mouth.

> One of the tricks performed by the Indian Jugglers now exhibiting their art in that city [Dublin], is the catching of a ball between the teeth fired from a pistol. At a recent exhibition, the pistol, according to the custom, was handed to a young Gentleman, one of the company, for the purpose of firing it. He did so, and shot the unfortunate Juggler through the head. It is supposed that a pistol accidentally loaded with powder and ball was, by mistake, substituted for that prepared in the usual way (*Star (London)* 8 December 1817)

Kia Khan was touring as a solo performer during 1817 and was not, as far as we can tell, ever in Dublin or otherwise within range of this particular Gentleman volunteer. This means that there was at least one other group of Indian Jugglers, if not more, in Britain at this time. Maybe the group in Dublin also included Ramo Samee, but we have no evidence of this.

The first mention of Ramo Samee by name in the British press came in November 1820[5], when he appeared at the Olympic Theatre in London, billed confusingly as 'Chief of the Indian Jugglers'. (The rival 'Chief', Kia Khan, was appearing in Chester at this time.) Zubrzycki records that Ramo Samee left England for America in 1817, returning to Britain a headline act some time in 1820. A piece in the *Salem Gazette* 5 October 1819[6] confirms his appearance in America; ...[after having been] for some time past in the metropolis of England and before all the crowned heads of Europe who have unanimously pronounced him to be the first master of the art in their dominions.

By 1822 he was well established and, like Kia Khan, he was working solo. The *Public Ledger and Daily Advertiser* 3 January 1822 gives a detailed account of his act at the Royalty Theatre in London;

> Ramo Samee, the Indian Juggler, will go through his extraordinary Feats of strength and agility; consisting of various Deceptions with Cups and Balls. After which a Series of Evolutions with four Brass balls; several Feats of Balancing, in which he will introduce the building a Canopy with his Tongue on top of his Nose, and removing the same with surprising ingenuity. Also, the Spinning of a Top on a Point as fine as a Needle, and balancing the same on his Chin. The wonderful Feat with large Knives, similar to that of Balls; swallowing a Stone the size of an Egg, and disposing of the same at pleasure. Also, his activity in throwing a large Ball, the size of an 18lb [pound] shot, to different parts of his frame with the greatest of ease. He will conclude with the extraordinary Feat of swallowing a Sword two feet long.

Not too dissimilar an act from Kia Khan but one that relies more upon physical skills much closer to 'juggling' in the modern sense rather than gimmick or deception. The building of a 'canopy' on his nose, using only his tongue, appears to have been an act peculiar to Samee. It is difficult to picture what this may have looked like, but the *Northampton Mercury* 28 April 1821 refers to the structure as a 'pagoda'. The *Newport and Monmouthshire Merlin* 11 November 1837 is a little more descriptive;

> Ramo Samee will perform his astonishing Feat of *Building a Grand Eastern Canopy* [sic], which he manages by the movement of Twelve Porcupine Quills, from the Mouth to the upper Lip, till the Canopy is beautifully erected; after which he will take out the Grand Supporter without the assistance of his hands, leaving the Porcupine Quills and the Top of the Canopy perfect, supported upon the upper Lip.

Juggling and balance activities made up the greater part of Samee's act, with the spectacular swallowing of the sword as the highlight. His act with the 'globe of stone' continued well into the 1830s[7] and he was also beginning to include acts of illusion[8]. Samee's juggling expertise astonished many of his audience. Hazlitt (1828), although he does not mention him by name, waxes lyrical over the skill of the 'Indian Juggler' who may well be Ramee;

> To catch four balls in succession in less than a second of time, and deliver them back so as to return with seeming consciousness to the hand again, to make them revolve round him at certain intervals, like the planets in their spheres, to make them chase one another like sparkles of fire, or shoot up like flowers or meteors, to throw them behind his back and twine them round his neck like ribbons or like serpents, to do what appears an impossibility, and to do it with all the ease, the grace, the carelessness imaginable, to laugh at, to play with the glittering mockeries, to follow them with his eye as if he could fascinate them with its lambent fire, or as if he had only to see that they kept time with the music on the stage - there is something in all this which he who does not admire may be quite sure he never really admired anything in the whole course of his life. It is skill surmounting difficulty, and beauty triumphing over skill.

Although Hazlitt was less than comfortable with the sword swallowing part of the routine, he confesses to being moved so much by Samee's performance that he questioned his own worth. The University of Bristol Theatre Collection holds an etching of Ramo Samee performing at the Royal Coburg theatre (now the Old Vic) in London in 1822. It shows him sitting cross-legged on the stage, dressed in traditional salwar kameez, and seemingly manipulating the brass balls for which he was famous. Around him lie other paraphernalia of his act and he is performing against a 'Looking Glass Curtain'.

This was a 'curtain' made entirely of large mirrors in which the audience could view itself during the performance. The theatre appears to be packed with an enthusiastic crowd, reflecting Samee's popularity.

Whereas other ethnic performers worked within the European aesthetic of the period, in the sense of what they did and how they presented it, Samee drew very much upon his own culture. He dressed in clothes that would have been usual for him, not in a stage costume as such. His performances were very much rooted in an ancient Indian performance tradition. He was not pandering to a racial stereotype as perceived by the British, in the way that blackface minstrels did. In simple terms, he was doing what he knew best.

Ramo Samee at the Royal Coburg Theatre *(Library of Congress)*

By the mid nineteenth century there were several solo Indian Jugglers, and still more group acts, performing throughout the country. Samee, like many others, was always billed as the 'Original', 'Chief', or 'Prince' of Indian Jugglers.

Not all of these performers were actually Indian, as we have seen with Kia Khan. A group of such jugglers appeared with *Adam's Circus* in Dublin in 1829[9]. A Monsieur Decour was appearing as an 'Indian Juggler' in Norwich also in 1829[10]. Earlier, a Mr Jameson, who claimed to be a 'pupil of the renowned Indian Jugglers' appeared in Hull[11] in 1821 and a Mr Vaulent, who stated that he was 'the first of the Indian Jugglers who exhibited their tricks in this country', was recorded leaving Britain in the same year[12]. M. Carl Rappo was performing in London in 1834[13] and a M. Ferdinand was appearing with *Batty's Circus* in Belfast in 1844[14]. A Mr Ryland also performed 'in the manner of Ramo Samee' with *Cooke's Circus* in Wakefield the same year[15]. These performers were only a few of the number of imitators that appeared during, and after, Samee's lifetime.

One can only assume that those non-Indian performers dressed the part and darkened their skin, thereby falling back into the tradition of minstrelsy. If imitation is the most sincere form of flattery then Samee was at the pinnacle of his career. When it came to popular variety entertainers his was a household name, and he was mentioned by several well-known writers of the time, including Hazlitt (1828) and Thackeray (1848).

Comparatively little is known about Samee's domestic affairs. We do know that Samee married a woman named Ellen, although no official record can be found of the marriage. By this time Ramo Samee had adopted the forename of George. They had three children before January 27th 1836. Two of the children, a boy named Thomas George, and a girl named Clara Elizabeth Sarah were baptised together in Lambeth on that day[16]. Some have suggested that this indicates that they were twins. This is not so, and it was not uncommon for siblings to be baptised together some years after their actual birth date. Thomas was actually born around 1826 and Clara around 1832. Their third child was a daughter named Ellen. Although there is no extant baptismal record for her, she does appear with her sister Clara and her mother Ellen in the 1861 Census returns[17], and from this it is estimated that she was born around 1831. Conflictingly, the 1881 Census[18] gives Ellen's age as 40, making a birth date of around 1841, though her birthplace remains the same. Mistakes were often made in these records and I am inclined to think that the former is more correct.

An article in the *Court of Exchequer Evening Chronicle* 30 June 1835 gives us a rare glimpse into their non performing lives. The piece makes reference to Samee's wife and children accompanying him whilst he was performing in Carmarthen 'some years since', and that they lodged together in the house of a Mrs Williams. Samee was wealthy enough to engage the services of a companion-housemaid for his family during the stay. According to a retrospective article in the *Manchester Times* 26 June 1850, entitled *Confessions of a Sword Swallower*, the writer states that;

> Six and twenty years ago I began to practise sword swallowing against the celebrated Ramo Samee, who was then getting £25 or £30 [pounds sterling] a week.

This was at a time when the writer himself was earning three or four pounds sterling a week. Samee's weekly income would have been equivalent to around 1,500 pounds sterling, a good amount as opposed to the writer's income of only 175 pounds sterling. Ramo Samee had a healthy income and yet, by 1840, his wife felt it necessary to write the following letter to *John Bull* 15 June 1840;

Sir – I have taken the liberty to address you, soliciting, a perhaps, unprecedented favour. I am perfectly aware that it is usual to pay for theatrical notices as an advertisement, but I am induced, through poverty, to solicit the favour of noticing Ramo Samee's approaching benefit on Friday, June the 19th, at the Victoria Theatre. Perhaps I need hardly point out he has been under the notice of the public for twenty-six years as the celebrated 'East Indian Juggler'.

I am Sir, very respectfully, E. Ramo Samee

The Editor added this footnote to the letter;

If this be the veritable 'Indian' who once excited our terror and our wonder, we shall be very happy to find the insertion of the above do him service.

We do not know if this letter was successful in drawing a larger crowd to support Samee's benefit night performance. By the end of June, he had concluded his engagement at the Victoria Theatre and went on to appear in Ipswich in the July[19] and then Bristol in the September[20]. Samee was clearly able to get engagements, so the question remains as to how his wife could plead poverty.

Many performers found that the travelling life led them towards drink. Certainly Ramee performed widely throughout the British Isles, appearing in some of the established theatres of the period, Variety Theatres, public gardens and other open air events, and private parties. Had this happened to Samee? According to newspaper entries he appears to have been in regular employment during the preceding decade, although in 1839 there is noticeable paucity in the press. In the September he was listed as performing in Vauxhall[21], and later in the month in Rochester[22]. Did something happen in that year that made it difficult for him to find work? We do not know, but it is interesting to note that another performer, a "Mr. Macauley", was very much in the public eye as an 'Indian Juggler' and, indeed, was invited to a dinner with

Queen Victoria[23]. Could it have been that Ramee now had other, more notable, rivals and imitators to his craft that, coupled with perhaps a growing drink problem, which led his wife to declare their poverty?

Whatever the reason, the reality was that Ellen had three children to feed. (Although, there is evidence that that one of the daughters worked with, or on the same bill, as Samee as a child performer in true circus fashion.) In 1835 we find at the Royal Pavilion Theatre;

> A Scotch dance by the Infant Ramo Samee, pupil of Mademoiselle Leoni (*Morning Advertiser* 26 October 1835)

And the following year at the Royal Beulah Spa in Norwood;

> The celebrated Ramo Samee, and his infant daughter, will exhibit their most surprising feats (*West Kent Guardian* 6 August 1836)

I believe that these two entries probably refer to the same child, but which daughter it was is not specified. It could have been either Clara or Ellen. There are no other references to him performing with his children as such but in 1837 there are several times when Samee appears with the 'Persian Youths'[24]. Who these youths were and what the act consisted of is not recorded, but it is not beyond the bounds of possibility that one or two of his children were involved. It is known that his son Thomas followed in his father's footsteps for a short period of time before his life ended prematurely in a tragic accident;

> DEATH FROM SWALLOWING A SWORD. On Tuesday last an inquest was held … on the body of Thomas Ramo Samee, the son of George, the celebrated Indian juggler, of that name, who met his death under the following peculiar circumstances;: - it appears that he had been in the habit for twelve months of emulating the example of his father (who first introduced in England the swallowing of the sword) in attempting to pass into his throat (oesophagus), a sword … On the 24th inst., while exhibiting his capabilities before some friends at a tavern in Long Acre, London, in this peculiar feat, which he executed

in the ordinary way, until the instrument had arrived about six inches in his oesophagus, when he felt an obstruction, and forcibly, though innocently, ;pushed it four inches further, instead of withdrawing it, as is usual when difficulties occur in its descent. He was immediately conscious of having injured himself, fell back, and after struggling for some time was brought in a collapsed state to the University College Hospital (*Manchester Courier* 3 February 1849)

The piece goes on in detail to explain that Thomas had managed to pierce the pericardium (the sac surrounding the heart) and died of intense inflammation some days later. It seems that his friends tried to dissuade him from doing it but a young man's bravado caused the 'Accidental Death' verdict.

This accident had a profound affect upon Ramo Samee. His health suffered and he appears not to have undertaken any performance work for the rest of 1849. However, in the June of 1850 he was engaged to appear at several Variety Theatre venues in Paris[25], such as here at Le Gamine theatre;

Le célèbre jongleur des Indes-Orientales Ramo Samee, exécutera des exercices inconnus jusqu'a ce jour (*Le Nouvelliste* 12 June 1850)

[The famous East Indian juggler, Ramo Samee, will perform exercises unknown until today. *Author's translation*]

Unfortunately, Samee could not complete his engagements and had to return home, having taken ill. His health declined and he died on the 20 August. His financial position had never improved and once again Ellen was forced to write to the newspapers;

MR EDITOR – I have taken the liberty of conveying to you the first intelligence of the death of my husband, the celebrated Indian juggler, Ramo Samee, with the hope you will kindly notice it in your widely circulated journal, for the sake of his family. There are thousands who have witnessed his performances who would now, I am sure, kindly give trifle to assist in procuring him a coffin, which we are unable to do ... he has lingered in the most painful state until yesterday, when death terminated his sufferings, leaving myself and two daughters to lament the kindest parent and friend in the world, without the slightest means of procuring him burial, our all being expended for his illness, and he from the nature of his performances being inadmissible to any theatrical club. If you then, sir, make such mention as you think fit, it will do an essential service to your obedient servant. Ellen Ramo Samee (*Bell's Life and Sporting Chronicle* 25 August 1850)

Times must have been difficult indeed if Samee's widow had to resort to what amounts to a begging letter in order to cover his burial costs. Victorian funerals could be an expensive affair, even for the poorest in society. Rosen (2008) refers to a mid-century advertisement in *The Times* that offered six classes of funeral, ranging from the most expensive at 21 pounds sterling to the least expensive at three pounds and five shillings [approximately equivalent today between 1,700 pounds sterling and 260 pounds sterling]. Even then, costs could be lessened by not having a funeral cortege through the streets. Did Ellen's letter generate any donations? A letter to *Bell's Life and Sporting Chronicle* the following week, 1 September, tells us more;

Sir; Your early insertion of the widow's appeal ... in last week's paper, reflects the highest credit on you, and in remembrance of the pleasure I experienced in early days of his performance, I beg to hand you 10s [shillings] from ten friends, collected in the neighbourhood of High Holborn, towards alleviating the sufferings of the poor widow and family, and should be rejoiced to hear if some 40 or 50 from amongst your numerous readers, who, in an hour or two, within their own circle of friends, could no doubt with little exertion do the same and scarcely miss it, thereby proving that the widow's appeal in the hour of need to a generous public has not been in vain. – Apologising for thus troubling you. I beg to subscribe myself, most respectfully, a widow's well-wisher. August 28th 1850. H.W.

(We have also received 5s from 'Two Jews', 1s from 'a Bishop', 2s 6d from 'a Bird' [sic], and add a trifle ourselves. Surely the managers of theatres and other establishments, who have derived so much advantage from the talents of the deceased, ought to contribute to lift his widow, a most respectable woman, from the severe gripe of absolute poverty. Poor Ramo is to be buried today, and his funeral expenses have to be defrayed by instalments. The trifle obtained has been handed to Mrs Ramo – Ed)

A poor response for such an esteemed performer. Donations amounted to 18s 6d plus anything more added by the newspaper. It would be interesting to know who H. W. was. Is it only a coincidence that if the initials were reversed that they could possibly be those of William Hazlitt who was so inspired by Samee's performances? I like to think that it was, despite the circumstantial nature of the evidence.

After the above letter was published, a further one pound sterling was donated by the circus proprietor William Cooke[26], and Samee was buried in the old St Pancras churchyard on 8 September 1850[27]. The coffin was followed to the grave by 'a large concourse of spectators'. The newspapers carried no obituary and the report of his interment was squashed between a pieces on the regulation of beer sales on Sundays and the erection of a lightning conductor on Salisbury Cathedral. A sad ending to such a celebrated performer.

And yet, his name lived on. In 1871, some twenty years after his death, his name was being used as a measuring stick for jugglers;

The clown, who has an unpronounceable name, is a regular Ramo Samee at juggling (*Bristol Daily Post* 27 December 1871)

Into the twentieth century he was still being referred to[28]. Even today he is discussed in juggling circles. For a man who died in relative obscurity, the fact that he is still talked about continues to celebrate his life. Although not purely a 'juggler' by today's definition, Samee was the foremost of his kind in the first half of the nineteenth century. His performances paved the way for many who followed him in the latter half; Paul Cinquevalli[29]; Paul Conchas[30]; Kara the 'Gentleman Juggler'[31], and many others.

Indian acrobats at the Jardin Zoologique d'Acclimitation. Postcard c. 1902 *(Author's collection)*

Notes

1. For a more detailed account of Paul Cinquevalli and the history of juggling I recommend reading Thom Wall's book *Juggling from Antiquity to the Middle Ages*

2. *The New Collins English Dictionary* p705

3. The Star Pagoda was a silver coin issued by Madras Mint for the British East India Company up until 1816, when the Rupee became the standard unit of currency in India. 1,000 Pagodas would have been equivalent to approximately 3,500 Rupees. That sum converts to approximately 37 pounds sterling today, which would have been less than one pound sterling in the early 1800s.

4. *The National Archive Currency Converter 1270-2017* has been used throughout this work. Online at; https://www.nationalarchives. gov.uk/currency-converter/

5. *Morning Post* 24 November 1820

6. Cited Banerjee S. (2011) p60

7. *Cheltenham Journal and Gloucestershire Fashionable Weekly* 21 August 1837

8. *Waterford Chronicle* 15 August 1835

9. *Saunder's News-Letter* 29 October 1829

10. *Norwich Mercury* 7 February 1829

11. *Star (London)* 9 August 1821

12. *Stamford Mercury* 2 March 1821

13. *London Courier and Evening Gazette* 21 May 1834

14. *Belfast Mercantile Register and Weekly Advertiser* 30 July 1844

15. Circus Poster 30/31 August 1844. Held in the Cryer Collection at Wakefield Library. Reference 2233-66. Online at; www.twixtaireandcalder.org.uk

16. *London, England, Church of England Births and baptisms 1813-1917.* Online at; https://www.ancestry.co.uk/interactive/1558/31 280_198055-00153?pid=3628945&backurl=https://search. ancestry.co.uk/cgi-bin/sse.dll?indiv%3D1%26dbid%3D15 58%26h%3D3628945%26tid%3D%26pid%3D%26useP-UB%3Dtrue%26_phsrc%3DAnq70%26_phstart%3Dsuccess-Source&treeid=&personid=&hintid=&usePUB=true&_phs-rc=Anq70&_phstart=successSource&usePUBJs=true&_ ga=2.179938284.914258114.1585754727-8519783.1584367827

17. *England and Wales Census, 1861.* Online at; https://www.familysearch. org/ark:/61903/1:1:Q2ML-WCFW

18. *England and Wales Census, 1881.* Online at; https://www.ancestry. co.uk/interactive/7572/LNDRG11_298_300-0732?pid=1 4503289&backurl=https://search.ancestry.co.uk/cgi-bin/ sse.dll?indiv%3D1%26dbid%3D7572%26h%3D14503289 %26tid%3D%26pid%3D%26usePUB%3Dtrue%26_phs-rc%3DAnq77%26_phstart%3DsuccessSource&treeid=&per-sonid=&hintid=&usePUB=true&_phsrc=Anq77&_phstart=-successSource&usePUBJs=true

19. *The Suffolk Chronicle* 11 July 1840

20. *Bristol Mercury* 5 September 1840

21. *Morning Advertiser* 9 September 1839

22. *Kentish Mercury* 28 September 1839

23. *Cheltenham Looker-On* 20 July 1839

24. For example, Morning Advertiser 18 May 1837

25. Listings for Ramo Samee appear in several French publications in June. Another example of these can be found online at; https://gallica.bnf.fr/ark:/12148/bpt6k46506080/f4.image. r=%22Ramo%20Samee%22?rk=21459;2

26. *Bells' Life in London* 8 September 1850

27. *Lloyd's Weekly Newspaper* 8 September 1850

28. *Pall Mall Gazette* 11 October 1901

29. For a detailed piece on Cinquevalli, I suggest reading The Greatest Juggler in the World which appears in *Holland* (1998)

30. As above, the piece on Conchas entitled A Heavyweight Juggler also appears in *Holland* (1998)

31. There are several accounts of Kara. I suggest reading *Michael Kara: King of Jugglers - Juggler to Kings* by Herman Sagemüller, which was reissued in 2020 by Niels Duinker.

CHAPTER 9
LOFTY TUMBLERS – THE BEDOUIN ARABS

Acrobatics, as a form of human physical expression, has a long historical tradition. Some of the earliest depictions of performing acrobats appear in wall paintings in the tombs at Beni Hasan, an Ancient Egyptian burial site some 150 miles south of Cairo. They date from the 21st to 17th centuries BCE. The art work of the Minoan culture, on the island of Crete, featured acrobats around 2000 BCE, and Chinese acrobats were prevalent between 200 BCE and 200 CE. In the Roman world, Petronius, author of the *Satyricon*[1], wrote about acrobats arriving at a dinner party, and in Greek culture acrobats were often depicted on vases and other artefacts. Vickers (2016) writes;

> There were acrobatic professionals in ancient Greece. There were acrobats who could contort their bodies, stand on their heads or hands, perform back-flips and somersaults, leap from horses, and dance among upright sword blades.

The desire for self-expression and self-discovery through the exploration of bodily physicality is truly a cross-cultural phenomenon that has endured and developed throughout history.

In Britain during the medieval era that extended from the post Roman 5th CE to the 15th CE, itinerant jongleurs entertained with performances of acrobatics and other physical skills (Speaight, 1980). The fact that acrobats, or tumblers as they were commonly called, were active into the

16th CE was well documented, even in official court papers. The *Calendar of State Papers for Queen Elizabeth I* 1584, records that;

> Certain foreigners to come over [to England] as tumblers, for spies and intelligencers

And Barrow (2005) also mentions that;

> Interludes, minstrels and tumblers were among the spectacles complained of by puritans in 1583

Clearly tumblers, like many other itinerant performers of the time, were treated with suspicion and scorn. Their world was one of scratching out a living wherever they could perform.

Southwark Fair by William Hogarth *(Public Domain)*

In Britain, and London in particular, Borough Fairs were popular venues for tumblers and acrobats. The 1733 engraving by William Hogarth, entitled *Southwark Fair*[3] or *The Humours of a Fair*, gives us an indication of the variety of entertainments on offer at these events. These Fairs, associated with vice and crime were situated outside the control of the City of London and were often bawdy and rowdy; riots and deaths amongst the crowd were not an uncommon occurrence, and did little to 'gentrify' tumblers and other related acts.

Although these entertainments may have been popular with the masses, it was not until the eighteenth century 'structuralisation' of such entertainments in the minor theatres and through the formulation of the circus as an art form. Many of the tumblers performing in these venues were British. In 1764, a Mr Matthews was reported as presenting 'Lofty Tumbling' and flying through ten hoops[4]. But there were also a growing number of European tumblers beginning to appear in Britain. In the same year that Astley inaugurated his equestrian performances at Halfpenny Hatch in London (Rendell, 2013) a company of Venetian performers were presenting acrobatic feats in Manchester;

Venetian Company of Performers

Sign. Colpi will balance his Children, in such a Manner as was never attempted by any one but himself ... also LOFTY TUMBLING
(*Manchester Mercury* 12 July 1768)

Colpi would be one of the performers that Astley introduced into his 'expanded' performances when he moved to his second site at the foot of Westminster Bridge, the venue that would be later known as Astley's Amphitheatre.

The influx of European acrobats into the embryonic circus continued into the nineteenth century. But it was not until 1836 that a new class of acrobats and tumblers appeared on the scene. At the end of April

1836, the *Windsor and Eton Express* announced the imminent arrival of a troupe of Bedouin Arabs[5]. The troupe had been performing in Paris[6] to great applause and had now been engaged to appear at the Colosseum in London. The British were already aware of the 'blood thirsty' Bedouin tribesmen from newspaper reports during the French invasion of Algeria and the subsequent conflict, but the circus was quick to capitalise on the exotic nature of the Bedouins long before they were actually seen in person. In March 1835, *Cooke's Circus* in Dublin presented an 'original Equitation Scene of Action and Evolution' entitled *The Bedouins of the Desert*[7]. This was a portrayal of the Bedouins by Cooke's company based entirely on the memoirs of a traveller – with not an actual Bedouin in sight!

> With new and appropriate Music, splendid and characteristic Dresses, and Accessories of the most correct and magnificent description, in order to give a full and efficient reality to the effects intended to be produced on one of the largest Arenas in the three Kingdoms (*The Morning Register* 14 March 1835)

Presumably Cooke and company 'dressed the part' and made to portray as best as they were able their interpretation of Bedouin life. Even when the real Bedouin performers arrived in 1836, the company members of the Colosseum took part as 'extras', dressed in 'Arab or Turkish costume'. These were little more than a backdrop to the feats of the Bedouin. *Bell's Weekly Messenger* 8 May 1836 gives a detailed account;

> The exhibition takes place upon the stage … which, with the addition of scenery, is made to represent the great desert of Zahara [Sahara]. To add to the effect a vast number of persons in the Arab or Turkish costume appear seated cross-legged around the stage, and form a very picturesque *tableau vivant*. An Arabian festival is then celebrated, in the course of which the evolutions, dances, and exercises so peculiar to Arabia are portrayed by the Bedouins … The strength and activity of these Arabs is almost beyond belief … The party consists of five – three young men, and a boy of about six or seven years of age, who are decidedly Arabs, with frames as tough and flexible as whalebone.

The fifth, who presents many features of negro organisation, is the 'strong man' of the party, and contents himself with running about with as many of his companions as pleased to mount on his and other's shoulders, and forming the base of a human pillar of 'three men deep'. His companions are rather slightly made, yet display extraordinary strength of limb – springing on high like monkeys, alighting on their hands instead of their feet, and thence throwing continuous turbillions [French for whirlwind] with as much ease as if it was all the same to them which end was uppermost. But all this is trifling when compared to the evolutions which the elder Bedouin goes through. He flings summersets [sic] in a race along the stage with a dagger in each hand and the points resting against his breast. He varies this feat with yatagans [a type of short sabre], single and double, receiving the points in his throat, mouth, and the angles of his eyes, so that a single slip or shake of the hand might inflict a mortal wound. He also fires a gun in the same airy whirl, apparently quite indifferent whether he takes it in his hand at the commencement of his race, whether he has to snatch it from the ground at the instant his heels are the uppermost (while his finger finds the trigger by intuition), or whether he has to fling himself and firelock over the heads and erect sabres of his brethren.

As daring and dynamic as this performance was, it is interesting to note how the performance was framed. Firstly, the director of the piece had tried to contextualise the performance of the Bedouin by creating an 'Arabian' festival, complete with many extras (presumably non-Arab) to dress the scene. It created a 'picturesque' scene, which was probably a romanticised interpretation of the reality dished up for a European audience; a chocolate box lid image. Then there is the language used to describe the Bedouin. They were, according to the writer, 'decidedly Arabs'. This only served to reinforce the 'otherness' of the troupe. The fifth member of the troupe, and presumably the older, was described as having 'many features of negro organisation'. What does this mean? Was the writer making reference to his skin colour, his hair, or his facial features? What purpose did it serve to separate this individual out from the troupe, apart from, again, to emphasise the 'otherness'? The writer's use of language further stereotypes the performers by describing them as springing like 'monkeys', thereby reinforcing the Anglo-Saxon perception of anyone from the African continent. Whilst the exploits of these performers appear to have been generally well received by the public, there were thankfully some, perhaps more liberal minded, who objected to the 'tableau vivant' being a distortion of the truth[8].

In most of the advertising for their performances the group was announced as the 'Bedouin Arabs'; they were an amorphous group of foreigners without individual identities. However, whilst performing in Birmingham in the December of 1836, *Aris's Birmingham Gazette* at last gave us their names;

> Those Wonderful Artistes, The Real BEDOUIN ARABS, SIDI ALI, ABDALLAH, AHMED, HOSSEIN, MOHAMMED, HASSAN, &c.
> (*Aris's Birmingham Gazette* 5 December 1836)

There are two interesting points in this advertisement. Firstly, there is an ampersand following the list of names. This implies that there were more in the group than the five named performers; perhaps a support group of spouses and an interpreter? The second point is that they are advertised as the 'Real' Bedouin Arabs. Is this to draw distinction from any other performing groups promoting themselves as Bedouin Arabs? Very possibly so, for an advertisement for *Samwell's Circus* appeared in the *Dover Telegraph*[9] announcing that 'the tribe of Ocrobats [sic] or Bedouin Arabs will appear'. Similarly, *Batty's Circus* in Cork, Ireland was presenting 'an entire, novel and interesting performance illustrative of the Customs and Manners of the Bedouin Arabs'[10]. Clearly, 'Bedouin Arab' performances were in vogue and I suspect that many of these Bedouin imitations involved few, if indeed any, actual Arabs.

This 'real' Bedouin troupe continued performing across Britain for the next two years, with other groups and individuals appearing at rival venues. In December 1837, an individual billed as an Arab, under the most un-Semitic sounding name of Merlo Rochelle, performed rope-dancing at the Royal Standard Theatre in Shoreditch[11], and across at the Pavilion the same newspaper reported;

> The wonderful performances of the Bedouin Arabs, BEN KALOCH, MULEY MUSTAPHA, and ABDEL SING ... proved one of the few attractive features. Such exhibitions, however, as even these extraordinary individuals present, however wonderful they may be as to mere feats of strength, we cannot consider pleasing at any time (*Morning Post* 27 December 1837).

Yet another group of 'Bedouin Arabs', one with a distinctly Sikh sounding name. They do not seem to have over impressed the reporter, although it seems to have a bit of a rough house and the audience came in for some criticism in the same piece;

> Of the crowd of non-descripts in the pit and gallery no adequate conception can be formed, nor of the constant war they carried on, by means of orange-peel, ginger-beer corks, apples, and old hats.

Abdallah, one of the 'Real' Bedouin Arabs who toured with the group, seems to have attracted some attention to himself while in London. The *Globe* newspaper of 6 December 1836 gave notice that he had married a Mrs Bill, a widow living near the Surrey Theatre, where he had been performing. This announcement was immediately refuted the following day in a letter;

TO THE EDITOR OF THE MORNING CHRONICLE

47 Prospect-place, West – square, Dec. 6th, 1836

> Sir – In the *Morning Chronicle* of this day there appears an announcement of the marriage of Abdallah, one of the Bedouin Arabs, to Mrs. Bill of the Shades coffee-house, Westminster Road. I am authorised by Mrs. Bill to state, that whoever has sent you that paragraph for insertion must be inimical to her interest, and has imposed a gross falsehood upon you. As Mrs. Bill states that it will be the means of doing her and

her family a serious injury in her business, she most respectfully relies on your contradicting it in the *Chronicle* of tomorrow.

I am sir, your obedient servant Jas. Riach

(*London Evening Standard* 7 December 1837)

It would be interesting to know why Mrs. Bill feared that an announcement of her marriage would have been so injurious to her business and family. Marriage to a 'foreigner', particularly one of colour, although legal was not always accepted; it was potentially subversive of the British sense of social and racial order. Mrs Bill certainly responded through her solicitor very quickly to quash the idea. Could this have reflected the prevalent attitude towards the Arabs? They were accepted as entertainment – but to be married to one was another matter; this was no Shakespearian paradigm of Desdemona and Othello. Added to this was the continuing newspaper reports of conflict between the Bedouins and the French. In the November it was reported that the city of Algiers, being held by the French, was under siege by Bedouin Arabs[12]. This might also explain racist attitudes towards the Arabs.

Another incident had happened to Abdallah earlier in the September. During a performance at the Surrey Theatre he was attacked by a member of the audience. William Marshall, a cabinet-maker, was charged with;

A most outrageous assault upon the Bedouin Arabs … by which Hassan Abdallah, one of the most dextrous of the party, had suffered the loss of three of his front teeth … the defendant, who had been permitted to sit in the orchestra [the theatre was crowded that night], made an attempt to force himself into the private box where Hassan was sitting, who immediately arose from his seat and made signs to the defendant that it was a private box, and he had no business there, upon which the defendant struck the Arab a most violet blow upon his mouth, and knocked out three of his teeth … the defendant put himself into a fighting attitude, and the other parties who had forced their way into the box also attacked the Arabs. By this time the other Arabs had come in to the assistance of their countryman, and speedily contrived to drive the whole of the parties from the box (*Sun (London)* 23 September 1836)

Although Marshall was the only person to be charged, it appears that there were others who were quite ready to back him up and join in the attack, which appears to have been in some part racially motivated. When the matter was brought before the Surrey Court of Sessions three weeks later, the troupe appeared before the Bench to give evidence. The news report of this hearing pointed out that they were dressed in the costume of their country and excited considerable interest[13]. Wearing their ethnic clothes served to maintain their identity, rather than adopting 'European' clothing. If this was a conscious decision on their part, or their Counsel's, then it might have served to emphasise their 'otherness' and thereby underline the racial motivation for the attack. Habbouch (2011) suggests that; 'Moroccan acrobatic performers were motivated by a cultural will to translate their sense of locality and peculiarity to global audiences'. But the fact that they were so dressed shows that even outside of their performance they were still being treated as an exhibition and entertainment. For the record, Marshall pleaded guilty and was ordered to pay a fine of ten pounds sterling with further sureties.

This was not the first time Abdallah had been before the Court. In June he had been the defendant, appearing before the Bench, with his companion Hamed (Ahmed), for causing an affray and assaulting several police officers when they attempted to arrest the two[14]. The Bedouin Arab troupe stayed touring in Britain until the summer of 1838, when they travelled to America—minus Abdallah. They arrived in Philadelphia on the 4 August, as reported in the *London Evening Standard* 22 August 1838. Even whilst the group was in America without him, Abdallah still managed to make the news;

Abdallah, the most expert and active of the troop of Bedouin Arabs (by whom the Surrey Theatre profited greatly) … is now on his return from

Arabia Felix [the Latin name formerly given to South Arabia or Yemen by the British and possibly his home country], whither he proceeded on dissolving [sic] partnership with his companions, previous to their leaving this country for America. From a letter received by Mr. Davidge [lessee of the Royal Surrey Theatre], it appears Abdallagh [sic] is bringing with him a new troop of Bedouins, who can jump so 'tarnation' high, that, as cousin Jonathan says, 'they fairly wear out their shoes before they come down again!' (*Clare Journal and Ennis Advertiser* 1 November 1838)

The original Bedouin troupe stayed in America until June 1839 and returned to Britain on board the steam-ship *The Great Western*. They arrived in Bristol on 26 June and the passenger list included Ali, Hossein, Hassan, and Moses[15]. If these were the original line up, minus Abdallah, then Moses may possibly have been Mohammed. On 8 July, the *Sun (London)* advertised their first performance since returning from America and the *Morning Post* of the same date bills them as the 'Real Bedouin Arabs'. This is interesting, because on 4 July the *Cheltenham Chronicle* carried this report on their performance at the Montpellier Gardens;

> The great novelty of the evening was the performance of the 'Bedouin Arabs', the excellence of whose surprising evolutions must be seen to be believed.

As well as this company of 'real' Bedouin Arabs, there were several other groups performing similar routines around Britain at the same time. The 'Bedouin Arabs and their Steeds' were appearing in Leeds with *J. Cooke's Circus*[16] on 3 August. A group calling themselves the 'Anglo-Bedouin Arabs' were appearing at the Thanet Ranelagh Gardens in Ramsgate between the 17 August and 4 September[17]. The advertising for their last night's performance gives;

> The celebrated ANGLO-BEDOUIN ARABS will go through the whole of their astonishing performances, consisting of Jeux de Gymnase [Gymnasium Exercises], Pas de Grenouille [literally from the French *Not a Frog!*], Feats of Strength and Agility on the suspended

line, forming a Grand Jeux de Balance in the air, Classical Pyramid on a pole 20 feet high, surrounded by a shower of fire ... (*Kentish Gazette* 4 September 1838)

The composition of the Anglo-Bedouin troupe is never defined but it is known that venue managers began placing Moroccan acrobats together with British gymnastic performances and also that British children were taken as apprentices by Arab troupes (Habbouch, 2011).

Yet another group just calling themselves 'The Bedouin Arabs' appeared at the Richmond Theatre around the 10 August[18]. Whether Abdallah was a part of any of these groups is unsure. In June 1843, a group calling themselves the 'Moroccan Acrobats' were performing at the Victoria Theatre in London. They were billed as being;

From the Great Mount Atlas, 12 in number, whose surprising Feats have been the wonder of the ages, in Africa, in Asia, and in different parts of Europe (*Morning Advertiser* 6 June 1843)

The *Illustrated London News* of 24 June gave a far more detailed account of these acrobats along with an illustration of their pyramid building or 'column of four persons'. In the September of 1843 this group was performing at Astley's Amphitheatre 'combined with the British acrobats'[19]. Could this combined group possibly have been the earlier billed Anglo-Bedouin group? William Batty was also touring his circus around Britain and Ireland at this time, featuring four acrobats who performed as 'The Enchanted Arabs'. These were possibly the four 'Persian Acrobats' who had been with the company throughout 1842.

Moroccan acrobats (*Illustrated London News* June 24 1843)

It was not until the March of 1847 that a distinctly new group arrived in Britain. With reference to the Royal Surrey Theatre, the *Sun (London)* announced on 25 March that the theatre would re-open on the Easter Monday with a performance of another 'Real Bedouin Arabs, twelve in number', although there would be larger groups to come in later years. The same newspaper on 7 April gave a little more information in telling the public that the group had come from the Theatre Port St. Martin, in Paris and that this would be their first appearance in England. The *Morning Advertiser* of 6 April gives far more detail about the group and its performance;

> They are twelve in number, including the director and the priest. There are also two very interesting little boys – one of pure Arab blood, the other having been born in France to a French mother. The ages of the party range from 20 to 40 years, the greatest number being under 30. It appears that they have performed at most of the principal theatres of Europe with great *eclat*. It is stated that their habits are exceedingly simple – coffee is their principal drink, and one substantial meal of meat and rice serves to supply them with sufficient nourishment. They are all small men, none of them exceeding five feet seven inches. Their frames are muscular, but owing to their spare and simple diet they are unencumbered with a single particle of unnecessary flesh. The performances of the Arabs consist of various feats of bodily agility – leaping, tumbling, standing on each other's heads, &c., all of which they accomplish with great ease and gracefulness. One of the most perilous feats was performed by one of the most active of the group, who, while standing in the centre of a hoop, about three feet in diameter, stuck round with bayonets, throws somersaults with such precision, as to alight in exactly the same place at each time. The bayonets are genuine ones, and the slightest failure here would be attended with serious consequences … They require to be seen to be appreciated.

The fascination that the British had with 'non–white' ethnic groups is reflected in the details given about their appearance, diet, and customs – as well as the performance. The itinerary of this group, performing across Europe, then at the Port St Martin theatre in Paris, and on to the Royal Surrey theatre in London follows a very similar pattern to the original 'Real' Bedouin troupe of the decade before.

(Right) The Bedouin Troupe at the Porte St Martin theatre in Paris. Print c. 1835 *(Author's collection)*

(Below) Extract from a poster for the Bedouin Arabs c. 1840 *(Victoria & Albert Museum)*

Although Abdallah is not named, it is plausible that he may have, himself, been the director of this group. It is also possible that this 'new' acrobatic troupe was built around the cast of his own 1838 troupe of Bedouin acrobats. The group were under an eight-month contract of engagement to Mr Wardell, the lessee of Vauxhall Gardens in London[20], and although they did perform there during the summer of 1847, they also toured throughout Britain. They had a brief engagement in Liverpool that May before returning to London, and whilst at Vauxhall Gardens there was a brief appearance at Rosherville Gardens, Gravesend, in August[21]. On the same bill was Ramo Samee. Perhaps the highlight of their 1847 performances was when they appeared at the St James's theatre in London before Queen Victoria, Prince Albert and the Royal children, who were accompanied by a large number of juvenile aristocracy[22]. The autumn saw them on the road again, appearing in Brighton, Birmingham, Manchester, and Sheffield before finishing the year at the Casino de Venise, alternatively known as the Holborn Dancing Saloon, in Holborn, London. The Casino had been a former swimming baths for the area.

There would seem to have been two groups of Bedouin Arabs performing at the same time. Press coverage shows that in early February, a group were performing in Hull. Mr Pritchard of the Theatre Royal announced that he had engaged a;

> TROUPE OF BEDOUIN ARABS, who's Performances before her Gracious Majesty the Queen … at the St James's Theatre, were received with most distinguished approbation (*Hull Advertiser and Exchange Gazette* 4 February 1848)

So we know that this particular group is the one that arrived in 1847. However, on the following day, this article appeared;

> On Tuesday, Mahmoud Ben Mohammed, one of the Bedouin Arabs performing in this city, through an interpreter, made an application to the magistrates under the following circumstances: - Mr. Davenport had made an agreement with Mr. Wardle [Wardell], of Vauxhall Gardens, London, for a troop of the Bedouin Arabs, eight in number, to perform for five nights [in Yarmouth and Norwich]. The sum of £50 [pounds sterling] was to be allowed for expences [sic], and all above that sum to

be divided between Mr. Davenport and Mr. Wardle. The Arabs were to have £30 [approximately 2,500 pounds sterling equivalent today] weekly from Mr. Wardle, the same to be paid weekly; but they had not been paid for the week ending on Saturday previous. On Monday night they refused to perform, unless they were paid, and they did receive £4 among them, which induced them to play on that night, there being a very full house. – They wished to be paid regularly according to agreement. The magistrates, having no power to interfere in what appeared to be a breach of contract, dismissed the case (*Norfolk Chronicle* 5 February 1848)

Was this a case of managers exploiting the performers? In a rival newspaper[23], coverage of the case claimed that box office takings for the group's performances had been so poor that there was not enough income to pay them, once the managers had taken their cut. Now it may be that this group in Norwich was the same group that appeared in Hull and that there had been a gap in the newspaper coverage. Alternatively, the Hull group could have been a small beak-away unit of the larger group. I do think it is unlikely, as in this particular case they were a completely different group – although rival imitators did still exist. At Astley's, in May, a Mr Henderson, 'the wonderful leaper' gave a performance of his 'Arab Flight'[24]. Although there is no description of this act, Henderson was a renowned acrobat of the period who could perform somersaults both on the ground and trampoline.

The Bedouin Arabs continued to perform around Great Britain during 1848, visiting Dublin, the north of England, and other regular venues such as Vauxhall Gardens and Rosherville Gardens. In May they were in Leeds and a local newspaper gave a full and detailed account of their performance, as well as giving us some of the names of the company;

Entrance of the Slaves before Abd-el-Kader [an Algerian religious and military leader who fought against the French], with their native music, used at the Arab Weddings; Arab Games; Great Leopard Spring, after the fashion of their country; Combat of the lion and Tiger, performed by El Hage Mohamed and Abd-Legrim; the Flight of Stags in the Forest, and the Whirlwind in the Desert of Damadji. Second part – Pyramids of Three Pillars; Tower of the Winds: FOUR persons standing on each other's heads; Leap from a massive Stone; the Leap of Death over a Band of Arabs with real Sabres; Giant Pyramids, on the shoulders of Hamet-Ben-Mohamed; Moving of the Mountain Waters by [H] Amet-Ben-Mohamed and the Little Lassem; Leap of the Bayonets, by Aboo-Ben-Ali; Tower of Babylon; Six Slaves on the Shoulders of Las-Gozonain at once; the Four Towers or Mosques of Abd-el-Kader (*Leeds Times* 6 May 1848)

Whilst they were performing in the Vauxhall Gardens in September the group was billed as 'the only troupe of Arabs in Great Britain'[25]. Coincidentally, also performing at the gardens was Isaac van Amburgh, the American lion tamer. However, *Batty's Circus* was offering a troupe of Bedouin Arabs during his performances in Scotland[26] around the same time as the group were performing in Bolton in the October. They presented more or less the same programme as they did in Leeds[27]. Although, all did not go well during their engagement in Bolton;

Mr. Sharples begs to apologise to parties who this week have been disappointed by the non-appearance of the Bedouin Arabs, which happened in consequence of them breaking their engagement by two of them being out of town at the time announced for them to perform on Monday afternoon, after which it seemed prudent to throw up the broken contract in order to prevent such serious disappointment in the future (*Bolton Chronicle* 4 November 1848)

For all their skill, daring, and bravado in performance, there does seem to have been a degree of volatility from some members of the group. From Bolton they moved on to Liverpool, where it was announced that they would shortly be travelling to America[28]. They completed their work in England by appearing at Astley's for the Christmas season[29]. When they actually travelled to America is uncertain, but they were certainly there in the December of 1849, as they were reported performing at Niblo's Garden in New York[30].

With their departure there appears to have been a lull in genuine Bedouin Arab performances. A group did arrive from America in the September to perform at the Vauxhall Gardens but this was not the group that had recently left Britain. They arrived with a tumbler named Said Ben Mohamed who was making his 'first appearance in England'[31]. The visit to Britain appears to have been short, with an engagement only at the Vauxhall Gardens. They cease to appear in any news reports after this date, although the name of Said Ben Mohamed does re-appear in 1857. It is possible that they moved on to France, as there is a brief mention in the *Exeter and Plymouth Gazette* of 27 July 1850, referencing a group of Bedouin Arabs performing in the circus in Paris. Indeed, for the next few years genuine Arab performers appear to disappear from Britain. A few mentions of purportedly "Arab" acts are made in the press but I suspect that these were imitations, rather than the real thing.

It was not until later in the 1850s that Bedouin Arabs and Arab tumblers reappear in Britain. In January 1857, the *North and South Shields gazette* announced the appearance of Sanger's, which offered a group of Bedouin Arabs. The following month they appear with *Macarte's Cirque Imperial* in Birmingham as Real Bedouin Arabs from Morocco[32]. By the May, the number in the group appears to have grown to 12 from an initial ten and Madame Macarte was fully exploiting their exoticism. As well as presenting them as tumblers and leapers, she had also acquired six trained camels.

> These animals have been procured at an enormous expense, with a view to give effect to the extraordinary feats of the Bedouin Arabs, in their exciting scene of THE HALT OF THE ARABIAN CARAVAN. The magnificent procession is of the most novel description; the carriages are new and elegant; the ladies habited in regal costume; and the Arabs in their picturesque national dress. Each camel will be ridden by an

Arab, the whole forming one of the most imposing processions ever seen (*Herts Guardian, Agricultural Journal, and General Advertiser* 9 May 1857)

This depiction of 'Arabness' was little more than exploitative. When the Bedouin Arab troupes had first performed in Britain they were largely hailed for their physical prowess and daring skills; they were acknowledged as acrobats. Now the performance was being subsumed by the spectacle of what the audience expected to see. Familiar echoes of minstrelsy, caricature, and stereotyping.

This troupe continued to tour with *Macarte's Cirque*, although *Hengler's Circus* boasted a 'tribe of Bedouin Araba acrobats'[33] when performing in Liverpool in early May. On April 18, *Howe & Cushing's Great United States Circus* arrived in Liverpool from America. They immediately set up and began their British tour in the city. Macarte's newspaper advertising was big but Howes & Cushing's was even bigger. The circus promoted itself as 'The Largest Establishment in the World' and performed inside an immense 'canvas amphitheatre' that could seat 5,000 people. Traveling with almost 200 personnel and a large array of animals, they included among their number the 'celebrated and original tribe of Bedouin Arabs, twelve in number who created so great a sensation in Paris and London'[34]. As the Bedouin Arabs were performing with *Hengler's Circus* in Liverpool when Howes & Cushing's arrived there, it is not inconceivable that the group sought an engagement with the larger American outfit.

A report of *Hengler's Circus* in the *Liverpool Mail* of 2 May 1857, lists these performers by name. The first name listed, and possibly the group leader, we have already come across; Mohamet Ben Said. Nine other names are listed; Assame, Molay Abdalah, Ali Ben Said, Ahye Abou, Brahieme, Ali Ben Brahim, Ahye Aussiene, (Le Noir) Grotesque de la Trupe – Monoy Benahi, Amani Ben Mohamet. In the same edition Howes & Cushing's advertise a mammoth British tour, announcing at least 40 different venues in May and June alone- and that was after they were to leave Liverpool on the 16 May. The first time that the 'tribe of Arabs' appears under the name of Howes & Cushing's is in a footnote to their advertisement of 30 May in the *Manchester Courier and Lancashire General Advertiser*. This announces them as a forthcoming attraction and by 13 June they were definitely performing with the outfit[35]. The performance is noted in one sentence at the foot of a review. By July they had moved up the pecking order of advertising and were appearing second on the bills. They continued with Howes & Cushing's through to January 1859, when they took a short twelve day re-engagement with *Hengler's Circus* in Liverpool before returning in the February. Hengler listed them by name again in his advertising so we can see that it is the same troupe. They appear to have taken several other engagements with different companies throughout the year. In the March they appeared with *Ginnett's Mammoth Circus* in Swindon and in May they were with *Wallett's Great Equestrian Company*, where they were billed as being 'lately with Howes and Cushing's Great United States Circus'[36]. In January 1859 they appeared in Belfast with *Mr. Hogini's Cirque Imperiale*, then for the rest of the year returned to Howes & Cushing's. The last mention that we have for them with this outfit is on October 13 1859 in the *Devizes and Wiltshire Gazette*. Howes & Cushing's appear to have gone into decline during the 1860s and the outfit was eventually sold at the beginning of October 1861[37]. The sale raised the sum of 2,000 pounds sterling [approximately 119,000 pounds sterling today]. The Bedouin Arabs cease to appear in any press reviews after 1859, but there was a distinct anti-Arab feeling across the country as problems still existed in Morocco. Newspaper reports, such as the following, only fuelled the situation;

> By the latest advices from Gibraltar it appears that the lawless Bedouins in Morocco are still driving the terror-stricken Europeans to desert the towns and take refuge on-board ship. The town of Mazagan has been attacked by these Arabs, in which they themselves lost thirty men (*Dover Telegraph and Cinque Ports General Adviser* 8 October 1859)

The first 'Arabian Circus' advertised for performers in the *Era* on 9 October 1864. This was based in Liverpool with the proprietor being named as Arrche Hassan. It certainly performed during that year in Liverpool but appears not to have toured. How 'Arabian' this circus actually was is not certain but as Hassan was advertising for all kinds of performers I think we can assume that it was not exclusively Arab. By 1866 advertisements start to appear for Cooke's Arabian Circus, and it may be that Cooke had bought out Hassan. This company toured for that year and it is not until 1873 that the *Great Arabian Circu*s appears on a tour of Ireland. It was announced in the press that the company would appear with 'the renowned troupe of Arabs'[38]. A further advertisement in the *Kilkenny Moderator* of 30 April states;

> The principal performers are announced as 'real' Arab acrobats, and undertake to perform the most wonderful feats of horsemanship &c.

However, there appears to have been some rivalry in the circus world in Ireland that year. William Batty was also touring with his circus, in which appeared 'the only troupe of real war Arabs'. He felt obliged to make note of this in the *Freeman's Journal* of 1 July 1873;

> There are only two Circus establishments travelling in Ireland - 'BATTY'S" and GINNETT AND HOPKINS, travelling under the name of 'The Arabian Circus. Mr, BATTY feel it is his duty to caution his country friends against being misled, and informs them that he, with his MAMMOTH PAVILION, are the largest company ever engaged in Ireland.

By January 1874, Batty had dropped the title of *Grand Arabian Circu*s and just billed it as *Batty's Grand Circus*, when he visited Norwich[39]. In fact, there is no mention of the word 'Arab' in any of his advertising.

By the 1860s, individual performers were beginning to appear, rather than as troupes. One such artiste, Saddi D'Jalma, was an equilibrist and contortionist and in 1864 appeared with *Barlow's Circus, Ginnett's*

Circus, and *Sanger's Circus* throughout the year, as well as taking short engagements in Paris. Another performer by the name of Aaron Hassan, a name very similar to that used by the proprietor of the Arabian Circus in Liverpool, appeared with *Newsome's Circus* in 1865 as the 'great Arab chief' and performed 'wonderful feats with a gun'[40]. Another, possibly the same, performer with the name of Alhi Ben Hassan was performing with a troupe of Arab tumblers in *Myer's Circus* in June 1879[41]. A Nubar Hassan advertised in the *Era* of 10 February 1883, describing himself as the 'celebrated wire walker and juggler, Arab tumbler &c.' In South Wales, in 1885, *Fossett's New Grand Circus* featured a performer named Aseiky (sometimes seen as Azeiky as there was no standard rules for transliterating Arabic to English) who was billed as 'the great Arab Tumbler, in his Marvellous Entertainment of Somersault Throwing with Knives, Swords, Bayonets &c.'[42]. In the same edition, across in Swansea were performing, 'Twelve Arabs, Escaped Soudanese, in their Stupendous Feats of Skill, Courage, and Daring'. Aseiky was still on the touring circuit in 1887 where, at the Varieties Theatre in Dundee, he was performing 'a number of daring feats, including the firing of a rifle while turning a somersault'[43]. The name Wallacini appeared in newspapers in 1888. He first appeared with *Newsome's Circus* and subsequent mentions of him in 1889 had him working with *Elphinstone's Circus*. He was described as an Arab, despite a decidedly Italian sounding name, and performed 'Arab bending' and tumbling. A report in the *Huddersfield Daily Examiner* of 27 January 1891 described him as being a;

> Wonderfully, elastic, smart, and clever tumbler, and his back somersaults, off from one to five tables are both daring and neatly accomplished.

He was variously described as 'the Whirlwind of the Desert', 'The Son of the Burning Sands', and 'the Ebony Wonder', clearly a reference to his skin colour. Whether or not he actually came from the Arabian peninsula is not recorded. To confuse the issue, he was sometimes billed as Signor Wallacini and on at least one occasion with the German honorific *Herr* Wallacini! He continued touring in circuses and variety theatres until 1895, after which time he disappears from news reports.

The end of the century and into the following one saw the re-emergence of performing troupes of Arab acrobats. At least two groups were operating in 1901. In the April it was reported that Abdullah's Bedouin Arabs were performing at the Pavilion in London[44]. Later in the year, Achmed Ibrahim presented his 'original troupe of real Bedouin Arabs, 10 in number' at the Blackpool Grand Circus[45] and other venues in the north.

We seem to have returned to the beginning with troupes of 'real' Bedouin Arabs performing acrobatic feats! It must be acknowledged that these performers made a great impact on the circus and variety industry of the Victorian period; a tradition that still exists into the 21st century. In 2007, the *Collectiff Acrobatique de Tangier* troupe performed at the London Roundhouse[46] and, at the time of writing, the *Tangier Acrobats* are advertising their work on the professional circus industry website *CircusTalk*[47].

Notes

1. The *Satyricon* is a satirical novel written by Petronius between 54 and 68 BCE. In the section entitled *Dinner with Trimalchio*, Petronius refers to the group of visiting acrobats at the sumptuous feast in Fragments 47 and 53. Online at; http://www.angelfire.com/art/archictecture/articles/trim.htm

2. Queen Elizabeth - Volume 175: December 1584, in *Calendar of State Papers Domestic: Elizabeth, 1581-90*, ed. Robert Lemon (London, 1865), pp. 214-222. *British History Online* http://www.british-history.ac.uk/cal-state-papers/domestic/edw-eliz/1581-90/pp214-222

3. William Hogarth's engraving is held at the Royal Academy in London. It can be viewed online at https://www.royalacademy.org.uk/art-artists/work-of-art/southwark-fair-1

4. *Manchester Mercury* 13 November 1764

5. *Windsor and Eton Express* 30 April 1836

6. 1835 Poster for *Les Bedoins at the Porte St Martin Theatre* in Paris. Online at; https://gallica.bnf.fr/ark:/12148/btv1b8436788h/f1.item.r=Les%20Bedouins.zoom

7. *The Morning Register* 14 March 1835

8. *Sun (London)* 23 August 1836

9. *Dover Telegraph and Cinque Ports General Advertiser* 19 November 1836

10. *Southern Reported and Cork Commercial Courier* 12 November 1836

11. *Morning Post* 27 December 1837

12. *Sun (London)* 26 November 1836

13. *The Examiner* 30 October 1836

14. *Globe* 15 June 1838

15. *Liverpool Mail* 29 June 1839

16. *Leeds Times* 3 August 1839

17. *Kentish Mercury* 31 August 1839

18. *Kentish Mercury* 10 August 1839

19. *Bell's New Weekly Messenger* 24 September 1843

20. *Brighton Gazette* 7 October 1847

21. *South Eastern Gazette* 17 August 1847

22. *Bell's Life and Sporting Chronicle* 27 June 1847

23. *Norwich Mercury* 5 February 1848

24. *Morning Advertiser* 1 May 1847

25. *Morning Advertiser* 25 September 1848

26. *The Scotsman* 18 October 1848

27. *Bolton Chronicle* 28 October 1848

28. *Era* 26 November 1848

29. *Era* 24 December 1848

30. *Era* 30 December 1849

31. *London Evening Standard* 27 September 1849

32. *Birmingham Journal* 4 February 1857

33. *Era* 10 May 1857

34. *Rochdale Observer* 6 June 1857

35. *Huddersfield Chronicle* 13 June 1857

36. *Monmouthshire Beacon* 29 May 1858

37. *Belfast Morning News* 2 October 1861

38. *Ulster Examiner and Northern Star* 27 March 1873

39. *Norwich Mercury* 7 January 1874

40. *Newcastle Daily Chronicle* 14 November 1865

41. *Lichfield Mercury* 6 June 1879

42. *Western Mail* 16 December 1885

43. *Dundee Courier* 19 April 1887

44. *London Evening Standard* 9 April 1901

45. *Lancashire Evening Post* 12 September 1901

46. *The Stage* 5 July 2007

47. This act can be seen on the *CircusTalk* website at https://circustalk. com/circus-acts/tangier-acrobats

Martini Maccomo *(Unknown photographer. Sunderland Museum Archives)*

CHAPTER 10
THE AFRICAN LION KINGS

Of all the different disciplines in the circus, the one that appears to have been seen as the most 'exotic' was that of the lion-tamer. This was man triumphing over nature and travelling menageries, in which these lion-tamers initially worked, were an embodiment of British imperialism showing how Britain had dominion over its empire and all that was in it. 'Big cat' shows also intended to thrill and excite as the lion-tamer faced nature, red in tooth and claw. This need for 'thrill' is something that all humans have, it stimulates the fight of flight response. Triggering such a response in a controlled situation allows a pure rush of energy and absence from rational thought, whilst all the time knowing that we are secure. The 'Big cat' shows fed the Victorian audiences' desire for potentially bloody spectacle.

This was the era when explorers were heralded for their courage and heroism as they toured far flung corners of the British Empire. The audience wanted visceral sensation, and daring was valued more than skill. Pascal Jacob, the noted circus historian, makes reference to this in the book *The Ordinary Acrobat* (Wall D, 2013:2765-2784);

> The new audience also lived in a different world – faster, harder, and more violent. The lion tamer in the cage, the *funambule* on his wire; they bring that violence to the circus ... a return to the ferocious energy of the past. In the opera, there is metaphorical violence. You die among the décor. In the circus, you die and it's for real.

To make lion-taming performances more 'exotic and primeval', many black performers began to appear. These were not portrayed as 'heroic British explorers', rather as the 'noble savage'. In this period, lion taming was the only circus discipline where ethnicity was specified in advertising for performers;

> Wanted for *Buff Bill's Menagerie*. Lion Tamer, Black or White. Black Man preferred (*The Era* 28 October 1893)

> Wanted, for *Sedgwick's Menagerie* ... also, Lion Tamer, to work Untameable Lion. A Coloured Man preferred (*The Era* 1 June 1895)

It is often said that the American-born Isaac Van Amburgh introduced the thrill of lion taming to the British public when he arrived in Liverpool in August 1838[1]. By the end of the month he was appearing at the famous Astley's in London[2] and soon became known as the 'Lion King'. There is evidence that lion-tamers had already taken the stage in Britain before Van Amburgh's arrival.

In an article in the *Northampton Mercury* of 7 October 1837[3], the writer records his witnessing a performance in France, making reference to a lion-taming act in England prior to this particular staging.

> Mons. Martin, the French lion tamer, who was at Brussels some months, has obtained a great celebrity in France from his feats with animals. I went more than once to witness his performances, which were got up in a theatrical manner; all things are in France; but I have seen Mons. Martin's exploits outdone by a man who had a travelling menagerie in England.

Although the article goes on at some length to describe the performance of this English lion tamer, unfortunately neither he nor the menagerie themselves are named. However, this character may well have been the 'Manchester Jack' who worked for *Wombwell's Menagerie*, referenced in an article in the *Monmouthshire Beacon* 13 January 1872.

Menageries were nothing new in Britain. Indeed, the Royal family had actively kept one at the Tower of London since 1204, when King John moved an existing menagerie from a palace in Woodstock to the Tower. During the eighteenth and early nineteenth centuries several menageries toured throughout Britain with a wide variety of exotic animals. In one particular instance a menagerie owner named Atkins promoted his menagerie as the only wild animal show at that year's St Bartholomew's Fair. At the time Wombwell had his menagerie on display in Newcastle upon Tyne but, with a supreme effort, he managed to strike his exhibition and move down towards London, arriving early on the morning of the fair. However, the journey had proved too difficult for his solitary elephant, which died shortly after he arrived. His rival Atkins saw this as a golden advertising opportunity and set up placards stating that he had the only living elephant at the fair. Not to be outdone Wombwell set up rival placards stating that he had the only dead elephant at the fair. Living elephants are a wonder, but a dead one was even more of a curiosity and Wombwell drew the larger crowd! It was one small step from keeping and displaying the animals to physically interacting with them, and menageries paved the way for the lion-tamers.

Although there were undoubtedly such performers working in Britain before the arrival of Van Amburgh, it is not recorded if any of these were black. The earliest record of a black lion-tamer was for a man named Maccomo (sometimes also written as Macomo). On 15 July 1853, the *Scottish Guardian* carried this piece;

> Maccomo, the Lion Hunter, in Jeopardy – On Monday last, a boy in Hylton's extensive collection of wild animal on the Green, was teasing the African lion, and punctured his nose with a needle … Maccomo, who was not aware of what had occurred, now entered the den for the purpose of exhibiting the animal's performances … The man [Maccomo] extracted the needle, when the animal seemed relieved from

pain, and with the affection of a spaniel, fondled his keeper, who then caused him to finish his wonderful performance.

Although he was appearing with *Hylton's Menagerie* during 1853, by February 1854 he was working with *Manders' Royal Menagerie* on its tour of Ireland[4]. On this tour he was often advertised as the 'Lion King' or the 'Lion Hunter'. His performance was largely one of playfulness with his African lions. Where he came from and how he came to work as a lion tamer has never been verified. The nearest contemporary account of his life that we have is in *Circus Life and Circus Celebrities* (Frost T, 1876:133-134), written five years after the death of Maccomo. Frost writes;

> One day, when the menagerie was at Greenwich fair, a powerful-looking negro accosted one of the musicians, saying that he was a sailor, just returned from a voyage, and would like to get employment about the beasts … Manders liked the man's appearance, and at once agreed to give him an opportunity to display his qualifications for the leonine regality to which he aspired. The negro entered the lions' cage, and displayed so much courage and address in putting the animals through their performances that he was engaged forthwith … This black sailor was the performer who afterwards became famous far and wide by the name of Macomo [sic]

This was written in 1876, and Frost states that this incident happened some twenty years previously. His memory is a little askew as we know Maccomo was working with *Hylton's Menagerie* in 1853. At the time Maccomo was working with Hylton, Manders was also there in an assistant manager role and he would later take over the running of the menagerie, taking Maccomo with him.

I suspect that Maccomo was not his given name but who he may have been is something of a mystery, as is very often the case with circus performers. He also sometimes appears with the first name of Martin or Martini. The name Maccomo was well known to the British public during the late 1840s and throughout the 1850s. During the so called 'Kaffir Wars' of 1851 – 1852, when tribal leaders waged a guerrilla war against the Boers and the British in South Africa, our lion tamer's real-life namesake was a highly respected Chief. He was imprisoned in November 1857[5]. A black lion tamer, by adopting this name could only enhance his 'exoticism'.

Some sources[6] suggest that this lion taming Maccomo's real name may have been Arthur Williams and that he came from the West Indies; the large group of islands between the Atlantic Ocean and the Caribbean Sea, many of which were part of colonial Britain. A piece in the *Newcastle Journal* of 21 January 1858 specifically places him in Sierra Leone, and the 1861 Census returns for Bath and Wells[7] give his place of birth as 'Africa Angola'. In this record he is given as being a 'servant' in the household of William and Rosina Manders, although his occupation is as a 'performer of lions and tigers'. In most of the advertising he is referred to as the 'African Lion Hunter' or the 'African Lion King', or simply as an 'African'. In the *Liverpool Mercury* of 18 January 1861, he is billed as 'Sable Maccomo – the African Lion Hunter', emphasising his ethnicity.

Coincidentally, in the 1861 Census, there is also a return for a seventeen-year-old George Macomo listed as being born in Africa. This is in the Warwickshire town of Nuneaton, east of Birmingham, and he is a visitor at the home of the local vicar, which is next door to a National School, and Macomo is given as a scholar. Was there a familial connection between these two? We will probably never know – but it is a strange coincidence that merits further research.

Maccomo is strangely absent from any advertising during 1855 and 1856. He appears to have left Manders after the 1854 tour, reappearing in Chesterfield in October 1857 with his own outfit;

FOR ONE DAY ONLY – MARTINA [sic] MACOMO the African Lion Slayer's Encampment and Monster Zoological Establishment of Wild Beasts, Birds, Reptiles, and Monsters of the Deep … The Lion Slayer begs to inform that having just arrived from Africa, where he has spent many years in hunting those wild and ferocious animals (*Derbyshire Times and Chesterfield Herald* 31 October 1857)

A lot of this is 'puffery' but it might explain his two year absence from the media. Did he spend those missing years in Africa, capturing animals for his own menagerie? A possibility. He also seems to have changed his style of performance. In 1854, although billed as the Lion Hunter he;

Fearless of danger, will enter the den of the Noble African Beast and cause him (forgetful of his savage nature) in playful gambols, to leap and bound and, as the tender Lamb, to crouch and fondle with his keeper; then, ever and anon, with a *Mysterious Performance*, will prove to the astonishment of all spectators his strength, sagacity, and highly trained endowments (*Waterford Mail* 8 February 1854)

By the 1857 tour he was advertising;

FAMILY OF LIONS of all grades, from the monster African King of Beasts to the tiny Cubs scarce a span in length accompanied by their sire an dam, the Tawny Twin Lions of the South, captured by the Lion Slayer, who in person will attend and fight his battles o'er again. Within the enclosure a circle will be formed, well secured by bolts and bars. The Lions will be loosened, and the Hunt, Attack, Defence, Capture, and Reconciliation will take place between the Monsters and the Man (*Leeds Times* 31 October 1857)

He had moved from being merely the Lion Hunter to the Lion Slayer! His 1854 act seemed quite 'cosy' and 'cuddly' but now it was dynamic, dangerous, and heroic. There was a thought at the time that;

It was riskier for him [Maccomo] than for a white man, if it be true as they say, that the beasts can nose a black man and are mad after the flavour of his flesh (*Monmouthshire Beacon* 13 January 1872)

His costume reflected a European image of the 'noble savage'. An 1860 poster[8] image shows him dressed in a Grecian style belted tunic, over which appears to be a leopard skin cloak.

This is topped off with a feathered head-dress. In his belt is a pistol and he wields a rifle as a club. A report in the *Cork Examiner* of 9 January 1862 also refers to him wearing a 'spangled dress', glittering with sequins and diamantes. This appears to have been his style of costume throughout his career. Unlike other white European lion-tamers who tended to wear military style costumes reflecting imperial might, Maccomo, regardless of whose decision it was, performed in an outfit that romanticised the concept of the 'noble savage'.

Although he appears to have been presenting and performing in his own menagerie in October 1857, an advertisement appeared in the *Leamington Spa Courier* of 5 December that links the 'African Lion King' to *Edmonds' Royal Windsor Castle Menagerie*. Edmonds took over the management of *Wombwell's Menagerie* on the latter's death in 1850. Although it does not mention Maccomo by name, the wording of his display is almost identical to that which ran in the Leeds newspaper.

In January 1858, Maccomo appears working for Manders again[9]. Here he is billed as the 'Lion Hunter' and his act contains the Hunt, Attack, Fight, Chase, and Reconciliation routine as in previous advertisements.

Maccomo's life as a lion-tamer was not without mishap. In that January tour of the north-east he had a run in with one of his lions, as here described in the *Newcastle Journal* of 2 January, 1858;

> Unfortunately, on the evening of Saturday last, he [Maccomo] met with an accident, which at one time, assumed a serious aspect. It appears, whilst exhibiting the lions and lionesses, one of the latter sprang upon him, and lacerated his right arm and cheek in a severe manner ... It may be stated that he is now recovering.

A few years later, in 1862, a similar incident took place while he was performing in Norwich[10]. He was attacked by a young lion and dragged to the ground. The lion seized his left hand in its jaws and when Maccomo was eventually freed it was found that part of the forefinger had been bitten off. The newspaper also commented that he had been attacked by a lion in a performance in Norwich two years earlier. Such encounters excited and thrilled audiences who, if truth be known, went to such exhibitions with an anticipation of something 'bloody' happening. The press often made comment on this public trait. In the *Stamford Mercury* of 26 March 1847 the reporter wrote;

> It is to be regretted that the taste of the public be so vitiated as to encourage the practice of performers placing themselves in situations of such great danger,

And in the *Birmingham Daily Post* of 21 July 1863, this comment appeared;

> ... the morbid and not too much to be reprehended taste for strong sensations, which disgraces English people in this nineteenth century.

In 1861, when Maccomo was in Liverpool he was again bitten on the hand, this time by a tigress. When the audience realised what had happened,

> The truth of his dangerous position flashed through the minds of those present, and created great excitement – one lady fainting, others running from the painful sight (*Illustrated London News* 19 January 1861)

Other such occurrences happened, seemingly much of an occupational hazard for Maccomo, and not only with big cats. In one instance in Portobello, Edinburgh, Maccomo was seized by an enraged dromedary[11] and had to be rescued by other keepers. Again, it was his arm that suffered. Outside of the cage he was a mild mannered man who drank nothing but coffee. But once inside with his animals his courage

Maccomo the African Lion Hunter. 1860 poster for Manders' Royal Menagerie *(Reproduced with permission of Leeds Libraries, www.leodis.net)*

could never be denied. For all this, it is a wonder that he was not actually killed in the pursuit of his profession.

Maccomo remained with the *Manders' Menagerie* for the rest of his career, touring widely throughout Britain to much acclaim. In 1877, a newspaper report appeared that indicates that he may have got married. The woman in question certainly claimed to have been his wife;

> A RELIC OF THE LATE MARTINI MACCOMO – Henrietta Bent, an unfortunate woman, was charged with assaulting and robbing Louisa Norman, another 'unfortunate', of a hat, feather, comb, &c. … the prisoner said her husband was a coloured man – Martini Maccomo – 'the great lion tamer' (*Liverpool Daily Post* 19 May 1877)

However, there is no record extant for Maccomo (or variant name) being married during his time in Britain. It is of course possible that he married before arriving in Britain or that his relationship with Henrietta was simply a common-law marriage. For such a sensational figure he was a very private man. Little is known about his personal life beyond this and a few other vague newspaper passages. Whether he had children at all is also a mystery.

Maccomo took to his bed with rheumatic fever and died on Wednesday 11 January 1871, somewhere around thirty years of age. Although he appears to have been ill for two weeks, he was still being billed to appear with *Manders' Menagerie* even on the day of his death. The first notice of his passing was given in the *Morning Advertiser* on 13 January.

> On Wednesday morning Maccomo, who was accompanying the tour through the north with Manders' Menagerie of wild animals, died at the Palatine Hotel, Borough Road, Sunderland, from epilepsy. Deceased had been ill for nearly a fortnight.

The Era of 15 January gave a fuller obituary, although slightly incorrect in places.

He was born in the year 1839, at Angola, in the South West of Africa …
At the age of sixteen Martini longed to distinguish himself as a tamer
of wild beasts. He accordingly made an appearance as a lion tamer at
the Circus of Messrs. Stone and McCollum, New York, in 1855, when
he achieved a triumphant success. After a successful tour through
the States he came to England, when he was engaged by Mr. William
Manders … He made his first appearance in England at Deptford in
1857, and since that time had travelled with Mr. Manders as the 'African
Lion King' … on the 2nd inst. He was attacked with rheumatic fever
in the legs, which, extending upwards, caused his death after a week's
illness.

This second account of his early life sounds complete but,
unfortunately, few of the facts match up with reality. *Stone and McCollum's
Great Western Circus* was only in operation from 1846 until 1850, after
which time Thomas Stone went to England[12]. I can find no reference
for *Manders' Menagerie* being in Deptford during 1857, although many
for other venues around Britain during that year, and we have also
seen that Maccomo was working in Britain as early as 1853. Martini
Maccomo was buried in the Bishopswearmouth cemetery, Sunderland,
and his headstone was commissioned by his long standing employer,
William Manders. Whatever the truth about his early life, there can be no
doubt that Maccomo was an iconic figure in the black cultural history of
Britain, and he paved the way for many others to follow him.

The use of an existing name was not an uncommon occurrence
within the circus and the name Maccomo reappeared in 1872 when
Manders' Star Menagerie performed in Chester. The *Cheshire Observer* of 23
March 1872 records that, 'The first caravan [in the procession] conveying
the African lion tamer, Maccomo …' But who was this new Maccomo?
A few years later, this appeared in an advertisement for *Bostock and
Wombwell's Menagerie*;

The manager has secured the services of YOUNG MACCOMO, 'The African Lion King' (son of the once famous animal trainer) (*Brecon City Times* 14 May 1881)

Although Bostock engaged several different lion tamers throughout the decade, by 1890 this new 'Young Maccomo' was still appearing with the outfit, where he was described as 'the giant negro' and 'the shapely black'[13]. In 1895, this second version of the Maccomo name acquires a first name – Orlando[14]. If this was the supposed son of Martini Maccomo, then one would have hoped to have found some record of his birth or even existence. But, like the suggested marriage to Henrietta, alas there is none. Maccomo was honoured by Bostock in 1896 with the award of a gold medal for his 'faithful and courageous services to the establishment'[15], but by 1898 Orlando is advertising for work[16]. There is no further record of him working the lions after this date. Tantalisingly, in 1899 the Bexhill Licensing Committee granted a hackney carriage [taxi] licence to an Orlando Maccomo[17]. Of course, there is no direct evidence that the Young Maccomo and Orlando Maccomo were the same person but, even so, it is clear that there were other black lion tamers working at this time. So successful was the original Maccomo that he established a trope within the mind of the circus-going public that managers were keen to capitalise on.

During the 1860s, at the same time as Martini Maccomo was performing, another black lion tamer was hard at work in Britain. His name was Joseph Ledger, although he performed under the name Delmonico (sometimes also written as Delimonico). His name first appears in 1865 in advertising for *Edmonds' Royal Windsor Castle and Crystal Palace Menagerie*;

DELIMONICO – THE ARABIAN LION CHIEF, in his daring and exciting Illustrations with his Excelsior Groups of Lions, Tigers, Leopards, and Panthers every hour during the Fair (*Birmingham Journal* 3 June 1865)

A little later that year, whilst in Reading, Berkshire, he is described as, 'The great 'sensational' lion hunter, Delimonico, a man of colour …'[18] Although not directly mentioned by name, it seems likely that Delimonico had been working for the company for many years, just not explicitly listed on playbills. Advertising going back to 1863 refers to an African lion keeper working for *Wombwell's Menagerie*[19]. Edmonds and Wombwell's were actually the same company at this time, operating under a second name. This company was often billed as *Edmonds' (late Wombwell's) Menagerie.*

So who was this Delmenico? In an exciting turn of events, we can actually hear his own version of events, as there exists a copy of his brief autobiography[20], written in French in his later years. In this work, Ledger Delmonico informs us that he was born in Milton, Delaware in the USA. His father had been a dealer in wild animals and had taken him on a visit to Africa when he was thirteen years old. He returned to Africa when he was fifteen and acquired two lions and four cubs. He began to train these and developed a talent for working with them. Having returned to America he then decided to sail to Europe, performing in Germany, Austria, and Hungary, and other countries before arriving in England. He writes that his first performance was in 1866 at the Crystal Palace in London, England but we know that he was named in the media earlier than this. Unfortunately, he does not give his age, but the 1871 Census returns[21] give him an age of twenty seven, making his prospective date of birth 1844. A little more about Delmonico can be gleaned from the following interview with him;

> In private life the 'lion tamer' is by no means a terrible person. Delmonico is a rather slim, but well set-up African, about 5 feet 11 inches, and if you met him in a train you might think him a shy, retiring man … I began when I was about fifteen. Have I been at it ever since? Yes, with breaks. I was in the American war; the only coloured man in my regiment. I came here in 1864, and left when the Franco-German

war broke out. I was in the ambulance with that (*New Zealand Herald* 4 October 1884[22])

Delmonico appears to have been quite an engaging figure. He certainly broke the perceived mould of how an 'African' should appear, which was quite a revelation for the writer of a piece that appeared in the *Cornishman* 27 October 1887.

> I encountered the first 'swell' black man I had ever met. I was fascinated and remained in the gangway, staring at this phenomenon in a beautifully-made, brown-velvet, get up – diamond rings and all. You see I had always hitherto associated a nigger with a sort of bed-trimming costume, *sans* boots, *sans* hat, *sans* everything but an apology for pantaloons and shirt of rainbow colours, with more patches than a person indulging in a game of Aunt Sally [a traditional fairground game involving throwing a stick at a model of an old woman's head] could 'shake a stick at' and hit a given mark. Thus was my delusion rapidly dispelled.

The writer's image of how an African should appear was very much predicated on popular stereotypical imagery that was advanced by people like this writer himself. Delmonico embraced European culture and dressed accordingly. Even his performance costume adopted the European perception of the valiant explorer having dominion over the beast. Unlike Maccomo, who posed as the 'noble savage', Delmonico dressed in quasi-military uniform[23].

Wombwell's Menagerie was sold by auction in Liverpool 1884. So his reference to coming here in 1864 therefore means to Britain, although he may have been a little flexible with the date. In September 1870 he was still working with *Edmonds' Menagerie* in Norfolk[24], the year that the Franco-German war broke out in the July. He must have left Britain after this date only to return the following year, after the war had concluded in the May. In June 1871 he was billed to appear with *Edmonds' (late Wombwell's) Menagerie* in Caernarvon[25]. As an American citizen why he

Delmonico at the Bal Valentino
Dance Hall, Paris. Poster 1874 *(BnF
Prints and Photographs Department)*

should have felt the need to serve in such a war is not recorded, although his wife, Anna Kreutzberg whom he had married in Norwich in 1866, was born in Prussia. However, there is a suggestion that he was with the French forces in this conflict[26].

Delmonico worked with quite a large number of animals, as here described when he was appearing in Southampton;

> The world famed Delmonico, the Arabian Lion Hunter, the only man in Europe who performs with twenty lions and the real Bengal tigers, and drives the only pair of domesticated Zebras ever known. These beauties of nature are driven round the interior by Delmonico, previous to each performance with the savage race [the big cats], as he appeared at the Crystal Palace in 1866, at which place he first performed in this country [not quite accurate as we have seen] (*Hampshire Advertiser* 13 July 1867)

He also worked with a group of 'Striped and Spotted Hyenas'[27], which he made to jump through hoops of fire, as well as leopards and wolves. Like many of his fellow animal trainers, his life was not without mishap, although perhaps not as many as Maccomo. In 1865 he was involved in an incident with a tiger[28] and later, in 1887, he courageously entered a cage of eight lions which were fighting among themselves;

> With only his professional whip Delmonico entered the scene of this Inferno, and succeeded – alone and unaided, without any outside hot irons, or pikes – to quell the battle (*Cornishman* 27 October 1887)

Carelessness, or misfortune, may have cause a panic at the menagerie in Bolton in 1884. There was a cry that a lion had escaped and as the crowd fled a young woman was carried to a nearby police station, her head covered in blood from a scalp wound. It appeared that;

> Delmonico, described as the Arabian lion chief, was going from den to den, in his usual performance, and was about to enter the den containing a group of young lions when one of them leaped over his head as he was opening the cage and alighted on the floor of the menagerie and in the centre of the people ... A panic ensued ... a woman ... was crushed beneath the ropes which surround the exhibition ... forced against a caravan containing a large full-grown lioness and next to the African lion 'Nero'. The lioness ... extended her paw beneath the wires of the cage and clutched at the woman's head. The attendants seized pikes and forks and struck the enraged lioness repeatedly before she would release her hold (*The Times* 3 January 1884)

At some point after October 1871 Delmonico moved to continental Europe. He is recorded as arriving in Paris, from Vienna, in November 1873[29]. And then came the news, reported in many newspapers across Britain that shocked everyone.

> (Special Telegram) DELMONICO, THE LION TAMER. Delmonico, the lion tamer, has been devoured at Berlin by one of his own lions (*Manchester Evening News* 30 December 1874)

Very strange! Because the following month, January 1875, he was appearing with *Coniselli's Circus* in Moscow[30]. I suspect that there may have been some sort of misreported 'incident' in Berlin because Delmonico continued to work across Europe until 1878, when he re-appears in Britain, working again for Edmonds[31]. Along the way he picked up some more injuries. At the Folies-Bergèr in Paris his hand was badly mangled by a lion[32] and in Hamburg in 1876 his thigh was bitten and his face clawed[33]. One bizarre incident occurred whilst he was in Paris. Although it did not directly involve Delmonico himself, it did result in four of his lions meeting their death. It seems that the lions managed to reach a stuffed horse, used as a theatrical prop, near their cage. Chewing their way through it they ingested a large amount of arsenic, which was used in taxidermy at the time, and subsequently died.

His attitude towards his animals leaves some questions. He was not averse, as were many others in his field, of using hot irons and steel bars to 'train' them. Unfortunately for him, these actions led to him being brought before the magistrates accused of cruelty to some of his animals.

> At the Derby Police-court, on Tuesday, Ledger Delmonico, a man of colour, who is known as the Lion Tamer, and travels with Edmonds menagerie was summoned … for having wilfully and unlawfully tortured four hyenas … when the defendant made his appearance they [hyenas] went into the corner of the cage, and seemed quite terrified … When he entered he took with him a stick about two and a half feet long, having a heavy knob at the end. When the defendant opened the partition, the animals were crouching in the corners, but he went to them and struck them violently several times, telling them to 'promenade'. The animals then ran forward, and screamed as though they were in pain. Having promenaded, defendant put up an iron rod, about the centre of the cage, and made the animals jump over it by hitting them … Defendant afterwards made them jump through a hoop, covered with tissue paper. An iron hoop was then handed to the defendant … the hoop was bound with tow and the defendant asked the man if he had put the naptha or

oil on it … the defendant took a match from his pocket, struck it, and applied it to the hoop, two-thirds of which was instantly enveloped in flames … the defendant held the hoop down to the animals' noses and beat them unmercifully. They appeared terrified by the fire, but they were compelled to pass through the hoop by the blows which he dealt them (*Derbyshire Advertiser and Journal* 29 October 1880)

This was a lengthy article in which the witness recounted how Delmonico had gone on to repeat the performance once more, with the fur of the hyenas being scorched and burnt. It is interesting to note that these performances elicited no applause and that several members of the public complained at the apparent cruelty. In fairness to Delmonico, there seems to have been several cases of cruelty to animals within Edmonds' menagerie brought before the magistrate that day. An attendant was fined one pound sterling for cruelty towards an argali (a breed of mountain sheep) and there were allegations made towards two other attendants for cruelty towards horses. These were dismissed, being more a case of carelessness and neglect rather than actual intentional cruelty. However, it was Delmonico who made the headlines and he was fined five pounds sterling plus costs, or one month's detention. The fine was paid.

Undeterred by this court case, Delmonico continued to work with big cats and other wild animals until an incident that almost cost him his life. While performing in Liverpool in 1891 he was badly mauled by a lion[34]. This seems to have put an end to his lion taming exploits but he did continue to work in Variety Theatres. By January the following year he was assisting a hypnotist who hypnotised a woman to enter a cage of lions. The lions of course were managed by 'Chevalier L. Demonico'[35]. These performances continued throughout the year and he appeared widely across the country. But how the mighty have fallen! In January 1893 he was still working the Variety Theatres, but now he was assisting a performer named Azellia in her snake charming act[36]. Snake charming was clearly not his forte because by the August he had become an 'actor' and was appearing in a performance of *Ups and Downs of Life*, a farcical comedy by F. A. Scudamore, in which he presented two 'fighting bears'. He continued with his acting career, appearing with the *Ups and Down* Company, and then with other theatre companies, such as the *Secrets of the Harem* Company, which toured the provincial theatres in Britain and lastly, in 1901, with the *Happy Days* Company. In the August of 1901, the last time he is mentioned as a performer, he gave perhaps the most detailed interview of his life[37], and if all the claims that he made are true then he had an extremely eventful life. By the time of the 1901 Census he was living with his son Victor in the Bournemouth area. He was widowed and gave his age as 59. He was still listed as an 'actor', although I suspect that he had by this time actually retired because, sadly for such a giant of a man, he is indicated as 'imbecile, feeble minded'[38]. Delmonico passed away on 31 July 1901. There were no great obituaries published in the press, merely a short report of the inquest into his death in the *Southern Times and Dorset County Herald* 3 August 1901. His cause of death was given as a cerebral haemorrhage caused by hitting his head after falling out of bed. For all the ferocious animals that he had faced in his life, all the danger, it was a simple fall that had finally taken him.

Fortunately for today's researchers, there was only one Joseph Ledger 'Delmonico' but, like Maccomo, a performer by the name of Alicamousa Sargano seems to have had several incarnations. Certainly there was a lion tamer by the name of Alicamousa performing with Sanger's company in 1881[39]. This individual would seem to be the same person who was interviewed as Sargano Alicamousa in 1886. The interview was lengthy and gave a detailed description of the man as well as much information about his life. The writer described Sargano as;

> A tall, full-featured, broad-shouldered, strong-limbed darkey of twenty-seven summers – there he was, undoubtedly a good-looking Indian. His woolly black hair was hidden by a hunting cap. His soft brown eyes and sweeping dark eye-lashes betokened an irresistible gentility of

spirit. His clean flat nostrils, determined mouth, and bold moustache showed his breeding and experience. He sported a Gladstonian collar, beautifully completed by a pink rosette, which came out with fine effect against his snow-white shirt and the natural colour of his neck. His tunic was of a greenish hue, all slashed with golden cord; his bosom was bedecked with a constellation of medals, and his body was encircled by a strong leathern [sic] belt, bearing the appendages of a dagger sheath and a pistol case. He stood above six feet in the bush boots and carried a leaden ranging whip in his hand. Truly a dashing fellow – the very type of a conqueror (*Dundee Courier* 4 September 1886)

Later in the interview, Sargano explained how he had been born of African parents in Kingstown, St Vincent, in the West Indies on 10 December 1859. He goes on to recount how he went to sea aged thirteen, his experiences with lion hunting in South Africa, and his arrival in Britain. Somewhere around 1876 he seems to have been taken on by *Sanger's Circus*, where he eventually became a lion tamer. At the time of the interview he was working with *Bostock's Grand Star Menagerie* and he appears to have been with that particular outfit on their tour of Scotland in since 1884[40]. Not only did he work with lions but he also seems to have presented venomous snakes!

Was Sargano Alicamousa his real name? Confusingly, an article appeared in the *Birmingham Mail* 26 January 1887, the year after the above interview. In this, the proprietor E. H. Bostock was found guilty of assaulting a 'negro' lion tamer in his employ, one by the name of William Dellah. Dellah claims to have been performing at the World's Fair in Bingley Hall two days previous to the hearing and had subsequently been dismissed by Bostock. He describes himself as being *the* [my italics] lion tamer for Bostock but that now he was working as a labourer since his dismissal. The implication of his statement is that he was the only lion tamer in employ. This seems to have been borne out by an advertisement in the *Islington Gazette* 28 January 1887, in which a Captain Dudley Vane is now listed as the lion tamer for Bostock's. So it seems quite possible that William Dellah was the first to use the later-popular name Sargano Alicamousa.

In February 1887, *Bostock and Wombwell's Menagerie* was in Preston. In their advertising they bill a Sargano Alicamousa[41]. Was this William Dellah being given a reprieve or was it a new incarnation? In December 1892, the death was announced of John Holloway Bright, who was 'for several years with Bostock and Wombwell's menagerie as an animal trainer under the name of Sargano' (*The Era* 31 December 1892). So, if William Dellah had been fired in January 1887 it seems quite plausible that the 'Sargano Alicamousa' that was advertised in the February could have been John Holloway Bright.

To confuse matters even more there was a third man associated with the name Alicamousa Sargano. Many references are made to a John Humphreys[42] but they also claim that this character was born in St Vincent – the same claim made in the 1886 *Dundee Courier* interview above. Compellingly, an advertisement seeking work appeared in *The Era* of 7 May 1892. The advert was for 'Sargano, or Humphreys, Coloured Lion Performer', so this certainly links the names Humphreys and Sargano. However, later that month an interview appeared in the *Aberdeen Evening Express* of 30 May. A lion tamer named Jan Sargano gives his age as thirty seven and claimed that he was born in Fiji. He was brought up by a missionary named Vernon and then travelled with him to South Africa and Bengal before ending up in Boston, USA. Here, after the death of Vernon around 1877, he joined *Barnum and Bailey's Circus* before travelling to Britain. Could 'Jan' Sargano be the same as John Humphreys Sargano? On 18 February 1893 a small illustrated article appeared in the *Penny Illustrated Paper* reporting on a 'plucky sable trainer' named Alicamousa who had an act wrestling with a lion.

Alicamousa and the Wrestling
Lion. *The Penny Illustrated Paper*
18 February 1893 *(Author's
collection)*

This act appeared in Variety venues in London and in Paris and seems
unconnected with any menagerie at the time – but which Alicamousa
was this?

As with many interviews given, I suspect that the interviewees were
prone to elaborate on their histories and exploits. Jan Sargano claimed
to have fought the lion named Nero, when it had escaped and hidden in
a sewer when *Bostock's Menagerie* was in Birmingham some years earlier.
However, newspaper reports of the incident[43] accord this exploit to a
'negro lion tamer' by the name of Orenzo. A couple of months later, still
in Birmingham, 'Marcus Orenzo, the lion tamer' had an incident with a
bear[44], something else that Jan Sargano claimed. This seems too much
of a coincidence but it is more than likely that Sargano and Orenzo were
different performers. In June 1892, just after the interview given to the
Aberdeen Evening Express, the following short piece appeared;

AN ETHIOPIAN LION TAMER HEAVILY FINED – Marcus
Orenzo, a 'gentleman of colour', with a profusion of curly hair, thick
rings, and watch chains, was brought up and charged with cruelly ill-
treating a horse … Prisoner, who was described as a lion tamer and

owner of a menagerie, was fined 20s [shillings] and costs (*Derby Daily Telegraph* 16 June 1892)

If, as is indicated, Marcus Orenzo was indeed the proprietor of his own menagerie then he was not the same person as Sargano. Reports indicate that he was later with *Biddulph's Menagerie*, which was owned by Perrari and Wombwell. The particular report[45] also gives an account of one of the few racially motivated assaults recorded against ethnic performers. Marcus Orenzo first appeared in the press with *Wombwell's Royal Menagerie* in the *Western Daily Press* of 9 May 1889. He was performing with lions and a variety of species of bears, including polar bears! His career effectively came to an end in February 1894 when he was severely attacked by a lion whilst performing in Stockport. By that May he was in hospital in Birmingham with blood poisoning and had undergone several operations to remove pieces of diseased bone from his arm. Because of this he is recorded as saying that he had 'turned his back on lion taming, having had enough of it' (*Leeds Times* 12 May 1894). But that was not the last heard of him. In 1896, with only one good arm, he was in charge of snakes at the Cardiff Exhibition. In recounting to the reporter how he had injured his arm, he went into great detail about the incident in Stockport, and the previous incident of the escaped lion in Birmingham. He claimed to have come from Sierra Leone and that, 'In '79 [1879] I went through Africa with H. M. Stanley hunting for Livingstone' (*Pontypool Free Press* 18 September 1896). Fact or fiction, I wonder? Showmanship was in his blood and he is last heard of in the performing world in 1905, where in June he was presenting a troupe of South African fire-eaters[46]. His reminiscences were recorded in a series of articles in 1910[47]. Much of the information he gave corroborates what we already know about him – but there are some interesting overlaps with John Humphrey Sargano in the fact that they both state they worked with Barnum and Bailey before coming to Britain. After that date no more is heard of Marcus Orenzo.

Although the names Maccomo, Sargano, and Delmonico appear in virtually every advertisement for lion taming at this time there were several other animal trainers of colour working at this time who also need a mention. For some the only reference of their existence in the field was their death notice. William Beaumont was badly mauled, and later died, in a Christmas Eve performance in the Agricultural Hall in 1895. He was referred to as a 'coloured lion tamer'[48]. There is no other reference to him other than this. In 1870, another animal trainer by the name of Charles Wood was attacked by a bear while performing for *Day's Menagerie* in Walsall. In this instance he survived and was described as 'a man of colour, from South America'[49]. As with Beaumont, little else is known about him. Joe Foster, another lion tamer of colour, this time with the *Buff Bill Menagerie*, was attacked by a lion in Sunderland in 1892[50]. Yet another one-article reference is for a man named Richard Jorgnis, who worked under the professional name of Dacona. He was 'a man of colour, described as a lion tamer engaged at the Aquarium, in Shoreditch'[51]. Apart from being in court on a charge of assault nothing more is known of him. Sadly, another lion and tiger trainer of colour was before the magistrates charged with theft. He went by the name of Martin Largue and worked at Sanger's Amphitheatre in London (formerly Astley's)[52]. Dellah Montarno (sometimes also written as Delhi Montarno) was appearing with *Wombwell and Bailey's Menagerie* near Wolverhampton in 1892. In the course of performance he was attacked by a bear and severely injured. He died from his injuries a few hours later. A little more information is given about him in the article, which appeared in the *Sheffield Independent* of 16 March 1892. He was described as 'an African negro' who had been with the menagerie for something like twenty years. It would seem that he had also worked with Marcus Orenzo at the time the lion escaped into the sewers in Aston some years earlier. He must have been a well-respected animal trainer because at his funeral several other lion tamers were present, including Marcus Orenzo[53]. Not to be confused with Delhi Montarno is a lion tamer by the name of Franco Montano. In *The Era* of 1 October

1898 a report was given of an incident with a lion, although his injuries were superficial. His age is given as thirty five. The following year a more serious attack took place whilst he was working with *Chipperfield's* in Preston[54]. As the surname is so similar it is not clear if there is any familial connection to Delhi Montano. He was still working in 1901, as advertised in the *Western Morning News* of 27 February. Two references are made to an African youth who performed under the name of 'Prince Cetewayo' with Wilson's lions at the Aquarium[55]. Exactly who this was has yet to be discovered.

The names of two other lion tamers of colour are worthy of mention, if for no other reason that they are often overlooked. Henry (Harry) Porter, who was said to have been an animal trainer from the age of twelve, wrestled with a lion at the Metropolitan Variety Theatre in 1893[56] and in 1894 he was described as working with Wilson's six lions at the Royal Aquarium[57]. And finally, Marquis Renzo, not to be confused with Marcus Orenzo, worked with *Day's Royal No. 1 Menagerie* in 1895. As well as working with lions he also performed with 'Tiger Wolves'[58]. By 1900 he was fairly destitute, not being able to work due to bronchitis, and was applying for assistance to return to Liverpool. This was granted and he did made it back but he died in the Workhouse in the April. He was only thirty two years old.

Black lion tamers continued into the twentieth century, although now there were far more Europeans and Americans dominating the field. Female lion tamers were also making a wider appearance. Characters such as 'Black Joe' (Albert May) continued to draw crowds for outfits such as Manders and Buffalo Bill. Born on a plantation in Spanish Town, Jamaica, Albert arrived in Britain around 1892 and, as a teenager, started out in boxing booths before moving into the lions' cage. He was yet another lion tamer to occasionally use the name of Maccomo (Hale, 2018).

We seem to have come full circle. We began with a Maccomo and ended with one but in between, during the nineteenth century, there were many lion tamers of colour performing throughout Britain. Some were well known and achieved their fame through daring exploits and notorious incidents with their animals, some achieved just a few lines of mention throughout their careers, and yet I am certain there were others who had no mention at all. Whoever they may have been, famous or not, we should recognise them all for roles that they played and the positions they had in a multicultural Victorian society.

Albert May (on the podium) in front of the show booth *(reproduced with permission of M. Hale)*

Albert May in front of the lion's cage *(reproduced with permission of M. Hale)*

Notes

1. *Sun (London)* 7 August 1838

2. *London Courier and Evening Gazette* 23 August 1838

3. The extract published in the newspaper was taken from an original paper entitled *Confessions and Opinions of Ralph Restless* by Capt. Marryat, first published in the *New Monthly Magazine and Humorist* (ed. Hook, T.) 1837, Part the 3rd, p175. Online at; https://books.google.co.uk/books?id=0HlHAAAAYAAJ&printsec=-frontcover&dq=Captain+Marryat+New+Monthly+Maga-zine+1837&hl=en&sa=X&ved=0ahUKEwi_gIDazfnoA-hUEu3EKHfLqABwQ6wEIKzAA#v=onepage&q=lion%20 tamer&f=false

4. *Waterford Mail* 8 February 1854

5. *Express (London)* 28 November 1857

6. This suggestion appears in an article entitled *Black lion tamers in Hull and East Yorkshire* as part of the African stories in *Hull and East Yorkshire Project*. This can be accessed online at; https://www.africansinyorkshireproject.com/black-lion-tamers.html#

7. *1861 England Census.* Online at; https://www.ancestry.co.uk/interactive/8767/SOMRG9_1682_1687-0604?pid= 19184942&backurl=https://search.ancestry.co.uk/cgi-bin/sse.dll?indiv%3D1%26dbid%3D8767%26h %3D19184942%26tid%3D%26pid%3D%26useP-UB%3Dtrue%26_phsrc%3DAnq79%26_phstart%3D-successSource&treeid=&personid=&hintid=&useP-UB=true&_phsrc=Anq79&_phstart=successSource&use-

PUBJs=true&_ga=2.185567209.1342941343.1587630165-8519783.1584367827

8. Poster for Manders Royal Menagerie of 9 July 1860 at the Cattle Market, Leeds. An original copy is held by the Leeds City Library. Not available online.

9. *Illustrated Berwick Journal* 30 January 1858

10. *The Times* 6 January 1862

11. *Cork Examiner* 4 March 1863

12. *Olympians of the Sawdust Circle Mac-Mc* on the Circus Historical Society website. Online at; http://www.classic.circushistory.org/Olympians/OlympiansMc.htm

13. *Boston Guardian* 10 May 1890

14. *Aberdeen Press and Journal* 23 May 1895

15. *Huntly Express* 13 June 1896

16. *The Era* 30 July 1898

17. *Bexhill on Sea Observer* 9 September 1899

18. *Reading Mercury* 23 September 1865

19. *Cheltenham Journal and Gloucester Fashionable Weekly Gazette* 7 February 1863

20. *Biographie du Dompteur Noir, Delmonico, Écrite par lui-même.* Online at; https://gallica.bnf.fr/ark:/12148/bpt6k8562898?rk=21459;2

21. *1871 England census.* Online at; https://www.ancestry.co.uk/interactive/7619/HAMRG10_1192_1194-0069?pid=466339&t

reeid=&personid=&rc=&usePUB=true&_phsrc=Anq122&_
phstart=successSource

22. Online at; https://paperspast.natlib.govt.nz/newspapers/
NZH18841004.2.60?end_date=15-10-1884&query=Delmon-
ico&snippet=true&start_date=01-10-1884

23. Poster for the Folies-Bergèr in Paris 1876/7. Online at; https://galli-
ca.bnf.fr/ark:/12148/btv1b90035177?rk=21459;2

24. *Norfolk News* 10 September 1870

25. *Caernarvon & Denbigh Herald* 17 June 1871

26. An account of his life is given in an online article by Phil Martin, a
volunteer researcher for the Milton Historical Society. Online at;
http://broadkillblogger.org/people/joseph-ledger/ A further
detailed interview with him appeared in the *Leigh Chronicle and
Weekly District Advertiser* 26 January 1894

27. *Yorkshire Post and Leeds Intelligencer* 2 November 1867

28. *Louth and North Lincolnshire Advertiser* 22 April 1865

29. *Aldershot Military Gazette* 29 November 1873

30. *The Era* 24 January 1875

31. *Lincolnshire Chronicle* 19 April 1878

32. *Leeds Times* 15 January 1876

33. *Middlesex Chronicle* 4 November 1876

34. *Gloucestershire Echo* 30 November 1891

35. *South Wales Daily News* 4 January 1892

36. *The Era* 28 January 1893

37. *Bedfordshire Mercury* 24 August 1900

38. *1901 England Census.* Online at; https://www.ancestry.co.uk/inter-
    active/7814/HAMRG13_1041_1042-0270?pid=996206&t
    reeid=&personid=&rc=&usePUB=true&_phsrc=Anq126&_
    phstart=successSource

39. *Aberdeen Weekly News* 22 January 1881

40. *Southern Reporter* 1 May 1884

41. *Lancashire Evening Post* 28 February 1887

42. Several websites link John Humphreys with Alicamousa Sargano.
    One of them being https://www.africansinyorkshireproject.
    com/black-lion-tamers.html

43. *St James's Gazette* 30 September 1889

44. *Birmingham Daily Post* 30 December 1889

45. *Sheffield Evening Telegraph* 21 June 1893

46. *Music Hall and Theatre Review* 9 June 1905

47. The reminiscences appear to have been serialised in the *Music Hall
    and Theatre Review* on the 11 and 18 August 1910, and the 1 Sep-
    tember 1910

48. *Manchester Evening News* 30 December 1895

49. *Birmingham Daily Post* 28 September 1870

50. *Lincolnshire Chronicle* 27 December 1892

51. *Lloyds Weekly News* 18 January 1880

52. *Manchester Evening News* 21 January 1879

53. *The Era* 26 March 1892

54. *The Era* 27 May 1899

55. These appear in the *Cornishman* 16 September 1886 and the *Illustrated Sporting and Dramatic News* 12 March 1887

56. *The Era* 28 October 1893

57. *The Field* 9 August 1894

58. *York Herald* 25 November 1895

CHAPTER 11
VICTORIAN ORIENTALISM – THE CHINESE AND JAPANESE TROUPES

Although there has been a Chinese presence in Britain from as early as 1687 (Price, 2019), it was not until the early part of the nineteenth century that we see the growth of Chinese communities in some cities. Liverpool and London were the main centres for incoming Chinese people, as these were major ports and ships belonging to the East India Company brought not only goods from China but countless sailors as well. Many of them settled in Britain and formed their own cultural enclaves, such as in the Limehouse area of London. It would not be until 1877 that formal relations were established between Britain and China, with the opening up of the first Chinese Legation in London.

As the Chinese arrived in Britain during those early years of the nineteenth century so Chinese jugglers and acrobats began to be seen in circuses and on the stages around the country. China itself has a long tradition of acrobatic performances dating back almost 2000 years. During the Qin and Han dynasties (221BCE – 230CE), beginning first as part of village celebrations such performances became popular at the Emperors' courts for several centuries, particularly during the Tang dynasty (618 – 917CE). These acrobatic performances embraced juggling, stilt-walking, knife throwing, fire-eating, and conjuring. Zhang Heng was a literary scholar and recorded an eye-witness account of a performance from that period (Chunfang Fei, ed. 2002);

A man of incredible strength lifts up a heavy cooking vessel. Like the tree-swinging folks from Dulu, performers climb up high poles. Some leap through wreathes spiked with knives. Some perform swallow dives in big water tanks. Hard chest muscles meet the challenge of sharp daggers. Jugglers, fencers, and tightrope walkers all show off their skills.

As European circuses, such as *Tourniare's*, *Charinni's*, and *Souliier's*, made inroads into China during the early nineteenth century, so there was a cross-pollination of ideas, with Chinese performers being brought to Britain.

Chinese strong-man act. Liebig Trade Card late C19th *(Author's collection)*

One of the earlier performers recorded was Quang Caoelis, who appeared at *Adams' Royal Hibernian Arena* in Dublin in 1829, where he was billed as the Chinese Positionist[1]. He later went on to work with *Batty's Circus*, where his act was described as follows;

> The postures which this individual assumes *ad libitum* [sic, Latin; as often
> as required], are truly wonderful; his limbs, particularly his legs, seem to
> move on universal joints; and we do not exaggerate when we say, that
> he appears to *handle* [sic] his legs with more ease and grace than does a
> *fugleman* [sic, a soldier expert in drill] his musket. To describe this young
> man's *contortions* [sic] were a vain task... (*Hereford Times* 3 August 1833)

After the 1834 season with *Batty's Circus* there are no more records
for this young man. In an 1830 advertisement[2] he is billed as 'from
Versailles'. One assumes that he was working in France before he
travelled to join Adams' outfit. There is also the possibility that he was
not actually Chinese, and that he had taken the name Quang Caoelis as
an 'exotic' sounding performance name. It was not unheard of at that
time for performers to appropriate Chinese sounding names.

As early as 1825 in Sheffield, Khia Khan Khruse, the Portuguese
'Indian' juggler, appeared with 'The Chinese Juggler from the Court of
Pekin'[4]. Ramo Samee, the genuine Indian juggler, did occasionally appear
as the 'Chinese' juggler and he did work with Khruse at one time. It is
conceivable that Ramo Samee may have been the 'Chinese' juggler in
Sheffield. There were several other Europeans who presented 'Chinese'
routines, one of whom was Ching Lau Lauro, who was appearing with
Cooke's Equestrian Company in 1827[4]. He was a Buffo, a comic character,
who exhibited 'Postures and Attitudes', in other word a contortionist.
Later in his career he became more of a conjuror and there is an
implication that he was actually a Cornishman[5]. He died in 1839.

It was not really until 1854 that a Chinese troupe made its mark in
Britain. Frost (1876:299) gives an account of their journey to England
via the USA, and a brief description of their act.

> They numbered eight performers, including women and boys, and
> their feats were of a varied character, embracing tumbling, juggling,
> balancing, fire-eating, besides conjuring, a specimen of a Chinese
> concert in the shape of a quartet for a gong, cymbals, and a couple

of stringed instruments, which was more curious than agreeable, and an attempt at a Chinese ballet, which provoked more laughter than admiration.

Again we can see here a further example of dismissive British Imperialism. The audience could cope with and accept demonstrations of physical skills; this was something that they were used to seeing and were comfortable with. However, anything that did not conform to the European aesthetic was to be laughed at or found curious. Presenting performances rooted in their own culture, the Chinese troupe should have expected a degree of respect from their British audience, not derision.

The troupe, with its leader Tuck Quy, began its tour of Britain in Scotland in January 1854. Here they were generally well received, and a report in the *Aberdeen Herald and General Advertiser* of 25 February gives a brief history of the group along with some details of the performance.

Natives of Nankin[6], and famous in that remote city for their juggling exploits, the revolution in China[7] has been the cause of their seeking refuge in a foreign land … They embarked for California, and have come thence to England … Their feats are said to be more astonishing than anything yet accomplished by European artists. Their precision of hand and quickness of visual power is marvellous in its perfection. One of their most astounding displays of the perfect training they have received consists in the father of the family, *Tuck Quy*, placing his daughter, a girl of about thirteen years of age, against the opposite wall of the room, and there encircling her with large knives, projected from a distance. The girl, with the utmost intrepidity, places her head and expanded hands against the wall, while the father, without seeming to take aim, and with the utmost *nonchalance*, flings at her a number of ponderous knives, which fix themselves in the wall between her fingers, on each side her face, and around her neck and shoulders, without grazing her skin … Nor are the other performances of these Chinese strangers less extraordinary. The boy is the most accomplished acrobat of his age; and the lady performs more wonders with her feet than the most expert necromancer ever accomplished with his fingers.

The 'impaling' act, as the knife throwing was known, became the signature act of the troupe throughout their tour of Britain, although in later performances Tuck Quy's daughter was replaced by a male performer.

The Chinese Troupe with their Impaling Act. *Illustrated London News* 8 April 1854 *(Author's collection)*

They were frequently billed as a 'family' of Chinese jugglers[8], although whether or not they were familial related is not certain. The *Poole and Dorset Herald* of 6 April 1854 gives a full list of the performers' names and, given that the reporter was probably recording these phonetically, there are similarities in some of the generation names (the first name written down). The names of the performers were recorded as Wan Sing, Yan Gyn, Zan Ban, Ar Cow, Ar Hee, Chang Moon, Ching Gan, Ar Ling, and Ar Sam. Tuck Quy is not specifically mentioned in the piece but it is to be assumed that he was there on the day as the leader and he was often referred to as the 'father' of the family. In addition to the Impaling Act with the knives, a further detailed account of their performances was given in the *Dublin Evening Packet and Correspondent* of 24 October 1854;

> The 'iron skull' displayed by Tuck Guy must have astonished any weak nerves that were present … and it consists of throwing a solid ivory ball from the hand into the air and catching it as it descends upon the forehead … the ball making a pretty loud noise as it struck his forehead … One of the best displays of skill during the evening, was the balancing of four or five wooden benches strung together, with a small table superadded, which had been taken at random from the stage, by the talented Tuck Guy, upon his shoulder, and afterwards upon his chin. A very singular part of the performance was that undertaken by the Chinese woman Wang Noe of balancing a heavy copper jar on her feet – a task seemingly difficult, but which she executed in a neat and precise manner. The Tumbling, by Ar Cow and Yam Poo, was extremely good; they displayed an agility and elasticity of body that seemed to declare the utter superfluousness of the ordinary springboard adjunct with which they so well dispensed. They were rivalled, however, in this department by the boy Tuim Hee, whose acrobatic evolutions were astonishing. He rolled about the stage like a ball, and bent and twisted his body as if it were of India-rubber, besides executing numerous difficult springs and pirouettes.

The group was appearing at the Drury Lane theatre in London during April but then disappeared from the British press. However, in September the following item appeared in several newspapers;

> THE CHINESE DWARF, CHIN GAN, forming part of the Chinese jugglers lately exhibiting at Berlin, died some days ago at the Charité Hospital, and was interred in the neighbouring cemetery (*Berkshire Chronicle* 9 September 1854)

A report in the French newspaper, *Le Nouvelliste*[9], confirmed that he died in Berlin on 20 August of a chest disease. He was thirty years old. This particular account goes on to record the circumstances of Chin Gan's interment in Berlin. Chin Gan was amongst the list of performers given above, so it is clearly the case that Tuck Quy and his troupe were in Europe between May and October, when they re-appeared in Ireland[10]. They toured throughout Ireland until March the next year, when they began a provincial tour in England. By July the group was back in London where, it seems, Tuck Quy was making plans to return home. However, he ended up in hospital after being viciously assaulted, as recorded here in *The Atlas* 7 July 1855;

> On Sunday night a row occurred in the purlieus [neighbourhood] of Rosemary Lane, among the Chinese jugglers … knives were drawn, and Tuck Guy received several severe wounds; his wife was also cut in the arm, and Ah Ling stabbed. *Afo* received a wound in his leg. *Assam*, *Afo*, and *Aking* were placed at the Thames Police-bar on Monday to answer for themselves … Tuck Guy lies at the London Hospital in a very precarious condition.

From an account of the court proceedings[11] that appeared in several newspapers, it appears that Tuck Quy had amassed a significant amount of money before making plans to return to China. Four named assailants, all sailors, approached him in his lodgings and demanded the money. He offered them a small amount but was then knocked to the floor and attacked with knives, receiving many wounds about the body. His wife and son intervened, receiving wounds themselves, and managed to call the police. The assailants were captured and indicted with 'cutting and wounding with intent to murder'. They were found guilty and each sentenced to four years penal servitude. What happened to Tuck Quy and his group after this incident is not recorded. They certainly were not in Britain for the rest of the year. There was a passing reference to a group of Chinese jugglers performing with Ducrow in the USA in March 1856[12] but there is no indication as to whether this is Tuck Quy's group or not.

Later that year an advertisement appeared in the *Staffordshire Sentinel and Commercial & General Advertiser* 25 October 1856 for the 'Celebrated Chinese Jugglers, who created such a sensation at the Theatre Royal

Drury Lane'. It mentions the Impaling Act, but no other details. The following month the group appeared in London, where they were billed as 'just returned from Copenhagen'[13]. That this is the same group as above is not in question, as reference is also made to them having been at Drury Lane. However, the performers are named in this piece; Arr Sanun, Ching Lau, and Tim Tamon. The implication is that there were only three members in the group. In another newspaper[14] the names were recorded as Arr Samm, Ching Lan, and Tim Tamm. I do not believe that these three were all from the original troupe of 1854. Arr Samm is the only name which correlates to both groups and I suspect that he was the leader of this new troupe. Throughout 1857 the three man Chinese troupe continued to tour throughout Britain, although the composition of the group seems to have changed by the September[15]. Arr Samm continues in the group, but now he was joined by Arr Hee and Arr Sang. It might be remembered that an Ar Hee was also a member of the original Chinese troupe in 1854. Favourable reviews continued through 1858, although at times the wording used to describe them still displayed the underlying British attitude towards ethnic performing groups. *The Era* of 11 July 1858, referred to the performance of the group as showing an 'amazing dexterity and cunning peculiar to their class'; and by class the writer is here referring to race. To praise the performers' amazing dexterity is admirable, but was it really necessary to qualify that by referring to their ethnicity in such a pejorative way? It adds nothing to the description apart from saying more about the writer than the performers.

Tragedy struck in September, when the sudden death of Arr San was announced in the *Shields Daily Gazette* on 30 September 1858. He died in Halifax and it was stated that he was a great opium smoker, although the exact circumstances of his death were not recorded. The surviving two, Arr Hee and Arr Sam, continued to tour together[16]. However, there are other 'Chinese' jugglers and individuals on the touring circuit at this time, and some of them were certainly not Chinese. On 2 August

1860, *The Era* announced that 'Dusoni and his Talented Pupils have now terminated their successful engagements, consisting of three first class entertainments, the Chinese jugglers ...' The Corelli Family of gymnasts was another non-Chinese group which performed a routine called the 'Chinese jugglers'[17].Other individual names that appear as individual performers are Ching Fan Lao[18] and Chi An Foo[19], but there is no evidence to suggest whether they were actually Chinese or not. Other names performing as Chinese jugglers were Ar Cone and Sam Ing[20], and Sam Ung and Chung Chan[21]. Given that names were often written down by journalists as heard, there may be some overlap of names but Arr Hee and partner were definitely still working together throughout 1861[22]. By 1862, the Chinese jugglers had returned to being three performers. They were the headline act in Leeds, 'for one night only', on the 20 December[23]. Arr Hee was now joined by Samung (possibly the same person as Sam Ing and Sam Ung above) and Ching Fong. The programme of entertainments was given in detail on the poster and included various conjuring, juggling, and acrobatic feats by Arr Hee, with fire eating and other effects from Samung. Arr Hee and Samung also perform the Impalement Act of knife throwing.

The lower portion of the poster includes glowing reports of the Chinese jugglers by the press. Ching Fong is not mentioned specifically in the programme details or in these reviews so what role this person played is not clear. However, a report in the *Kelso Chronicle* of 5 December 1862 gives a review of the Chinese jugglers and states that Ching Fong was the 'target' for the Impalement Act for that particular programme. Arr Hee was named as the thrower so maybe the other two rotated as the target during their tour. In 1864, the Chinese jugglers were working at the Cirque Napoleon in Paris. *Le Temps (Paris)*[24] of 19 January 1864 gives a full account of their performance. But things were not well between them.

The Paris Chamber of Commerce gave judgement the other day in a suit between the two Chinese jugglers engaged at the Cirque Napoleon. Sam Ung, the plaintiff, stated that he had been engaged by Arr Hee, for two years, at a salary of 50f. [Francs] a week, besides board and lodgings, but that the contract had not been fulfilled with regard to the latter particulars, and he accordingly demanded the annulment of hid engagement, with 600f. damages. He alleged that, owing to the ill-feeling entertained towards him by the defendant [Arr Hee], he (the plaintiff) could not with safety continue one part of his performance [being the target for the Impalement Act] (*Penny Illustrated Paper* 19 March 1864)

Not the best position to be in if you are at odds with your boss! The Tribunal agreed with him and ordered that the contract be annulled and that Arr Hee pay 200f. damages plus costs. One assumes that they parted company after that because Arr Hee appears performing solo at a Working Men's Hospital Fete in Bath the following August[25]. No mention is made of Ching Fong and the report of the Chamber of Commerce case above refers to *the* two Chinese jugglers rather than two *of* the Chinese jugglers. This implies that Ching Fong was no longer with them when they went to Paris.

Arr Hee disappeared from the British press after his appearance in Bath but he does re-appear in Paris again in 1867. He was appearing with Ah Sam at the Elderado venue[26] and an earlier report in the French press gave the information that Arr Hee and Ah Sam were brothers[27]. It seems that the Elderado was almost a permanent venue for Arr Hee over the next few years. Certainly he was there in 1871, as confirmed in *The Era* of 17 December 1871. By 1873 he had gathered a new troupe together and was touring Britain again as *The Great Original Chinese Troupe*. With all the bluster of advertising it was announced that;

This is the only real Troupe of Chinese travelling or that have ever travelled in England (*Manchester Evening News* 31 March 1873)

Chinese Entertainment.
1862 poster *(Reproduced
with permission of Leeds
Libraries, www.leodis.net)*

Arr Hee seems to have conveniently forgotten the original touring troupe he was a member of almost twenty years previously. But, in fairness, he was drawing the distinction between his troupe of 'genuine' Chinese artistes with other groups who performed as 'Chinese'. In the early 1870s the Brothers Lavatus and the Ricardos performed as 'Chinese acrobats'[28]. Arr Hee's troupe toured Britain that summer and the *Derbyshire Times and Chesterfield Herald* of 14 June gave names to the performers. Four were listed as follows;

> Arr Hee; The famous Knife Thrower of Pekin. Sing Song Zou; Champion Chinese Sword Swallower. Arr Saen; the Chinese Leotard. Taen Hee; The daring little Nankeen Wire Walker.

By the October Arr Hee was back at the Elderado in Paris[29] with a group, although the names listed were different from the group that he toured in Britain.

> L'avaleur de sabre – le petit chinoise, Hee Teu, âgé de 10 ans – les petits Ada Ferlaudy, Arr Cutz, Lan Hoo, sont autant de prodigies que, dècidément, on ne trouve qu'en Chine (*Revue Artistique* 16 October 1873)

> [The sword swallower - the little Chinese, Hee Teu, age of 10 - the little Ada Ferlaudy, Arr Cutz, Lan Hoo, are as much prodigies as, decidedly, we find only in China. *Author's translation*]

Nothing more is heard of Arr Hee in Britain after 1873, either working solo or with a group. He seems to have stayed in France and the last record of him was in 1877[30] when he was working at The Casino in Paris with a troupe of ten Chinese performers. After this date he disappears from all advertising and revues.

There was a 'craze' for 'Oriental' performances of all kinds in Britain during the latter half of the nineteenth century. As Habbouch (2011) records; 'popular entertainments of the Oriental Other were celebrated to satisfy audience attraction to images of the exotic'. In July 1869 the *Bolton Evening News* of 24 July announced that;

> CHE MAH. THE SMALLEST MAN IN THE WORLD HAS ARRIVED, and will give his unique entertainment, and afterwards appear in a ball of fire. He will also take his terrific flight on the back of the GREAT FLYING FISH, accompanied by the CHINESE TAME SALMON.

His age was given as forty four years and he was stated to be from Mingpo. This may or may not have been the city of Ningbo, south east of the city of Hangzhou in China. At least one person maintained that he was possibly a Malay[31]. He toured throughout Britain, very often appearing as a knock-about clown and able to quip with the audience in very good English.

Che Mah. Carte de Visite late C19th century *(Author's collection)*

In 1875 he made his debut in Paris[32] but he was back in Britain again in the following year, working with *Powell's Circus*[33]. Although there is no record of him in Britain after this date, we do know that he travelled to the USA because an article in the *Central Somerset Gazette* 3 November 1883 gave a copy of a report from the *Philadelphia Press*. It would seem that a fellow Chinese person visited his exhibition and spoke to him in various Chinese dialects, none of which Che Mah responded to. Che Mah eventually replied, in perfect English, 'Oh, give us a rest, you make me tired. I've been so long away from China that I forget the language'. The visitor declared him a fraud and walked off. Fraud or not, Che Mah lived to be eighty eight years old and died in Chicago. His death was announced in the French newspaper the *Excelsior* on 24 March 1926[34].

The fashion in Britain for all things from the Far East was further increased by the arrival of Japanese performing groups in the country.

Japan has a long history of circus style entertainments, particularly acrobatics and juggling that flourished almost in isolation during the *Sakoku* period (1639-1853). During this time Japan closed its doors to the outside world, although the Dutch East India Company still maintained a presence in the country, and there was ongoing trade between Japan and its neighbours China and Korea. When the *Sakoku* period came to an end it became possible for Japanese performance groups to travel outside of the country.

The British were already aware of the presence of individual Japanese people in the country, especially in London. A small number of students and officials had made their way to the capital. But in November of 1863, *Ginnett's Circus* in Southampton was advertising the 'Japanese Troupe of Moon Worshippers'[35]. This group also presented the Impalement Act of knife throwing, in the same manner as Arr Hee and his Chinese troupe were performing. However, I suspect that these were possibly

Japanese Acrobats. Print 1891 *(Library of Congress)*

not genuine Japanese performers because the Correlli Family name immediately precedes that of the Japanese Troupe, and, as we have seen earlier, the Correlli Family had already been performing as a group of 'Chinese' jugglers as early as 1861. The imminent arrival of the first genuine group of Japanese performers to Britain was announced widely throughout January 1867. They made their first performance at the Great St Martin's Hall in London on February 11, and included 'Gaensee the unrivalled Top Spinner to the Tycoon', Asi-Kitchi-San the 'original performer of the great Japanese Butterfly Trick', and several Japanese actresses[36]. Although the group was generally and genuinely well received by most reviews, with full descriptions of the acts involved[37], there were others who resorted to the usual xenophobic cant embodied in a general review of the performance;

Accompanied by Japanese music of a quality so barbarous that it could not have been worse in the days of Sungt, this new *troupe* of about a dozen yellow-skins exhibit feats of oriental skill ... During the performance a young Japanese girl entertained ... with one of the popular songs, doubtless, of the metropolis of Japan. But if she intended to enchant her hearers, she must have reckoned extravagantly without her guests, for not one of the music hall comic songs could excite much more laughter ... The young songstress is very good looking for a Japanese ... those persons who are very excitable should stay away. They might laugh themselves into fits ... The instrumental music consists of guttural guitars, discordant drums, and something that clatters like 'bones' (*South London Chronicle* 16 February 1867)

It is completely unnecessary to have couched the review in such a racist tone. The same reviewer then goes on to give a more detailed account of the performance.

One of them makes out of pieces of paper butterflies that fly about, alight wherever the author likes, and then fly about and travel along the edge of his fan as though they were real butterflies whom the Japanese had taught to perform in public. Another [Asi-Kitchi-San] is a top-spinner, the most wonderful of top-spinners, who makes his top spin along a bamboo, or along the edge of a sabre, or run over his arm and shoulders, as though it also had been conjured into vitality. Then he flings it into the air 14 or 15 feet above his head, and catches it several times on his thin stick, while it spins along like the king of tops. The Japanese acrobat [Gaensee][38] is wholly unlike all European acrobats. He lies along some scaffolding near the top of the hall ... , and holds on end of a thick bamboo pole ... , while the chief acrobat glides along it in every kind of dangerous posture holding on sometimes only by his naked feet.

What benefit was there to highlighting the 'otherness' of the Japanese performers when the description of the acts should have superseded the performers' ethnicity? Similar to the Chinese performers, who performed as Chinese people and not within the European aesthetic, the Japanese troupe performed within their own cultural aesthetic.

Having taken London by storm, the group embarked on a provincial tour, taking in most of the major cities across Britain. During this time the group performed to Royalty, for the Prince of Wales on the occasion of his birthday[39], and before Queen Victoria and her children at Windsor[40]. It was always the intention of the group to travel to Paris for the International Exhibition of 1867, as was stated in the *Southern Reporter* 21 February 1867. However, they were not alone in these plans and they appeared to have a rival group also heading to Paris. 'Professor' Risley, the well-known American gymnast and acrobat, had first visited Japan with his circus in 1865 (Schodt, 2012). This was the first time the Japanese had experienced a western circus. By the autumn of 1866, Risley entered into a financial contract to finance the taking of the *Imperial Japanese Troupe* to the Paris Exhibition via the United States of America. At that time at least three Japanese performing troupes were being organised to go abroad, and later there would be five.

Risley and his troupe arrived in Liverpool on 24 July 1867, en route for Paris[41]. However, by this time it had been announced in the *Sheffield Daily Telegraph* 23 July 1867 that the Japanese Troupe from Britain (the *Gensui Troupe*) had already opened at the Theatre Prince Imperial (Cirque de l'Impératrice). Faced with competition, Risley's group opened at the Cirque Napoleon and proved to be a huge success, soon eclipsing the performances of the *Gensui Troupe*. The Gensui audiences began to dwindle as the *Imperial Japanese Troupe's* increased. By mid-August the successes of the 'Imperials' were so great that the *Gensui Troupe* left Paris to work in Brussels, Belgium. They had also appear to have lost one of their prime performers. Before they left England for Paris, Der Hang had parted company with group and was working a solo top-spinning and butterfly act with *Quaglieni's Circus* in Newcastle[42].

The *Imperial Troupe* intended to travel to England in the December but before they arrived there was yet another Japanese troupe touring

Britain, the *Great Dragon Troupe of Japanese Performers*. This group opened in Dublin in early August 1867 and included;

> HAROSAN – in his Great Jar Pyramid (his first appearance)

> SINTARO BUNGO –the Japanese Winship – in his immense Feats of Strength

> FONDI KEIDJIE – in his Terrific Ascent of a Bamboo Pole, suspended from the Ceiling (*Saunder's News-Letter* 12 August 1867)

The *Dublin Evening Post* 15 August 1867, expands on the list of performers and details;

> KINZO-GORO – The Marvellous Jongleur and Illusionist; HAROSAN – in his great sensational Awe-inspiring Flower-pot Pyramid, with 'Little Tommy' on top; METARO – The Curious and Intrepid Tiger Polanbulant; TORA KEETCHE – In the most Graceful Fetes of Posturing; BOMBI-GOREE – The Oriental Leotard; MASA-KUTCHE – The Wizard of Top-spinners.

The Royal Imperial Japanese Troupe. *Illustrated London News* 2 May 1868 *(Author's collection)*

The *Great Dragon Troupe* continued to tour throughout Britain for the remainder of the year before leaving for continental Europe. So it was into a Britain well-versed in Japanese performance that the *Imperial Japanese Troupe* arrived in early December. The *Morning Advertiser* 7 December 1867 announced;

> IMPERIAL JAPANESE TROUPE – Directors, Messrs. MAGUIRE AND RISLEY. This, the most extraordinary Troupe of Japanese Artistes from the empire of Japan, and holding in their own country a position above that of any other company of performers, will appear at Her Majesty's Theatre on MONDAY Dec. 16. The public are respectfully notified that the Imperial Japanese Troupe have never appeared in Europe, except at Paris, where their success has been inordinarily great. They have nothing in common with any company which has previously visited England. Unequalled in their own land, they come to invite English criticism in one of the largest theatres of this country.

However, disaster struck when the theatre they were due to perform in was destroyed by fire. All other London theatres were committed to December productions so Risley took the decision to open the British tour in the provinces, to return to London at some later point. The Imperials opened their tour at the Curzon Hall in Birmingham on 26 December 1867, to a packed audience. The following day, the *Birmingham Daily Gazette* gave a very detailed account of the troupe that is worth reading in full as it tells us so much about them.

> The leader of the troupe is Hamaikari Sadakichi, a grave and senatorial-looking personage, and among the rest of the company are Hamaikari Mikichi (or Little All-right," as he was called in America), Denkiohi, Tjokicbi, Zumidangarva Wamingaroo, Yonekiohi, Shintharo, Matzuikikujiru, Swa'kichi, Linzoa, Dieksan, Zaundangawa Matzungoro, Shingtamatzu, Mikichisan Maseangoto, Hanekicbi, and three ladies, Mesdames Komong, O'tho'o, and Ozunei. Perhaps the most interesting feats in the whole entertainment, though not perhaps the most difficult of accomplishment, are those performed by the gentleman bearing the remarkable name of Matzuikikujiru, the top-spinner. He makes his top

spin in the air, on the edge of a sharp sword, or on thread, and finally makes it travel up a sort of incline to a tower. The "tower" is made of pasteboard, and in shape and appearance is not unlike a coffee-mill, but it is supposed be a clock. The top enters by the roof, and by some unseen process causes the clock to strike the hour, and then it comes out from the bottom and travels along another incline, still spinning. One of the acrobats of the troupe dances on a tight rope, 20 or 30 feet from the ground, and performs some most outrageously daring "feats of feet." The other tumblers—and there are six or seven of them—are no less remarkable for their strength and their cat-like suppleness. Let the reader imagine—or, better still, let him go and see—a not over-robust looking Oriental lying on his back, and balancing a long and apparently heavy ladder on the soles of his feet. At the top of the ladder a second ladder is placed crosswise, and a third ladder is suspended from the end of the second—the whole resting on the feet of the tumbler. A Japanese lad [Little All Right[43]], about ten years of age, ascends the main ladder, performing on his way a series of acrobatic evolutions that would distance the most daring tumblers at the Alhambra. Arrived at the top, the sweet little cherub sits—or rather squats—Japanese fashion up aloft, unconcernedly fanning himself, looking as meek as a toad, and in other respects rather resembling that animal, but withal keeping a watchful eye on the movements of him whose slightest error or mischance would send him into the middle of the audience, and perhaps into eternity. He then passes over on the other ladders, and after a continuation of daring tricks he alights safely, and the curtain falls … The celebrated butterfly trick is done to perfection, and there are a dozen other feats which no European could be trained to do so as admirably as the Japanese gentlemen now at Curzon Hall go through every night.

After a relatively short engagement in Birmingham, the troupe moved on to Belgium and the Netherlands before returning to London in the April. Sadly by this time, Matsui Kikujiro the top-spinner had died (Schodt, 2012:212-213) but the group made their first appearance in London at the Lyceum theatre on April 13.

(Left) A page from the 3D pop-up book *Internationaler Circus* by Lothar Meggendorfer, showing a Japanese Troupe (possibly the Royal Imperials). Originally published 1889 *(Author's collection)*

(Right) Unknown Japanese girl on the tightrope. Early C20th Postcard *(Author's collection)*

But fire still plagued the group. On April 18, while the group were performing, a fire broke out in their lodgings in Gerard Street[44]. Fortunately, much of their belongings were saved but Little All Right's pet dog died in the fire. As much as the group were a triumphant success in performance, off stage they were not so lucky. In early May, 'Ha Swakicke' [Hirohachi] was involved in a fracas in a house of ill-repute where he had nine sovereigns stolen from him[45]. Apparently he frequently visited sex workers. But there was also a joyous occasion when it was announced by Risley in the press that;

> Professor Risley, who brought over the Imperial Japanese Troupe to this country has announced the birth of the first child of pure Japanese blood ever born out of Japan (*The Era* 14 June 1868)

267

This event seems to have been a novelty for the British and the story was carried in many newspapers across the country. It was shortly after this that the Troupe left England for an extended tour of Europe, taking in Spain, Portugal, and France before returning to America at the beginning of 1869. Shortly after that, in the February, Hirohachi and eight other members of the original troupe left to return to Japan. Risley offered a new contract to the remaining nine members and still operated as the *Imperial Japanese Troupe*.

But, as the Imperials left Britain so another Japanese group arrived. On March 3 1869 the *Newcastle Daily Chronicle* advertised the *Royal Tycoon Japanese Male and Female Performers* under the direction of Tannaker Buhicrosan. This group offered;

> New and Astonishing Feats of TOP SPINNING, BAMBOO BALANCING, ARCHERY Shooting a lighted match from the top of a Man's Head (*a la* William Tell), YEDDO FLYWHEEL Turning summersaults [sic] on the Points of Sharp Swords, BRICK BALANCING, EGG SPINNING, Butterfly Fanning &c. &c. CONCERT BY THE JAPANESE LADIES.

Tannaker himself was an exponent of the Butterfly act and also acted as the group's interpreter. Although a relatively small company, there were initially ten in total including Tannaker, they also delighted in 'illustrating the Manners, Magic, and Music of their so little known Nation'.[46] *Tannaker's Royal Tycoons* toured widely and by 1871 had expanded to fifteen performers[47]. The continued touring in Britain but Tannaker himself was not without controversy. In December 1872, he was charged with child cruelty. He had unnecessarily and cruelly punished his 'son' by restraining him and locking him in a cupboard for many hours because he would no 'learn his lessons'[48]. Tannaker was fined ten pounds sterling.

Tannaker continued to work throughout Britain with an ever changing troupe of Japanese performers but he was also heavily involved in promoting Japanese culture. As early as 1876 he was using merchandising as a way of attracting the crowds to his performances. When his Japanese Troupe visited Brighouse, Yorkshire;

> Every person paying for admission to the hall receives an article ostensibly of Japanese manufacture. Some of these which we saw on Wednesday evening were very neat and valuable, but of course the bulk of the presents were mere trifles. The presents comprised fishing rods of bamboo cane, fans, whips &c. &c. (*Brighouse News* 11 March 1876)

This focus on Japanese culture lead him to establish the Japanese Native Village Exhibition and Trading Company Limited in 1883. It was housed in Humphrey's Hall, an exhibition hall in Knightsbridge, London. It was intended to be a replica of a Japanese village centre, complete with Japanese craftsmen, villagers, and entertainers. Officially opened in 1885, it attracted over 250,000 visitors in its first few months of operation. It continued until 1887. Tannaker was the managing director and chief promoter and this placed him in a very advantageous position to attract visiting Japanese performers to bolster his touring company. Tannaker Buhicrosan died on 10 August 1894 at his home in Lewisham, Kent. His effects of 302 pounds sterling were left to his widow Otekasan Ruth Tannaker[49].

It may be remembered that Risley's *Imperial Japanese Troupe* had left Britain at the end of 1868 – but they had returned by June 1869. The new group, along with 'Little All Right', opened in Liverpool on 23 June 1869. There was rivalry between Risley and Tannaker, with each claiming to be the 'original' troupe of Japanese performers. Tannaker even went as far as taking on a young performer and naming him 'Little All Right'. The Imperials began to tour England but when they were in Nottingham Risley became the centre of a scandal that was broadcast throughout the British press. He was charged with assaulting Maria Mason, a girl of about eleven years old. He had followed the girl and attempted to take her into various coffee-shops as well as asking her to go with him to his rooms, on the promise of a present[50]. The case was brought to trial at the Old Bailey[51] and after a lengthy hearing Risley was acquitted but the damage to his reputation had been done, and by association so was that of the Imperials. They continued to perform in England but on 6 March 1870, *The Era* reported that the troupe were setting out for St Petersburgh in Russia. After this date little more is heard of them.

During the latter part of the nineteenth century there were several other 'Japanese' groups performing throughout Britain.

Most of these were imitations but one group that was genuine and spent several years in Britain was the *Royal Yokohama Troupe*. There were six members, male and female, and they specialised in juggling with knives and rings. One particular part of their act was for a member, by means of a fork held in the mouth, to catch various objects thrown from the audience[52]. By this stage in the century Japan was less of a mystery to the British public, there had been so many Japanese performance troupes throughout the country for almost forty years. But both the Chinese and Japanese performers had made an impact on British culture.

Yamagata Troupe. Postcard c. 1904
(Author's collection)

The Royal Japanese Troupe. Poster 1892 *(Library of Congress)*

Notes

1. *Dublin Morning Register* 27 October 1829

2. *Leeds Intelligencer* 22 July 1830

3. *Sheffield Independent* 9 July 1825

4. *Morning Advertiser* 12 July 1827

5. A brief biography is given on the Magicpedia website; https:// geniimagazine.com/wiki/index.php?title=Ching_Lau_Lauro

6. Presently known as Nanjing, it is the capital of Jiangsu Province in Eastern China

7. The revolution referred to here was the Taiping Civil War (sometime also known as the Taiping Rebellion) and lasted from 1850 – 1864. Tianjing (Nankin) was the capital city of the Taiping rebels.

8. *Dundee Courier* 8 February 1854

9. *Le Nouvelliste* 1 September 1854. Online at; https://gallica.bnf.fr/ ark:/12148/bpt6k6272842b/f3.image.r=Chin-Gan?rk=42918;4

10. *Saunders's News-Letter* 24 October 1854

11. *The Globe* 24 August 1855

12. *The Era* 30 March 1856

13. *The Era* 9 November 1856

14. *Morning Advertiser* 12 November 1856

15. *Newcastle Guardian and Tyne Mercury* 19 September 1857

16. *The Era* 27 May1860

17. *The Era* 25 August 1861

18. *Staffordshire Sentinel and Commercial & General Advertiser* 2 June 1860

19. *Norwich Mercury* 30 December 1857

20. *The Era* 7 June 1861

21. *The Era* 14 July 1861

22. Arr Hee's name is mentioned in *The Era* 24 February 1861 and in the *Leeds Times* 25 May 1861

23. Poster for the Victoria Hall in Leeds, 20 December 1862. Two original copies are held by the Leeds City Library and an image of the poster can be viewed on www.steve-ward.net

24. *Le Temps (Paris)* 19 January 1864. Online at; https://gallica.bnf.fr/ark:/12148/bpt6k221907k/f1.item.r=%22Arr%20Hee%22. zoom

25. *Bath Chronicle and Weekly Gazette* 11 August 1864

26. *Le Café- Concert* 19 May 1867. Online at; https://gallica.bnf. fr/ark:/12148/bpt6k5484268p/f1.image.r=%22Arr%20 Hee%22?rk=42918;4

27. *Le Pays* 1 March 1867. Online at; https://gallica.bnf.fr/ark:/12148/bpt6k4683889w/f3.image.r=%22Arr%20 Hee%22?rk=278971;2

28. The Brother Lavatus are advertised in the *Leeds Times* 2 September 1871, and the Ricardo troupe in the *Derbyshire Courier* 15 January 1870

29. *Revue Artistique* 16 October 1873. Online at; https://gallica.bnf.fr/ark:/12148/bpt6k54530965/f3.image.r=%22Arr%20Hee%22?rk=21459;2

30. *La Dépêche* 16 March 1877. Online at; https://gallica.bnf.fr/ark:/12148/bpt6k4107890c/f3.image.r=%22Arr%20Hee%22?rk=85837;2

31. *Bolton Evening News* 6 August 1869

32. *L'Orchestre* 7 September 1875. Online at; https://gallica.bnf.fr/ark:/12148/bpt6k1204031/f24.image.r=%22Che%20Mah%22?rk=21459;2

33. *Bolton Evening News* 5 April 1876

34. Online at; https://gallica.bnf.fr/ark:/12148/bpt6k4603218j/f2.item.r=%22Che%20Mah%22.zoom

35. *Hampshire Advertiser* 21 November 1863

36. *Sun (London)* 5 February 1867

37. There were several descriptions of the Japanese Troupe's performances, such as in the *Field* 16 February 1867, and the *London Evening Standard* 11 February 1867

38. This is probably a phonetic corruption of the name Matsui Gensui. Schodt (2012) refers to this Japanese Troupe as the 'Gensui Troupe'. A photograph of Gensui and his family is available online at; http://www.19thcenturyphotos.com/The-Gensui-family-122208.htm

39. *Morning Post* 9 April 1867

40. *Reading Mercury* 20 April 1867

41. *Liverpool Daily Post* 24 July 1867

42. *Newcastle Daily Chronicle* 14 June 1867

43. Little All Right reputedly got his nickname through his declaring loudly at the end of each figure in his act "All Right!"

44. *Lloyd's Weekly Newspaper* 19 April 1868

45. *Lloyd's Weekly News* 17 May 1868

46. *Greenock Telegraph* April 15 1870

47. *The Era* 19 February 1871

48. A full report of the case was given in the *Exeter and Plymouth Gazette Daily Telegram* 17 December 1872.

49. *England & Wales National Probate Calendar.* Online at; https://www.ancestry.co.uk/interactive/1904/31874_221853-00313?pid=3447630&treeid=&personid=&rc=&usePUB=true&_phs-rc=Anq198&_phstart=successSource

50. *Liverpool Daily Post* 3 September 1869

51. A full transcript of the case can be viewed on-line at; https://www.oldbaileyonline.org/browse.jsp?id=def1-903-18691025&div=t18691025-903#highlight

52. *Nottingham Evening Post* 29 August 1899

CHAPTER 12
THE UNSUNG AND UN-NAMED

In researching this book it became evident that there were many artistes from a wide range of ethnic backgrounds performing in the circuses and halls during the nineteenth century. Only a relatively small number of them were documented well enough to give details of their lives. They were well represented in the media of the time, even if at times that representation was distorted. For others there are is only a small amount of information to be gleaned, but often just enough to give us an idea of their acts. Paul Pietro was one such character. He was predominantly an equestrian and he worked with *Cooke's Circus* during the 1820s, coincidentally often on the same bill as Pablo Paddington. His exact ethnicity was not clear but he was severally referred to as the 'Flying Peruvian'[1], the 'Sable Hero'[2], or just simply the 'Indian'[3]. In 1826, Pietro got himself into a bit of trouble that resulted in him being in court. The press coverage gives us a little more inferred information about him.

> TUESDAY – *The Wild Indian* – Paul Pietro the Wild Indian, of the New Olympic Circus [Cooke's], was brought before the sitting Alderman … on the following charge. A watchman stated that between one and two o'clock this morning, he was obliged to assist other watchmen in clearing the New Circus Tavern of a number of persons, among whom was Mr. Paul Pietro, who was comfortably smoking [sic] a pipe, affixed to his tomahawk; upon being ordered to depart, he refused, and attempted to strike the watchman with his tomahawk; the watchman therefore took him into custody (*Gores Liverpool and General Advertiser* 2 March 1826)

Pietro claimed that the tomahawk was only used in performance and that he had not intended to strike the watchman. It seems that he was acquitted with a warning and his tomahawk was returned to him. Clearly, Pietro was appearing with the trappings of a native American and in other advertisements he was referred to as an 'Indian'. That he was dark skinned is implied by the reference to being a 'sable hero' but his exact ethnic heritage is not known, and possibly may never be.

Tom Handford was a black clown who worked the circuses and halls during the middle of the century. He was born in Manchester around 1835, his father, also born in Lancashire, being a publican[4]. He is first mentioned in *The Era* of 12 August 1860, where he is invited to apply to Mr. George Levy's Mammoth Concert Hall in Dublin. As he is specifically named it is to be assumed that he was already performing 'on the circuit' at this time. A one line entrance places him at Astley's in May 1861[5], although there is no reference to his style of performance, he was celebrated. The *Newcastle Daily Chronicle* of 28 October 1861 gives us a little more detail;

> Mr. Tom Handford, the celebrated 'black cure' continues to be a source of great attraction ... He is really a clever man, and in his line of business the best I ever saw ... Mr. Handford's voice is both sweet and strong; but the chief attraction of his singing is the inimitable pantomime with which he accompanies his songs.

Handford was also known as the 'Black Diamond'[6] and his act appears to have been a mixture of comic song, dance, eccentricity, and physical pantomime. There were shades of minstrelsy in his acts and he was, on occasions, billed as a 'negro eccentric'. He was well respected and by February 1863 he was the proprietor of his own Concert Hall[7]. As well as working the halls, Handford formed his own company of entertainers and also worked with *Barlow's Circus*, *Pinder's Circus*, and with *Swallow's Circus* throughout his career. He died on 2 June 1876, after a long illness. The *Sunderland Daily Echo* of 3 June 1876 printed this obituary;

This well-known vocalist and comedian died yesterday morning at Penrith … Handford, we believe, was a native of Sunderland and few men in the profession were more thoroughly liked in this district, when he appeared in his prime as 'The Black Diamond'.

Another black clown of the nineteenth century was professionally known as 'Chocolat'. He was born of African-Cuban parents in Cuba around 1866, and took the name Rafael Padilla. As a boy, he was sold by the elderly woman who raised him, and was taken to Spain. Eventually he made his way to Bilbao where he was 'spotted' by an English clown, Tony Grice. The pair began working together at the Cirque Nouveau in Paris in 1886. It was Grice who gave Padilla the professional name of Chocolat. They parted company in 1888 and Chocolat went on to work with other clowns over the next five years. It was in 1895 that the manager of the Cirque Nouvau partnered Chocolat with the English clown George Footit. They went on to work together for twenty years. Working in France, the British press rarely mentioned them but they did occasionally appear in professional 'stage' newspapers[8].

Chocolat and Footit. Au Bon Marché Trade Card, late C19th *(Author's collection)*

Much of their action was comedic and slap-stick. Footit was the classic clown figure, white-faced and sometimes resplendent in gold and silver trimmed costume. By contrast, Chocolat was the Auguste of the act but not as we might expect to see today. He was always well dressed as a Dandy, sometimes in tail coat and knee breeches. We are lucky in that there is a film clip, in colour, of Chocolat and Footit working in 1900 which can be viewed online[9]. This gives an excellent idea of how they appeared and of their act. That Chocolat was always well dressed is reflected in Nohain (1907:pp113-114);

> sous les yeux, une superbe photographie du joyeux nègre en habit de soirée, gilet et cravatte blanche, gardénia à la boutonnière, et raie partageant par le milieu ses cheveux crépus;

> [in front of me, a superb photograph of the merry negro in evening dress, waistcoat and white tie, gardenia in his buttonhole, and a parting in the middle his frizzy hair; *Author's translation*]

Chocolat was frequently on the end of the knocks and kicks dished out to him by Footit. In this respect Chocolat was conforming to the prejudiced and stereotypical role of the down-trodden negro scapegoat. But, as often with 'Auguste' characters, Chocolat was able to turn the tables on Footit and end up the 'winner'. Chocolat died while on tour in Bordeaux in 1917.

> Sombrant dans les affres de l'alcohol, il finira ses jours dans la misère à Bordeaux au 43 rue saint-Sernin. Sur les registres du cimetière protestant de la rue judaïque, on relève que Raphaël Padilla, décédé à 49 ans, a été inhumé dans la partie réservée aux indigents, carré M rangée 7 numéro 2 (*Les Lettres Sud Ouest* 2010)[10]

> [Sinking into the throes of alcohol, he ended his days in misery in Bordeaux at 43 rue Saint-Sernin. On the registers of the Protestant cemetery in the Jewish street, it is noted that Raphaël Padilla, who died

at 49, was buried in the part reserved for the destitute, square M row 7 number 2. *Author's translation*]

A French language film entitled *Chocolat* was released in 2016, directed by Roschdy Zem, and celebrates the rags to riches story of the poor boy from Cuba who made it to the big time of nineteenth century Parisian circus.

In 1861, the *Bridlington Free Press* of 19 October carried an advertisement for Edmonds Royal Windsor Castle Menagerie. As well as an extensive collection of animal and birds, the exhibition was;

> Accompanied by that extraordinary Race of Men, the ZULU KAFFIRS. The only Men of their Race ever brought to this Country, who will go through their wonderful and extraordinary Performances at each Exhibition, representing in their Native Costume the MANNERS and CUSTOMS of KAFFIR LIFE, viz. the War Signal, Modes of Warfare, War and Club Dances and Exercises, Songs of Peace, War &c.

Not exactly accurate, as Dickens witnessed a troupe of Zulus in 1851 and there was a group that performed in London in 1853[11].

The 1861 edition also carries a very detailed report of the Zulus on their visit to St George's Hall, Hyde Park Corner in London. It expands upon the performances of the group, as well as giving personal details about some of the chief performers. However, with typical British arrogance of the time aspects of the performances are considered somewhat quaint and amusing.

> The performance has its comic features; for the Zulu poet laureate wears a leopard's head and collar of tigers' tails, when he chants the king's praises, and the entrance of the witch-doctor, in pursuit of the sorcerer who caused the illness of a sick man … is more amusing than anything in a farce. The cries, songs, and dances of these extraordinary people are extremely amusing.

The British public had little concept of ethnography so these displays of Zulu culture were treated as exploitative entertainment, as discussed in Chapter One.

Groups of Zulus visited Britain frequently, even during the period of the politically motivated Anglo-Zulu war of 1879.

Zulu Kaffirs at St George's Hall. *Illustrated London News* 28 May 1853 *(Author's collection)*

However, after British defeats at the battles of Isandlwana and Intombe, feelings towards the Zulus who performed in London that year were running high. When they performed at the Crystal Palace Concert Hall in Birmingham;

> The warriors drew a crowded, but by no means altogether a friendly, audience, as while they occupied the stage there was a hissing heard from various parts of the Hall (*The Era* 20 April 1879)

One wonders as to how these performers felt about the reception they received, whether it be laughter or jeering. We know how British audiences received, and perceived, ethnic performers but there are very few occasions when we know how the artistes felt. Their opinions are few and far between, and are very often given second hand through reported incidents.

Young Zulu Chief. *Illustrated London News* 27 April 1878

Little is known about the many 'artistes of colour' and their place in the circus is often evidenced by only occasional mentions. At *Keith's Circus* in Dewsbury in 1878 there appeared, for the first time;

TILLIDU, THE LITTLE AFRICAN PRINCESS The only Coloured lady rider in the profession. Her extraordinary feats on a bare-backed horse are marvellous (*Dewsbury Reporter* 20 July 1878)

There were other 'African Princesses' who would appear during the nineteenth century. At *Tayleur's Circus* in Hastings in 1881 there appeared another such Princess;

> The African Princess Zambezia next appeared on the 'corde elastique' and her performance was one of the most clever of the kind we have ever seen. Her dancing on the tight-rope was finished and firm, indicating long practice and decided adaptability (*Hastings and St Leonard's Observer* 29 January 1881)

Transfield's Great American Troupe appeared in Cheltenham, also in 1881. They too had an 'African Princess';

> ZOO, THE AFRICAN PRINCESS. Daughter of the Zulu King. Brought to England by Capt. Purvis, who will introduce her famous NATIVE DANCE – a great novelty (*Cheltenham Mercury* 4 June 1881)

At least with the previous two Princesses their performances had been hailed as 'marvellous' and 'most clever'. But for Zoo, she was nothing more than a novelty to be gawped at. It is worth mentioning that on the same bill were 'Barton & Hart, Negro Comedians'. Zoo appeared on the billing between June 1880 and June 1881. After that date nothing more is heard of her. The only indication that we have of her ethnicity is that she is billed as the 'daughter of the Zulu King' and a brief mention in the *Norfolk News* of 5 June 1880, where she is referred to as a 'little half caste girl', inferring that she was not very old and may well have been of mixed heritage. In Chesterfield in 1877, an un-named[12] circus presented;

> Mdlle. Flora (the fascinating *equestrienne*), the African Princess, who sings and plays the guitar while riding on horseback (*The Era* 8 April 1877)

A Mdlle. Flora was appearing with *Adam's Grand Circus* in 1874, but there is no indication of her act so we cannot say with any certainty that the two Floras are the same person. Another Mdlle. Flora appears in the late 1890s as a wire-walker[13] but, again, there is no indication that this was the same person. The *Congleton and Macclesfield Mercury* of 29 May 1869 references, very briefly;

THE LATEST MUSIC HALL NOVELTY is a female negro performer
on the trapeze

The same insert appears in the *Tipperary Free Press* of 4 June 1869, and many other newspapers throughout May and June. No other information is included so we do not know her name. It is unlikely to have been Miss La La as this predates her visit to Britain by ten years.

Like the Zulus mentioned previously, as late as 1900 individuals were being exhibited for entertainment. At the *Scottish Zoo and Circus* in Glasgow[14];

Fatima and Smaun, two perfectly formed Burmese dwarfs, who are 20 and 23 inches in height respectively, and weigh something under one stone each [approximately 6.5 Kilos each] … Their acrobatic and gymnastic performances are greatly appreciated by a large number of spectators (*Airdrie and Coatbridge Advertiser* 30 June 1900)

Two years earlier, Bostock had exhibited Aaron Moore, 'the largest negro giant known to civilised nations', at the *Scottish Zoo and Circus*[15].

Sometimes, unfortunately, the only reference we have to an individual person of colour's involvement with the circus comes through negative press. One such instance was given in the *Mid-Sussex Times* of 6 October 1885. Alexander Munroe, who was a 'negro lion tamer' was stabbed to death by a man in the same lodging house. According to the report, Munroe had been heard to say, several times, 'You English are dirty dogs' and that 'White men were dirty dogs'. He appears to have been arguing with another man outside of the room before he was stabbed. What prompted the argument and whether it was racially motivated we do not know, nor do we know the circumstances of his comments but clearly a white Englishman had upset him. Another incident occurred in

1888, when Joshua Taylor, 'a coloured man travelling with the Olympia Circus'[16] was charged in Doncaster with having assaulted a young girl. Another reported assault case took place in 1899, when a circus worker of colour going by the name of 'Black Bill', who worked with Sanger's Circus was charged[17]. In 1893, *Sanger's Circus* visited Motherwell and this prompted a recollection of five years previous when a fight broke out between an iron worker and 'one of the coloured circus men'[18]. A riot had ensued after the arrest of the circus worker. Sanger clearly employed more than worker of colour because, in a report given earlier in the *Ardrossan and Saltcoats Herald* of 26 May 1893;

> Harry Washington, a coloured man, foreman circus assistant, was charged with having on the 28th April, in a field near Beith, assaulted James Campbell, circus labourer.

Sanger's Circus also appeared in the press earlier in 1867, when it was reported that;

> Wright, a coloured person, belonging to Sanger's Circus, was tried at Dundee Circuit Court … or the murder of a farm servant (*Fifeshire Journal* 19 September 1867)

In 1899, a twenty five year old circus groom of colour by the name of Edward Frappier, who was working with *Anderton's Circus*, was sentenced to one month's hard labour for theft from his employer[19]. Similarly, in 1885, Alexander Young, another man of colour who worked with the circus was charged with committing a burglary and theft in Merthyr[20].

There are references to many more individuals in the press throughout the nineteenth century. In 1891, two circus workers of colour with an un-named circus were involved in a knife fight[21]. The assailant was named John James (Jummy) and the victim named Hicks (Frisco). A few years later in 1898, again with *Sanger's Circus*, Nathaniel Gibson, a coloured man employed at Sanger's Circus, pleaded guilty to biting another labourer, and also stabbing another coloured labourer named Collins (*Dundee Evening Telegraph* 8 June 1898)

In 1867, a former rider in an equestrian troupe with Sanger, who was nicknamed 'Snowball' had to be subdued by no less than five policeman when he caused a fracas after being teased by some boys[22]. Joseph Edward Forster was a circus worker of colour with *Howe and Cushing's Circus*, who was involved in a fight in Leeds in 1870[23]. The news was not always about violence. In 1893, a girl named Annie Anderson ran away with the circus when it visited Kirkaldy in Scotland. She seems to have become enamoured with a circus worker of colour[24], but his name was not given. Another 'elopement' was reported in 1878. It seems that;

A girl of somewhat respectable appearance, only seventeen years old, and who it is stated came from Kingston-on-Thames, had fallen in love with a coloured man connected with the circus and proposed to follow him wherever he went (*Bury Free Press* 9 November 1878)

She was later found guilty of theft! Joseph Austin, a bare-back rider of colour with *Elphinstone's Circus*, was charged with being drunk and disorderly in the circus in 1889[25]. In 1866, a strong-man of colour fell and broke his thigh during a performance with *Haye's Grand Troupe* in Burnley[26], again unfortunately no name is given. *Sanger's Circus* employed a man of colour by the name of Richard Hopewell. He was the victim of an assault reported in the *Hampshire Advertiser* of 19 August 1871. Peter Michin, 'a tall coloured man', was employed by *Wombwell and Bailey's Circus* in 1895[27]. Another named circus worker of colour was Charles Demorst, who was employed as a watchman accompanying a circus[28]. In Banbury in 1866 there was performed;

Feats of Strength by Sampson Hercules, the strongest coloured man known, and his clown 'Joey' (*Buckingham Express* 27 January 1866)

Sampson Hercules may possibly have been the same strong-man who broke his thigh in Burnley in 1866, as referenced above.

Violence, murder, theft, and abductions were commonly reported in the British press. It made good reading for a sensation seeking public, and sold newspapers. However, the blatant reference to an individual's ethnicity in these reported cases, especially those of a 'negro' heritage, only reinforced the popular, but erroneous, perception of the 'black man' as being violent, dishonest, and a sexual predator. Yet the history of the nineteenth century circus shows that this was not true. There were many more well-respected and applauded performers of non-white heritage than these reported cases would have us believe. And, it must be emphasised that, there were many more of the indigenous Anglo-Saxon population, not circus workers, who were equally responsible for such crimes. Their ethnicity was never labelled, thereby by omission, underlining the 'difference' of anything non Anglo-Saxon.

Circus has always been seen as having an 'otherness'. It became, and indeed still is, a place where the audience entered a world that was both real and illusory at the same time.

> The audience knows that what they see, in terms of the physical actions presented, is real but when they enter the circus space they accept that they are entering the world of the other; different from the reality of everyday experience, something beyond the norm (Ward 2019:12)

The Otherness of the Victorian circus was, in part, embodied in the large number of performers of non-white heritage involved, from all parts of the world. They were 'exotic' and part of the illusory nature of the circus. The circus has always been, and still is, more progressive and accepting by nature than other fields. The 'modern' circus, founded by Astley over 250 years ago, was underpinned by the wealth of talented performers of non-white heritage involved. Some became famous in their own right, and were very much in the public eye. Some were just a single named reference in an advertisement, and others were just mentioned by their ethnicity. What has to be remembered, applauded, and celebrated is that in the circuses, music halls, and other performance venues of the Victorian era, 'artistes of colour' were a very real presence.

Notes

1. *Sheffield Independent* 23 April 1825

2. *Sheffield Independent* 30 April 1825

3. *Manchester Courier* 25 March 1826

4. *1841 England Census*. Online at; https://www.ancestry.co.uk/interactive/8978/LANHO107_569_570-0101/6011590?back-url=https://www.ancestry.co.uk/family-tree/person/tree/46211521/person/6494918672/facts/citation/13926418814/edit/record

5. *London Daily News* 28 May 1861

6. *Aberdeen Press and Journal* 18 December 1861

7. *Newcastle Daily Chronicle* 21 February 1863

8. One earlier British example appears in *The Era* 26 June 1897

9. https://www.youtube.com/watch?v=qpYTanqDzvc

10. Online at; https://www.sudouest.fr/2010/07/05/le-clown-noir-en-terre-a-bordeaux-132597-2780.php

11. *Illustrated London News* 28 May 1853

12. From other news reports of the same time it appears that Mddle. Flora was working for Weldon's Circus, cf *Derbyshire Times and Chesterfield Herald* 28 April 1877

13. *Music Hall and Theatre Review* 14 July 1899

14. For a brief history of the Scottish Zoo and Circus refer to *Scotland's First Zoo*, published by History Scotland magazine May 2020. Online at https://pocketmags.com/history-scotland-magazine#popup1

15. *Glasgow Herald* 19 April 1898. Moore stood at seven feet three inches in height.

16. *Sheffield Daily Telegraph* 29 March 1888

17. *Kilburn Times* 10 March 1899

18. *Motherwell Times* 17 June 1893

19. *Nottingham Journal* 6 January 1899

20. *Cardiff Times* 5 December 1885

21. *Hartlepool Northern Daily Mail* 18 August 1891

22. *Islington Gazette* 16 July 1867

23. *Bradford Observer* 25 June 1870

24. *Newcastle Courant* 23 September 1893

25. *Staffordshire Sentinel* 25 April 1889

26. *Burnley Advertiser* 14 July 1866

27. *Grantham Journal* 5 October 1895

28. *Cheltenham Chronicle* 20 October 1894

SELECT BIBLIOGRAPHY

Adams, W. (1975). Civilizations, Barbarians, and Savages : The social and political nexus of diffusion. *Civilisations*, *25*(3/4), 319-324. Online at http://www.jstor.org/stable/41229295

Armistead, W. (1848) *A Tribute for the Negro: Being a Vindication of the Moral, Intellectual and Religious Capabilities of the Coloured portion of Mankind, With particular Reference to the African Race*. William Irwin, Manchester. Online at https://docsouth.unc.edu/neh/armistead/armistead.html

Armistead, W. (ed), (1853) *Five Hundred Thousand Strokes for Freedom*. Leeds Anti-Slavery Tracts. The First Half Million Issue. W & F Cash. London

Armistead, W. (1853) *A Cloud of Witnesses against Slavery and Oppression*. Wm. Tweedie, London

Assael, B. (2005) *The Circus and Victorian Society*. University of Virginia Press, Charlotteville & London

Banerjee, S. (2011). The Mysterious Alien: Indian Street Jugglers in Victorian London. *Economic and Political Weekly*, *46*(14), 59-65. Online at www.jstor.org/stable/41152053

Barrow, J. et al, (2005), Leisure and culture: Plays, sports and customs before 1700. *A History of the County of Chester: Volume 5 Part 2, the City of Chester: Culture, Buildings, Institutions*, ed. A. T. Thacker and C. P. Lewis (London, 2005), pp. 247-255. Online at http://www.british-history.ac.uk/vch/ches/vol5/pt2/pp247-255_

Blanchard. P, Bancel. N, Boëtsch. G, Deroo. E, Lemaire. S, Forsdick C, (Eds) (2008) *Human Zoos; Science and Spectacle in the Age of Colonial Empires*. Trans. Bridgeman, T., Liverpool University Press

Best, G. (1979) *Mid-Victorian Britain 1851 – 1875*. Fontana Press, London

Bethencourt, F. (2013) *Racisms; From the Crusades to the Twentieth Century*. Princetown University Press

Brent, L. (Harriet A Jacobs) (1861) *Incidents in the life of a slave girl*. Boston. Online at https://play.google.com/store/books/details?id=1R-wEAAAAYAAJ&rdid=book-1RwEAAAAYAAJ&rdot=1

Brown, M. (2007) Miss La La's Teeth: Reflections on Degas and "Race". *The Art Bulletin December 2007*. Online at https://www.mutu-alart.com/Article/-Miss-La-La-s--Teeth--Reflections-on-De-g/4ECE634E323FBB3D

Buoiu, I. V. (2007) *Contributions to the history of aeronautics in Romania*. PhD extract. Online at https://old.utcluj.ro/download/doctorat/Rezumat&Ioan_Buiu.pdf

Cannadine, D. (2017) *Victorious Century; The United Kingdom 1800 – 1906*. London, Allen Lane

Chunfang Fei, ed. (2002) *Chinese Theories of Theatre and Performance from Confucius to the Present*. University of Michigan Press, pp24-25. Online at https://books.google.co.uk/books?id=Ci-QegTh99-wC&pg=PA24&redir_esc=y#v=onepage&q&f=-false

Davies, G. (2017) *Pablo Fanque and the Victorian Circus*. Poppyland Publishing

Dickens, C. (1853) The Noble Savage. *Household Words, a Weekly Journal*. 11 June 1853 No. 168, London

Desbonnet, E. (1911) *Les Rois de la Force*. Berger-Levrault, Paris. Online at https://archive.org/details/4908148.0001.001.umich.edu/page/I/mode/2up

Frost, T. (1874) *The Old Showmen and the Old London Fairs*. Tinsley Brothers, London

Frost, T. (1876) *Circus Life & Circus Celebrities.* Tinsley Brothers, London. Online at https://books.google.co.uk/books?id=i0ozAQAAMAAJ&printsec=frontcover&dq=thomas+frost&hl=en&sa=X&ved=0ahUKEwjWxcbAi_7oAhVQU-MAKHbHVApMQ6wEINDAB#v=onepage&q=thomas%20frost&f=false

Frost, T. (1876) *The Lives of the Conjurors.* Tinsley Brothers, London

Groneman, W. (2019) Women of the Alamo. *True West magazine* 4 February 2019. Online at https://truewestmagazine.com/women-alamo/

Habbouch, L. (2011) Moroccan acrobats in Britain; oriental curiosity and ethnic exhibition. *Comparative Drama.* December 22, 2011. Online at Moroccan acrobats in Britain: oriental curiosity and ethnic exhibition. - Free Online Library (thefreelibrary.com)

Hale, M. (2018) Albert May. *African Stories in Hull and East Yorkshire.* Online at https://www.africansinyorkshireproject.com/albert-may.html

Harris, J. (1993) *Private Lives: Public Spirits. A Social History of Britain 1870 – 1914.* O.U.P.

Hazlitt, W. (1828) The Indian Jugglers. *Table Talk.* Online at http://www.juggling.org/papers/hazlitt/#fn1

Holland, C. (1998) *Strange Feats and Clever Turns.* Holland & Palmer. London

Kerr, M. (2017) The Psychology of Thrill; Why we love to terrify ourselves. *XPRESS Report* November 2017. Online at The psychology of thrill: Why we love to terrify ourselves | Lifestyle – Gulf News

Laryea, R. (2019) The Untold Story of Europe's First Black Female Circus Star. *The Voice* 3 September 2019. Online at https://archive.voice-online.co.uk/article/untold-story-europe's-first-black-female-circus-star

Locker A. (2014).The social history of coarse angling in England AD 1750-1950, in Thomas R. & Fothergill B. T. (eds), *Animals, and their Bones, in the 'Modern' World (AD 1750-1900)*. Anthropozoologica 49 (1): 99-107. Online at http://dx.doi.org/10.5252/az2014n1a07

Low, E. (1895) Acrobats and how they are trained. *The Strand magazine*. Vol X. July – December 1895

Maddra, S. (2006) *Hostiles? The Lakota Ghost Dance and Buffalo Bill's Wild West*. University of Oklahoma Press

Manjara, K. (2018) When will Britain face up to its crimes against humanity? *The Guardian*, 29 March, 2018. Online at https://www.theguardian.com/news/2018/mar/29/slavery-abolition-compensation-when-will-britain-face-up-to-its-crimes-against-humanity

National Geographic. (nd) *Genographic Project – Map of Human Migration*. Online at https://genographic.nationalgeographic.com/human-journey/

Nohain F. *Les memoires de Footit et Chocolat clowns*. Pierre Lafitte & Co. Paris 1907. Online at https://gallica.bnf.fr/ark:/12148/bpt-6k312620x/f7.image.r=%22Footit%20et%20Chocolat%22

Nowrojee, J. Merwanjee, H. (1841) *Journal of a Residence of 2 ½ years in Great Britain*. W. H. Allen & Co., London. Online at http://access.bl.uk/item/viewer/ark:/81055/vdc_000000051912

Price, B. (2019) *The Chinese in Britain: A History of Visitors and Settlers*. Amberley Publishing

Rediker, M. (2007) *The Slave Ship; A Human History*. London, John Murray

Rendell, M. (2013) *Astley's Circus; The Story of an English Hussar*. Createspace Independent Publishing Platform

Richardson, J. (2002) Degas and the Dancers. *Vanity Fair*, October, 2002. Online at Degas and the Dancers | Vanity Fair

Rosen, B. Dr (2008) Victorian Funerals and Mourning. *Victorian History*. 3 June 2008. Online at https://vichist.blogspot.com/2008/06/victorian-funerals-and-mourning.html

Rutherford, A. (2016) *A Brief History of Everyone Who Ever Lived. The stories in our genes*. Weidenfeld & Nicolson, London

Schodt, F. (2012) *Professor Risley and the Imperial Japanese Troupe*. Stonebridge Press, Berkley, California.

Speaight, G. (1980) *A History of the Circus*. Tantivy Press

Stewart, J. (2012) *The Acrobat. Arthur Barnes and the Victorian Circus*. McFarland & Co.

Stoddart, H. (2000) *Rings of Desire, Circus history and representation*. Manchester, Manchester University Press

Strausbaugh, J. (2007) *Black Like You; Blackface, Whiteface Insult and Imitation in American Popular Culture*. Tarcher Perigee

Tait, P. (2005) *Circus Bodies; Cultural Identity in Aerial Performance*. Routledge Chapman & Hall

Thackeray, W. M. (1848) *The Book of Snobs*. London

Toulmin, V. Prof. (2018) Miss La La – Olga Albertina Brown. *Circus250; Circus Show of Shows*. University of Sheffield

Turner, .J M. (2000) *Victorian Arena – The Performers. A Dictionary of the British Circus Biographies Vol 2*. Longdales Press, Formby

Usherwood, S. (1981) The Black must be discharged – The Abolitionists' Debt to Lord Mansfield.

History Today Vol 31 Issue 3

Vickers, J. R., (2016) *The Acrobatic Body in Ancient Greek Society*. Electronic Thesis and Dissertation Repository. 3834. Online at https://ir.lib.uwo.ca/etd/3834

Wall, D. (2013) *The Ordinary Acrobat*. Vintage Books. Kindle edition online at https://www.amazon.co.uk/Ordinary-Acrobat-Journey-Wondrous-Present-ebook/dp/B00957T5A0/ref=tmm_kin_swatch_0?_encoding=UTF8&qid=&sr=

Wall, T. (2019) *Juggling from Antiquity to the Middle Ages; the forgotten history of throwing and catching*. Modern Vaudeville Press, Philadelphia, USA

Ward, S. (2019) *The Art of the Circus*. PhD Exegesis. University of Hull

Wild, N. & Remy, T. (nd) *Le Cirque, Iconographie. Catalogues de la bibliothèque de l'opera*, p.107, Bibliothèque Nationale de France

Will & Testament. Ducrow A. Online at https://www.ancestry.co.uk/interactive/5111/40611_309656-00537?pid=340250&backurl=https://search.ancestry.co.uk/cgi-bin/sse.dll?indiv%3D1%26dbid%3D5111%26h%3D340250%26tid%3D%26pid%3D%26usePUB%3Dtrue%26_phsrc%3Dsbc1265%26_phstart%3DsuccessSource&treeid=&personid=&hintid=&usePUB=true&_phsrc=sbc1265&_phstart=successSource&usePUBJs=true&_ga=2.77057501.91645169.1580288256-1986502099.1539097385#?imageId=40611_309656-00538

Wilson, B. (2016) *HEYDAY. Britain and the Birth of the Modern World.* Weidenfeld & Nicolson, London

Zubrzycki, J. (2017) The Jadoowallah from Madras. *The Indian Quarterly* January-March issue 2017. Online at http://indianquarterly.com/the-jadoowallah-from-madras/

General Notes

In researching this book a variety of archives have been consulted, both physically and online;

The National Fairground and Circus Archive. Western Bank Library, Sheffield, S10 2RN, UK and online at https://www.sheffield.ac.uk/nfca

The National Archive. Kew, Richmond, TW9 4DU, UK and online at https://nationalarchives.gov.uk

The British Library. 96 Euston Road, London, NW1 2DB, UK and online at https://www.bl.uk

The British Library Newspaper Archive at Boston Spa. Thorpe Arch Park, Wetherby, LS23 7BQ, UK and online at https://www.britishnewspaperarchive.co.uk

The Bibliothèque Nationale de France in Paris and online at https://www.bnf.fr/en/gallica-bnf-digital-library

The National Library of Australia digital newspaper archive online at https://trove.nla.gov.au/newspaper

Some readers may be unfamiliar with pre-decimal British money. Prior to 1971, the pound sterling (£) was divided into twenty shillings (s) and each shilling into twelve pence (d). So, 12d = 1s and 20s = £1. There is another unit that is sometimes mentioned, and that is the Guinea. A Guinea was worth twenty –one shillings.

Every effort has been made by the author to locate the copyright holders of images reproduced within this book.

INDEX

ABOUT THE AUTHOR

Steve Ward has a background in theatre and clowning. Moving into teaching he soon recognised that as well as an artistic activity, circus could play an important role in the educational and social development of young people. From his early days in experimenting with circus in the classroom, and projects linking the professional circus, schools, and youth groups he went on to run his own award-winning youth circus, as well as establishing the original National

Photo Credit: Richard Babbs

Association of Youth Circus in the UK. Steve has created and directed many youth circus festivals in the UK, as well as in Germany and Brazil.

With a deep rooted interest in the circus, he now writes about its fascinating cultural history. He has a PhD by Published Works from the University of Hull, and is a member of the Circus Research Network and the Circus Arts Research Platform, both international organisations. To date, he has written five books and many articles on the subject. Steve also lectures on aspects of circus history and has appeared on television and in many radio interviews. He also advises on educational and youth circus matters – and he still finds time to occasionally perform as a clown!

His previous Circus publications are;

Beneath the Big Top; A Social History of the Circus in Britain, Pen & Sword 2014

Sawdust Sisterhood; How Circus Empowered Women, Fonthill Media 2016

Father of the Modern Circus; Billy Buttons; The Life & Times of Philip Astley, Pen & Sword 2018
Circus Notes & Jottings, Amazon 2017
Nineteenth Century Circus Poster Art, Amazon 2018

Other books by Steve Ward;
Robin's Wood, Createspace Publishing Platform 2013
The Indentured Man, Createspace Publishing Platform 2014
Tales from the Big House; Temple Newsam, Pen & Sword 2017

OTHER WORKS BY MODERN VAUDEVILLE PRESS

Juggling: From Antiquity to the Middle Ages
Thom Wall
ISBN 978-0-578-41084-5

As with dance, so with juggling—the moment that the performer finishes the routine, their act ceases to exist beyond the memory of the audience. There is no permanent record of what transpired, so studying the ancient roots of juggling is fraught with difficulty. Using the records that do exist, juggling appears to have emerged around the world in cultures independent of one another in the ancient past. Paintings in Egypt from 2000 BCE show jugglers engaged in performance. Stories from the island nation of Tonga place juggling's creation with their goddess of the underworld—a figure who has guarded a cave since time immemorial. Juggling games and rituals are pervasive in isolated Inuit cultures in northern Canada and Greenland. Though the earliest representation of juggling is 4,000 years old, the practice is surely much older—in the same way that humans were doubtlessly singing and dancing long before the first bone flute was created.

This book is an attempt to catalogue this tangible history of juggling in human culture. It is the story of juggling, represented in art and writing from around the world, across time. Although much has been written about modern jugglers–specific performers, their props, and their routines–little has been said about those who first developed the craft. As juggling enters a golden age in the internet era, Juggling: From Antiquity to the Middle Ages offers a look into the past—to the origins of our art form.

Juggling: or How to Become a Juggler (the annotated edition)

Rupert Ingalese, Thom Wall
ISBN 978-1733971201

Rupert Ingalese, born Paul Wingrave, was a British juggler who worked in the first half of the 1900s, both as a juggler and as a producer and manager of variety shows across England. In 1917, he published the very first "learn to juggle" book, teaching in detail the methods used to learn traditional toss juggling as well as a variety of more esoteric juggling skills.

This edition offers complete annotations that add context to Ingalese's writing as well as asides that explain the work of other jugglers in the same time period.

Body Talk: Basic Mime
Mario Diamond
ISBN 978-1-7339712-1-8
MSRP: $15USD / €13EUR

Body Talk is Mario Diamond's detailed introduction to the art of mime. Body axes, illusions, and exploratory games are laid out accessibly for any learner.

The Midwest Book Review calls this book "...a highly recommended 'must' for any theater or drama reference collection and for producers and actors who want to translate mime's basics to better acting and cognitive results."

Games for Circus Educators, Organizers & Innovators
American Youth Circus Organization, compiled by Lucy Little
ISBN 978-1-7339712-2-5

With over 100 games organized for optimal use in cooperative, movement-based settings, this book is a must-have for every circus school, teaching artist, and arts education program! Games are organized by age, number of participants, energy level, and social/emotional learning outcome, and include special notes for working with a variety of populations that may require adaptation or modifications.

Pottery in Motion: A practical guide to the impractical art of plate spinning
Sam Veale
ISBN 978-1-7339712-3-2

Judging by the books already available with the words "Plate Spinning" in the title, there is a good chance that you picked this up because you are a working parent trying to balance your home life with a busy career. If so, I can't help you. This book deals with plate spinning in the strictly literal sense. Unless you are interested in spinning ceramic plates on sticks, I won't waste any more of your precious time, save to say, best of luck with the kids and the job.

If you are actually interested in spinning actual plates on actual sticks, then this is the book for you (but if you end up struggling to balance your home life with your busy career as a plate spinner, then don't say I didn't warn you).

Juggling: What It Is and How to Do It
Thom Wall; ft. Jay Gilligan, Fritz Grobe, Benjamin Domask-Ruh
ISBN 978-1-7339712-5-6
www.JugglingBook.com

Juggling: What It Is and How to Do It is the result of six years of work by former Cirque du Soleil juggler Thom Wall. This book teaches learners of all ages how to juggle – one of the world's oldest artforms. With a kind demeanor, humor, and enthusiasm, Wall explains the process of juggling through four different modalities, bolstered by the latest physical education research.

The practice of juggling has been proven time and time again to benefit the body and mind: it reduces stress, increases the brain plasticity and density, and is an age-old form of active meditation. *Juggling: What It Is and How to Do It* is a timely and accessible primer that even a middle-schooler can hit the ground running with, or one that families can enjoy together. But make no mistake, this book isn't child's play. With guest chapters by some of today's modern juggling masters, *Juggling* provides a wealth of content to span years of study for even the most serious adult learner.

Mongolian Contortion: An Ethnographic Inquiry
Mariam Ala-Rashi
(eBook only)

This ethnographic research proposes an introduction to the performance art form Mongolian contortion by examining its theories and functions before and after the establishment of the Mongolian State Circus in 1941. Through qualitative research methods it further investigates different repercussions that lead to the transformation and decline of *Traditional Mongolian Contortion* in Mongolia and the West in recent years. By examining the genesis and history of body flexibility prior to the establishment of the Mongolian State Circus, it explores parallels between Mongolian folk dance and folk acrobatics and the establishment of Mongolian contortion as the international "brand" we know today. It discusses the categorization of different styles within Mongolian contortion, discovers the development of aesthetics and how religious symbolism is incorporated in contortion performances. Lastly, it examines the numerous challenges contortionists with traditional aesthetics and presentations, a style referred to in this paper as *Traditional Mongolian Contortion*, face and proposes solutions for the safeguarding of this art form.

Lightning Source UK Ltd.
Milton Keynes UK
UKHW010716020322
399440UK00001B/17